Chekhov

THE EARLY PLAYS

Smith and Kraus *Books for Actors*

GREAT TRANSLATIONS FOR ACTORS SERIES

Anthologies and Collections

Chekhov: Four Plays, tr. by Carol Rocamora

Chekhov's Vaudevilles, tr. by Carol Rocamora

Ibsen: Four Major Plays, tr. by R. Davis & B. Johnston

Ibsen Volume II: Four Plays, tr. by Brian Johnston

Ibsen Volume III: Four Plays, tr. by Brian Johnston

Marivaux: Three Plays, tr. by Stephen Wadsworth

Arthur Schnitzler: Four Major Plays, tr. by Carl Mueller

Villeggiatura: The Trilogy by Carlo Goldoni, tr. by Robert Cornthwaite

Classics

The Coffee Shop by Carlo Goldoni, tr. by Robert Cornthwaite

Cyrano de Bergerac by Edmond Rostand, tr. by Charles Marowitz

Emperor and Galilean by Henrik Ibsen, tr. by Brian Johnston

A Glass of Water by Eugene Scribe, tr. by Robert Cornthwaite

Mercadet by Honoré de Balzac, tr. by Robert Cornthwaite

The Sea Gull by Anton Chekhov, tr. by N. Saunders & F. Dwyer

Spite for Spite by Agustin Moreto, tr. by Dakin Matthews

The Summer People by Maxim Gorky, tr. by N. Saunders & F. Dwyer

Three Sisters by Anton Chekhov, tr. by Lanford Wilson

The Wood Demon by Anton Chekhov, tr. by N. Saunders & F. Dwyer

Zoyka's Apartment by Mikhail Bulgakov, tr. by N. Saunders & F. Dwyer

If you require pre-publication information about upcoming Smith and Kraus books, you may receive our semiannual catalogue, free of charge, by sending your name and address to *Smith and Kraus Catalogue, P.O. Box 127, Lyme, NH 03768. Or call us at (603) 643-6431, fax (603) 922-3348. WWW.SmithKraus.Com*

Chekhov

THE EARLY PLAYS

Platonov
a new translation/adaptation

Ivanov
a new translation

The Wood Demon
a new translation

by Carol Rocamora

Great Translations Series

SK
A Smith and Kraus Book

A Smith and Kraus Book
Published by Smith and Kraus, Inc.
PO Box 127, Lyme, NH 03768
WWW.SmithKraus.com

Copyright ©1999 Carol Rocamora
All rights reserved
Manufactured in the United States of America

Cover and Text Design by Julia Hill Gignoux, Freedom Hill Design

First Edition: September 1999
10 9 8 7 6 5 4 3 2 1

The Library of Congress Cataloging-In-Publication Data

Chekhov, Anton Pavlovich, 1860–1904.
[Plays. English. Selections]

The early plays / Chekhov ; "Platonov" translated and adapted by Carol Rocamora ; "Ivanov," "The Wood demon" transltated by Carol Rocamora.
p. cm. — (Great translations series)
Includes bibliograhical references.
ISBN 1-57525-152-3
1. Chekhov, Anton Pavlovich, 1860–1904 Translations into English. I. Rocamora, Carol. II. Title. III. Title: Chekhov — the early plays. IV. Series: Great translations for actors series.
PG3456.A19R63   1999
891.72'3—dc21   99-38692
CIP

Contents

"It is too early
for me to begin writing plays…"

Chekhov, to Suvorin, 12/30/88

Preface

An untitled manuscript, never finished... A melodrama, inciting both praise and condemnation... A romantic comedy, deemed a failure. The first, he tore to pieces; the second, he rewrote till he was sick of it; the third, he forbade to be published. "Stick to short story writing," his critics advised...

These are three early full-length plays of young Anton Chekhov, written in his twenties: rich, bold, exciting, flamboyant plays...flawed plays...youthful plays... The stories of how they were written, and how they were first perceived by Chekhov's public, read like pure melodrama, providing more theatre histrionics than theatre history!

The purpose of this collection is threefold: 1) to introduce lovers of Chekhov to the early plays, with a new translation/adaptation of the unfinished *Platonov* (1880–81), and new translations of *Ivanov* (1887) and *The Wood Demon* (1889); 2) to introduce readers to the young Chekhov, with a short biographical portrait of his twenties; 3) to offer insight into how these early plays served as rich and vital sources for the later, mature works.

This collection is intended to complement my other two volumes of translations published by Smith & Kraus: *Chekhov: Four Plays* (1996) and *Chekhov: The Vaudevilles* (1998). Together, these three volumes constitute the complete collected, translated plays of Anton Chekhov.

While I have titled this collection *The Early Plays,* in my heart I think of it as *The Young Chekhov* — because of the energy and ambition of these exuberant works, and the passion and determination with which its young author dedicated himself to making his mark on his beloved theatre.

ACKNOWLEDGMENTS

To my publishers, Marisa Smith and Eric Kraus, I wish to extend my heartfelt thanks for their love of theatre and of Chekhov, and for their endorsement and support of my work. In addition, I wish to express my deepest appreciation to the following: for editorial assistance and dedication, Matt Cheney and Maria

Headley; for important support, Janet Neipris and all my colleagues and students in the Dramatic Writing Program at New York University's Tisch School of the Arts; for their resources, The Bryn Mawr College Library and Head Librarian Anne Slater; for comments, Andrey Shenin, Julia Smeliansky, Michael Hollinger, D. B. Gilles; for production and design, Julia Hill Gignoux; for additional support, Elizabeth Monteleone and all the others at Smith & Kraus.

I am further indebted to the following actors who participated in the first reading of *Platonov* in March, 1999: Pearce Bunting, Forrest Compton, Julia Gibson, Mira Kingsley, Chris McFarland, Katie McNichol, Joel Rooks, John Rothman, Todd Weeks, Susan Wilder, Bill Wise, Frank Wood. Thanks also to Hilary Missan for casting the reading, and to NYU's Graduate Acting Program, Anne Matthews and Anne Washburn for hosting the reading. Further thanks to the People's Light and Theatre Company in Malvern, Pennsylvania, for hosting a reading of *Ivanov* in October, 1996, and to the following actors who participated: Jeff Bleam, Alda Cortese, Eric Hissom, Louis Lippa, Mary Matthews, Steve Novelli, Kathryn Peterson, Marcia Saunders, Tom Teti, Juanita Vega, Doug Wing.

Notes from the Translator

Bringing *Ivanov* and *The Wood Demon* to life for the contemporary stage requires straightforward translations from the original texts, respectful of the language, the intent, and the spirit of their author. As in my other two published volumes of Chekhov's plays, I have sought to create living translations for the purposes of reading and performance that are faithful to the original Russian language, while at the same time fluid for the contemporary English-speaking actor and accessible to modern audiences.

Bringing Chekhov's first extant play to life for the contemporary stage poses a different challenge. There are so many questions for the translator to address. How does one approach a play that, in its original form, would fill 137 pages of this book? It would run over seven hours long if translated and performed uncut. What is its genre? Its tone is wildly uneven: at times farcical, then broadly comedic, then melodramatic, then moralistic. What about its structure? It is written in four acts, but one act has two long scenes — therefore, in actuality, it is more like a five-act play. Its first act alone would run over two hours in playing time, making it almost the length of the entire *Uncle Vanya!* What about its format? Unlike the later, mature plays, which are rich in ensemble, this youthful endeavor consists primarily of an endless sequence of two-character scenes, one after the other, for most of the 137 pages! And what about the cast? With its twenty characters, it is an embarrassment of dramatic riches, and yet, given some of these portrayals, one might also say it is rich in dramatic embarrassments.

Then there is the confusing issue of the play's identity. Is it the first or second play that Chekhov wrote: the one entitled *Fatherless*, which he wrote alone in Taganrog at the age of seventeen and sent to his brothers in Moscow? Or is it the sprawling, untitled manuscript with a leading character named Platonov, which he wrote while in medical school at the age of twenty-one? And what difference does it make to the translator? In the 1974–82 Soviet edition of Chekhov's *Complete Collected Works and Letters in 30 Volumes* from which I translated this play, the editors title it *Fatherless.* But I agree with most Western literary historians, who argue that the text in the Soviet edition is the later play, not the earlier one, and that, therefore, *Fatherless* is *not* its proper title. If so, then how do I title the play for this collection? *A Play Without a Name,* as some critics refer to it? That seems far too academic for a collection of translations dedicated to keeping the plays of Chekhov alive on the stage...

In truth, any adaptation of *A Play Without a Name* is, ultimately, a "version" of the play. There can be no "standard," definitive adaptation... What to do, then, with this manuscript, in terms of this collection, to keep it consistent and compatible with the faithful translations in my other two collections? Offer it as a straight translation, uncut, unshaped, so that it may serve as resource material, a dramaturgical museum piece? Or adapt it, so that it can live on the contemporary stage? And if so, how?

There arises a tantalizing literary hypothesis: What if Chekhov himself had returned to this untitled play at a later date, in the same secretive way in which he returned to *The Wood Demon* (1889) and quietly, discreetly transformed it into *Uncle Vanya* (1896)? What would he have done? Why not approach the task that way?

I began the daunting work by completing a straightforward translation of the massive, overwritten, uncut manuscript. What a discovery! It is a treasure trove of characters, settings, themes, and leitmotifs — riches from which to draw upon over the years. Perhaps he never rewrote this particular play because it served him better as a resource for all the later ones! And in any event, how can any contemporary adaptor presume to place himself or herself in Chekhov's place?

Ultimately, I found an approach to the text...I chose to celebrate the youthful Chekhov, and to preserve the exuberance, the excess, and the energy of the original manuscript. I did so in order to keep alive the spirit and the intent of the fledgling dramatist, that passionate, ambitious, young medical student so determined to make his debut in the Moscow theatre scene. I set out, first of all, to pare the play down to a playable size, to cut back on what seemed to be superfluous and what didn't quite "work" dramaturgically, so as to show its strengths in high relief. And there are so many strengths! Imagine, for one, a *plot* in a Chekhov play! How important it is to preserve that! The plot in *A Play Without a Name* is a lively one — involving intrigues, seductions, celebrations, dancing, singing, games, drinking, fireworks, trains roaring onstage, fighting, shooting, murder... "Action-packed" is hardly a word one would associate with a Chekhov play — why not preserve this aspect in all its excessive splendor! Secondly, the play is a comedy. It has a vaudevillian energy, complete with numerous entrances, exits, pratfalls, fisticuffs, and excessive physical action. All this must be preserved and celebrated.

This approach also means preserving some of the imperfections of the play: its sharp swerve at the end from a lively comedy to a tragedy, and its moralistic ending, for example. These imperfections don't impede its "playability," and I think the roughness makes it interesting and all the more valuable. After all, preserving some of the dramaturgical immaturities is important in helping us to appreciate both the author's intent and the progress he made in the later years. Why presume to paint over the young portrait with the alleged brush of the mature master, if the master didn't do it himself?!

Here is a summary of my changes: Firstly, I reduced the length of the play from 137 pages to 58, omitting numerous secondary plot lines to the principal story that impaired its lively comedic flow. Secondly, I reduced the cast of characters from twenty to twelve — not for the sake of contemporary production costs, but rather for the sake of graceful and effective playability. I omitted characters who seemed to be doubled and tripled in the original, reducing the numbers of excess suitors, merchants and their sons, servants, and so on.

In this process of paring down the cast, I inevitably made some judgment calls which reflect my own personal taste — in doing away, for example, with Vengerovich Sr. and Jr., two somewhat distastefully drawn characters who resemble a "Shylock and son." (Chekhov and the attitude toward Jews in his day is a topic that merits exploration in another context; suffice it to say, I omitted these characters because they seemed superfluous.) I also don't regret omitting one of the merchants, Bugrov, a rather crude character who seemed more Ostrovskian than Chekhovian. I do regret two omissions: Shcherbuk, a colorful and blustering suitor, whose best lines I gave to the other two remaining ones; and Marko, a tiny, ancient courier. Thankfully, this charming, eccentric creature reappears again in a future incarnation — as old Ferrapont, the watchman in *The Three Sisters*.

What stands before us now is a full-length, youthful, exuberant comedy, markedly different from all the other full-length plays, distinct in the Chekhovian canon.

There are two adaptor's liberties I took that bear mentioning here. I made one slight adjustment to strengthen the play's cumulative energy, with respect to the unities of time and action. In the original manuscript, Chekhov set the first three acts during the afternoon, evening, and night of the summer solstice — and then set Act IV three weeks later. I adjusted the time of Act IV to occur the next morning, thereby unifying the action of the play into a twenty-four-hour period. As such, we can appreciate the cumulative effect of the summer solstice, and the urgency of that exhilarating Russian midsummer night.

The second liberty pertains to the ending. Chekhov intended for Platonov to perish, comedy notwithstanding — and of course I have preserved his original intent. However, I made an adjustment in the choice of the character who brings about the final demise of our hero. My choice is based on a plot line that Chekhov left somewhat unresolved, pertaining to Osip, the play's demonic character. My choice is also in keeping with the Don Juan legend and its moralistic ending, which I believe is the inspiration for Chekhov's comedy. (Chekhov refers to the Don Juan legend in the text of this unfinished play, and later in *The Wood Demon* as well; it is one that clearly intrigued him. He was undoubtedly familiar with Mozart's *Don Giovanni,* probably from a production he saw either in Taganrog or in Moscow.) In the legend, Don Juan is done in, at the end, not by the women he has wronged, but rather by the *commendatore* — the statue of a lover's father whom he has murdered, a dark *deus ex machina* who brings justice down upon the sinner. My adjustment is based on the spirit of this legend, as well as on Chekhov's clear intent to have a moralistic ending of retribution. I leave it to the reader to judge the effectiveness of my choice.

Finally, the title: "Platonov," the name of the central character, is how biographers refer to his first extant play. I thought it would be the simplest, clearest choice for the title of this adaptation. Hence, *Platonov...* May it serve, in this three-volume collection, as the example of the youthful, exuberant Chekhov, the twenty-one-year-old medical student newly arrived in Moscow, in love with life and the theatre.

A Russian *Midsummer Night's Dream...* A Russian *Hamlet... Scenes from Country Life* of earlier, halcyon days... May the three early plays of young Anton Chekhov bring the surprise and delight of discovery to all...

Introduction

For decades, scholars, biographers, literary historians and critics have pored over what they call the mature years of Anton Chekhov — his thirties and early forties, corresponding to the 1890s and the early 1900s. The writing of the major plays *(The Seagull, Uncle Vanya, The Three Sisters,* and *The Cherry Orchard)*, the founding of the Moscow Art Theatre, his relationship to Stanislavsky, his marriage to the actress Olga Knipper, his declining health, his tragic and untimely death — these theatrical and biographical events are universally known, minutely scrutinized, and lovingly re-examined. No moment, no letter, no story, no detail has been overlooked during this period of his life and work.

Less attention has been paid to the early years — Chekhov's twenties, corresponding to the decade of the 1880s. The reason is apparent: The plays he wrote in this period — the vaudevilles and the early full-lengths, *Platonov, Ivanov,* and *The Wood Demon* — are deemed less worthy, less weighty. They are seldom performed in this country, largely overlooked, and therefore unfamiliar to most. To some extent, this is understandable: *Platonov* is unfinished, *Ivanov* is a flawed melodrama whose success today relies heavily on the charismatic casting of its protagonist, and *The Wood Demon* was deemed unfit for publication by none other than the author himself. And, in any event, he later transformed this early work into *Uncle Vanya* — why perform the former if we have the later masterpiece!

Despite their major flaws, however, the revisiting of these three plays will prove to be a rewarding effort for theatre artists, scholars, and lovers of Chekhoviana. Firstly, they reveal the young Chekhov in all his glory — bipolar in his artistic endeavors, mercurial, daring, and extreme. Secondly, they are blueprints for his mature work, containing the seminal characters, settings and themes that appear again and again in his later masterpieces. Thirdly, they are surprisingly stageworthy in their own right, and merit new productions and exploration. Particularly in the case of *Platonov*, which is rarely rendered from the Russian into English, there is the discovery of a vibrant, youthful, irreverent comedy that will surprise all lovers of the mature Chekhov.

How markedly different these early plays are! It is startling and noteworthy, when we consider all three plays together. *Platonov,* an exuberant comedy inspired by the Don Juan legend, differs markedly from the dark, melodramatic *Ivanov* with its complex Russian-style Hamlet figure, which in turn contrasts sharply with the romantic comedy of *The Wood Demon*. These differences attest to the youthful energy, to the boldness he felt in those days of experimentation, to a flamboyance and a sense of theatrical adventure, as his passion for theatre burned bright. He was determined to make his mark on the Russian stage, and he was searching for the form in which to do it. It was not until much later, in his thirties, with *The Seagull*, when he realized, in the words of his character Treplev, that

> It is not about forms, old forms, new forms, it's about writing freely…from the soul.
>
> The Seagull, *Act IV*

For those of us whose lives have been enriched by the later plays, the early plays will come as a surprise, a delight, and an epiphany. Above all, they will give us insight into the growth and development of the mature dramatist.

Portrait of an Artist as a Young Man

We all know the portrait of the mature Chekhov. Familiar paintings show him, typically, seated in an armchair, head thrown back slightly, the pince-nez giving him a reserved, almost unapproachable look. Photographs reveal a gentle, reserved, self-effacing man, modest and wise, a quietly suffering invalid and martyred doctor elevated almost to literary sainthood — and yet at the same time elusive, aloof, inscrutable, mysterious. Note the oblique titles of studies of his life: *The Real Chekhov, A Spirit Set Free, Observer Without Illusion,* and so on. Biographers are still searching for "the true Chekhov," his shadow lurking behind his plays and stories, his true identity always out of reach…

What a contrast, then, to catch a glimpse of the young Chekhov — the exuberant, gregarious, mischievous, almost hyperactive Chekhov of his twenties; the young doctor Chekhov of comedy, author of hundreds upon hundreds of humorous short stories and a dozen vaudevilles; the darling of Moscow; the blithe spirit who, had he not contracted consumption, may never have experimented with the darker tones in his work. Here is a brief overview of the youthful years…

1860–1879: The Taganrog Period

> In my childhood, I had no childhood…
> *Chekhov to friends, from Aleksandr's memoirs*

The most important spiritual and intellectual development of Anton Chekhov — the one that was to shape his course as a dramatist — occurred during the least-documented period of his life, from the ages of sixteen to nineteen. For an understanding of Chekhov the artist, one must revisit his years in Taganrog, to appreciate the difficult circumstances in which he grew up and how his character was formulated in spite of them.

I always relish reading the scant information available about Chekhov's childhood — especially the reminiscences of his brothers, Aleksandr and Mikhail. From these personal accounts, one receives a vivid portrait of a chaotic, crisis-laden childhood of poverty, pressure, and family strife — an abusive, rigid, disciplinarian father; a meek, ineffectual mother; and six cowering children in abject, impoverished circumstances. Anton's father was a shopkeeper, and he forced his five sons and one daughter to work in the shop whenever they were not in school. A devout zealot, moreover, he would wake them at two in the morning to practice for church choir.

As an antidote to this childhood suffering, Anton developed compensatory survival tactics that were to become the foundation of his love for the theatre. An exuberant comic and ham performer, he organized his brothers and sisters in parlor theatricals to diffuse the tension of the authoritarian home atmosphere, himself playing all the lead parts.

One can feel the palpable relief of young Anton, age sixteen, when his maelstrom of a family left their home in Taganrog for Moscow. Chekhov lived on his own — facing the creditors from whom his father had fled, begging and borrowing from remaining relatives, tutoring, taking in boarders to make ends meet. It was during the years from age sixteen to nineteen (1876–79), according to Mikhail, when Anton spent hours in the library reading voraciously, and above all, indulging in his supreme passion — the theatre, attending productions of Shakespeare, French farce and vaudeville, and other stock theatrical fare of the day. He saw *Hamlet, King Lear, The Merchant of Venice,* numerous Ostrovsky plays, Gogol's *The Inspector General,* Griboedov's *Wit Works Woe,* and even a dramatization of *Uncle Tom's Cabin,* among many other productions. As young boys, Anton and his brothers used to steal into the provincial theatres, wearing a variety of outrageous disguises. Now, free from parental scrutiny, he could attend openly.

Most significantly, Chekhov began writing plays during this period — youthful attempts that he sent to his brothers in Moscow. Mikhail mentions a handful of vaudevilles and a serious drama entitled *Fatherless (Bezotsovshchina)*. According to his reminiscences, Mikhail kept these works in safekeeping, but when Anton arrived in Moscow after finishing secondary school, he tore the full-length drama to pieces. The vaudevilles were lost amidst the chaos of the family's frequent relocations. Thus, no theatrical writings from this early period survive.

1879–1890: "To Moscow! To Moscow!"
Irina, in The Three Sisters.

> As soon as I finish school, I'll fly to Moscow on wings. I do love Moscow so much!
>
> *to cousin Mikhail, 11/4/77*

Vibrant, exciting, hectic — these were the Moscow years. They were crammed with activities of all kinds, including family, educational, medical, literary, and theatrical. During these ten years, living with his chaotic family, serving as its sole financial supporter, attending medical school, practicing medicine, writing hundreds of short stories, all at a feverish tempo, Chekhov also managed to write three full-length plays and eleven short ones, thus launching his career as a playwright as well!

When young Anton arrived in Moscow in 1879 at the age of nineteen, full of dreams of the glamorous Moscow theatre life, he moved into the family's two-room basement flat in the Drachovka quarter and found himself almost immediately in the role of head of the family. His two elder brothers were seldom at home, and his father had a shopkeeper's assistant job that kept him away, except on Sundays. Anton assumed these responsibilities, first by moving his family from the tenement and helping to raise his three younger siblings as best he could — even though the family quarters also served as temporary lodgings for visiting relatives and various lady-friends of the two older brothers. Anton entered medical school in September, 1879, following a rigorous academic program, but spending more time with his brothers' art school friends than with his own medical school classmates.

Within months after his arrival, young Anton began submitting sketches and stories to numerous Moscow publications with colorful names such as *Dragonfly, Fragments,* and *Splinters.* Several hundred of his pieces, ranging from one-line cartoon captions to humorous short stories to novellas, were published in these popular magazines throughout his medical school years. He wrote under the name of "Antosha Chekhonte" (a nickname given to him by a Taganrog secondary school teacher), as well as other *noms de plume,* including "My Brother's Brother" and "A Doctor Without Patients." At first, his publishers paid the eager young student with theatre tickets or pairs of trousers in lieu of money. Eventually, he would be given a certain number of kopeks per line, and his income from short story writing eventually became the main source of financial support for his family. It was thus that he developed his craft as a writer of humorous short stories, a skill that would soon gain him fame.

During these years, however, Chekhov's dream of writing for the theatre was still his greatest passion. He submitted a sprawling, untitled manuscript of a full-length play to Yermolova, the leading lady of the prestigious Maly Theatre. The identity of this manuscript is cloaked in obscurity and confusion — indeed, its determination reads like a mystery story, one that will be told later in this introduction. In any event, this massive, unfinished work was rejected by the theatre and returned to its offended author, who destroyed it.

Thus passed Anton's medical school years — engaging in his studies, shouldering the responsibility for the support of his family, and still finding time to write! And indeed, the conditions were desperate:

> ...in the neighboring room howls the child of a distant relative who is living with us now, in another room father reads aloud to mother from *Angel of My Memory...* Someone has wound up a music box, and I hear "La Belle Helene."...I feel like running away to the country, but it's already one in the morning... There couldn't be more vile conditions than these for a writer. My bed is occupied by a relative who's just arrived, who keeps on trying to start a conversation with me about medicine. [...] The conditions are incomparable.
>
> *to Leykin, 8/21–22/83*

A portrait of the young doctor Chekhov emerges from family and friends' reminiscences: a tall young man, with a kind, open face, curly chestnut hair and hazel eyes, vital, lively, witty, gregarious, and mischievous. In his reminiscences, the writer Korolenko observed that young Anton's eyes sparkled with wit and gaiety, and yet, at the same time there was something much deeper there as well, something that would find expression in a different way. Evidently he was quite attractive to women and had a great number of female admirers — an aspect of his youth that would continue throughout his life. Some biographers imply that he was quite a "ladies' man," providing insight into the portraits of Platonov, Ivanov, and later, Trigorin.

Chekhov graduated in the spring of 1884, and he began practicing medicine that summer in the provincial town of Voskresensk, where a military troop was stationed (providing material for *The Three Sisters* that he was to write years later). It was also in that year that he experienced his first lung hemorrhage. From 1884 on, he suffered serious lung hemorrhages once or twice a year, as well as attacks of dysentery, hemorrhoids, and bronchitis. The taste of blood was often in his mouth. A less optimistic spirit might have succumbed to these vicissitudes, but in the case of Chekhov, his capacity for *joie de vivre* was boundless. He adored Moscow life, his summers in the country, fishing, the company of friends and artists; he loved champagne, women, oysters, soirées, music. He rarely complained, and he avoided talking about his health. Instead, he threw himself vigorously into his literary career, which was indeed blossoming.

The years 1884–87 marked Chekhov's ascent to the status of Russia's most famous short story writer, and one of the most eminent young authors in all of Russia. His productivity was remarkable — he wrote almost 300 stories during this period, and he graduated from his *nom de plume* of Antosha Chekhonte, author of humorous sketches, to Anton Chekhov, contributor to the most prestigious publication in Russia, the St. Petersburg *New Times.* Suvorin, its venerable publisher and Chekhov's newfound mentor, introduced him to the most famous writers in Russia, and Chekhov became the darling of both the Muscovite and St. Petersburg *literati*, protegé of the great literary figures of the 1880s, and the object of admiration of his contemporaries.

With all this praise and recognition at such a young age, Chekhov began to feel the pressure.

> All my hopes lie in the future. I am only twenty-six. Perhaps
> I shall manage to do something…
>
> *to Grigorovich, 3/28/86*

Serious literature is what he wanted to write, but what he was producing, and with such facility and alacrity, was humorous and popular fare. This was not enough for him. He wanted to write for the theatre, his continuing and abiding passion. He had written several one-acts during this period, but it was drama he longed to write.

So when the offer to write a full-length commissioned play came from the prestigious Korsh Theatre in 1887, no wonder he leaped at the invitation! Finally, a point of dramatic focus had presented itself, and the theatre had given him *carte blanche!* At last, he had the opportunity to make his mark as a serious dramatist, "to create a type of literary significance," to be the Russian Shakespeare, to accomplish on the stage what Pushkin, Lermontov, and Turgenev before him had accomplished in novels! He threw himself into the task of writing the play, *Ivanov,* referring to it as his first full-length play (he hadn't recovered from the rejection of the earlier manuscript in 1881). The premiere caused a sensation: There were wildly divergent responses, from ecstatic critical praise to fist fights in the lobby to vociferous condemnation. Chekhov was now catapulted into fame as a dramatist as well as a writer of short stories. He was the toast of Moscow.

The opening of *Ivanov* unleashed a whirlwind of feverish theatre activity. Chekhov was transported, seduced by the fame, the recognition, and the glamour of the theatre. During the eighteen months following the opening, he plunged into a feverish bout of writing vaudevilles, turning out no less than five, while at the same time rewriting *Ivanov* for the St. Petersburg opening. "Vaudevilles spout out of me like oil from the depths of Baku," he wrote (to Suvorin, 12/23/88). The most famous among these, *The Bear* and *The Proposal,* were widely praised by all, including Tolstoy and the czar himself. They brought Chekhov increased acclaim and even unexpected financial remuneration. "I shall live on my *Bear* and on mushrooms," Chekhov wrote years later to Suvorin (8/16/92).

The years 1887–88, a period of feverish theatre activity, were also ones of sharp mood swings for Chekhov. The euphoria of recognition alternated with attacks of self-doubt as to his abilities as a serious dramatist. Even as he struggled to rewrite *Ivanov,* he knew that it was not entirely successful. The comedic vein was still where he was most comfortable and confident, and this caused him great frustration, ambivalence, and self-doubt. He feared he was not yet ready to write serious plays.

If 1887–88 were years of intensely theatrical activity, then 1888–90 were the years of taking stock. In October, 1888, his colleagues and his country, in the form of the Imperial Academy of Sciences, acknowledged his accomplishments with the prestigious Pushkin Prize in Literature. Here was an occasion for him to pause and gain perspective.

From 1888–90, the euphoria was tempered, and Chekhov became more contemplative and introspective about his life and the theatre. It was in those years that he wrote his most beautiful letters about art and about his craft. While he philosophized in his letters about writing for the stage and the role of the writer, he continued turning out his public-pleasing vaudevilles, almost as an aside: *Tatyana Repina, A Tragedian in Spite of Himself,* and *The Wedding,* all in 1889. A darker tone, however, began to creep into his prose, with serious stories, including *A Dreary Story* and *The Bet.* He also sustained the two greatest failures of his literary career; a long novel — *Stories from the Lives of my Friends* — that never passed the censor and was subsequently destroyed by its author, and his fourth full-length play, *The Wood Demon.* While it was a fairly productive period, Chekhov clearly lacked a strong literary focus.

In 1889, a cartoon appeared in the literary journal *Oskolki (Fragments).* The drawing depicted Chekhov driving a cart drawn by three figures — Ivanov, a bear, and a wood demon. The cart stood at the crossroads whose signs indicate "Road to Prose" and "Road to Drama." Reports were that Chekhov took it good-naturedly, but clearly it depicted the literary intersection at which he stood. He was writing, he was moving in a direction…but which one? Comedy or tragedy? The short form or the long form? Prose or drama?

The death of his brother Nikolai of consumption and the failure of *The Wood Demon* in 1889 were two traumatic events, serving as catalysts for the end of "the Moscow Years." Tired of the glamour of Moscow theatre life, smarting from the bad reviews of *The Wood Demon,* frustrated by his feelings of inadequacy as a dramatist, facing the reality of his own progressing illness, Chekhov left Moscow and writing altogether for almost a year to make his legendary trip across Russia to the island of Sakhalin, to study the penal codes of the prisoner's colony there. He knew he wasn't ready yet to become a serious playwright — but at least he could perform serious philanthropic duties. The bright, youthful Moscow years — the hectic years of success, fame, and glamour were over. He began a long journey and a slow spiritual conversion… The results, to be seen years later, were a series of four great plays, plays of his mature years, plays that changed writing for the theatre in the twentieth century.

The Plays

Platonov: A Play Without a Title

No issue in Chekhov's *oeuvre* is more mysterious, obscure, and confusing than the identity of his first extant play, herein called *Platonov.* Scholars cannot even agree upon its title, let alone when it was written, its place in the Chekhovian canon, or even its literary value! Indeed, not until recently is the attention that it truly deserves being paid to this manuscript.

First, there are the mysterious circumstances surrounding the discovery of the manuscript. (The most recent comprehensive account of these circumstances can be found in Michael Frayn's introduction to his own version of *Platonov,* entitled *Wild Honey* [see Bibliography].) The story goes that in 1920, sixteen years after Chekhov's death, officials from the Soviet Literary Committee opened a safe-deposit box in Moscow belonging to one Marya Yegorovna Chekhova. In it they found papers, photographs, and a manuscript of an unproduced, full-length play. The manuscript consisted of 134 closely handwritten pages. The title page was missing and the lower half of the last clean page had been torn off. The text had been corrected many times in black and blue pencil, as well as ink. It was not dated.

The process of identifying this newly found manuscript reads like a detective story. The question, to this day definitively unresolved, is whether *Platonov* is the *first* or *second* full-length play that the young Chekhov wrote — or were these two manuscripts in fact one and the same. His youngest brother, Mikhail, sheds most light on the mystery in his *Reminiscences*. According to Mikhail, there were indeed two separate early manuscripts: The first, entitled *Fatherless*, is one which the schoolboy Anton sent to his brothers in Moscow some time around 1877–78 from Taganrog, where Anton had been left by his family to finish his secondary schooling. Mikhail writes that he kept the manuscript in safekeeping, but when Anton arrived, he destroyed the only existing copy. End of mystery…or is it?

In these same *Reminiscences*, Mikhail also refer to a second, unproduced full-length play. This one he remembers as a voluminous, untitled manuscript that Anton wrote after his arrival in Moscow while in medical school, in the early 1880s, living with his parents, three younger siblings, and other extended family members in their impossibly cramped quarters. Eager to have it produced, Anton asked Mikhail to copy it out by hand. Mikhail remembers it as a cumbersome play in the manner of a French melodrama and extremely overwritten, with "a railway train, horse thieves and a lynching scene." According to Mikhail, the plot was so exciting that while copying it out, it "stopped his heart"! (Knowing the plotless nature of Chekhov's later plays, this response is especially noteworthy!)

Anton had great dreams for this sprawling, unfinished work, according to Mikhail. He sent it to Yermolova, the leading lady of the preeminent Maly Theatre, with the high hopes of securing a production and thereby making a dramatic debut in the Moscow theatre. According to Mikhail, it came back to Chekhov with a rejection note. Crushed, Chekhov tore this manuscript to pieces, but his sister fortunately had saved the rough draft from which Mikhail had made the copies for the Maly Theatre. This is the copy that the devoted Masha, on the eve of the Russian revolution, sequestered away in the safe-deposit box with other memorabilia, at great personal peril.

Fatherless…A Play Without a Title… We have the title of the former and the text of the latter… Are they, therefore, one play or two plays? According to the

Soviets, they are one and the same. The second, untitled play, whose leading character is named Platonov, was first published in 1923 under the title of the first play, *Fatherless,* the editors thereby subscribing to the one-play theory. To compound the confusion for contemporary translators, including myself, the editors of the *Complete Collected Works and Letters of Anton Chekhov in 30 Volumes*, published in Soviet Russia in 1974–82, perpetuate the one-play theory as well. However, thanks to the careful research of British scholars and translators, most notably David Magarshack and Michael Frayn, the current consensus of opinion in the West is that there were indeed *two* plays, that the text of the adolescent *Fatherless* is lost to us, and that the second, untitled manuscript, most commonly referred to in scholarship as *Platonov* after its central character, was written during the winter of his second year of medical school (1880–81).

Versions of *Platonov* have appeared in the West sporadically over the decades since its discovery. It was first translated into English in 1930 in a recklessly edited version entitled *That Worthless Fellow, Platonov.* Other English versions since then have been entitled *A Play Without a Title, A Play Without a Name, Don Juan in the Russian Manner, A Country Scandal.* British translators Ronald Hingley and David Magarshak offered complete uncut translations in the 1960s. Recently, thanks to the fine stage version by British playwright Michael Frayn entitled *Wild Honey* (1985) and the charming film adaptation by Russian filmmaker Nikita Mikhalkov entitled *An Unfinished Piece for Player Piano* (1977), the richness of this marvelous, youthful creation has again been brought to light.

Fatherless is lost to us forever, but its contents haunt us, like a ghost from Chekhov's past. "In my childhood, I had no childhood," said Chekhov about his years in Taganrog. In the mature plays of Anton Chekhov, the character of the father is conspicuously absent. We can only imagine what the contents of the play might have been. As it is, we are left to the daunting task of dealing with *A Play Without a Name* — a. k. a. *Platonov* — assessing its literary value, and preparing it for the contemporary stage.

The Value of *Platonov*

In its original state, *Platonov* is, quite simply, unproduceable. With its uncut length it would play over seven hours on the stage! Its twenty characters and clumsy, immature structure (an interminable sequence of two character scenes, one after the other, with hardly any ensemble scenes) render it unwieldy and awkward. The first act alone is almost the length of the entire *Uncle Vanya!* With such malleable clay in the hands of the adapter, no wonder there are so many divergent "versions" of Platonov!

And yet, in its original form, what rich raw material there is! What a treasure trove! In this youthful, massive, disorganized work lies the source of all the later, full-length plays — the characters, the settings, the themes, the tonalities. It contains the many "voices" of Chekhov: the farcical, the comedic, and the melodramatic all in one sprawling draft. Moreover, it presents an articulated view of the times, in which the fledgling dramatist reveals a passion for his country, a sense of literary tradition, and a precocious insight into his world and its changes at the *fin de siècle*. Above all, it reveals a youthfulness, a vibrancy, an eagerness, a flamboyance, a sense of adventure, and a bold appetite for experimentation.

Let us first savor the endless parade of characters — twenty in number! — who reappear throughout the Chekhovian canon. At first glance, we instantly recognize the prototypes who inhabit the later, greater plays, the gallery of portraits of all strata of Russian society: the impoverished lady of the estate, the local landowner, the village schoolmaster, the doctor, the emerging capitalist, the elderly eccentric, the ancient servant, the knavish lackey... There is Sergey, son of a general, a spoiled, over-educated, privileged, foolish young man, whose estate is being auctioned out from under him, who will never know the meaning of work — predecessor of Tusenbach in *The Three Sisters*. There is his young wife, Sofya Yegorovna, fresh, innocent, and young — predecessor of the sheltered, radiant Irina in *The Three Sisters,* full of naive notions of work and idealistic causes, oblivious to the realities of the world. Then there are the landowners Glagolyev and Shcherbuk, predecessors of Sorin in *The Seagull* and Pishchik in *The Cherry Orchard.* There is the delightful eccentric, Ivan Ivanovich Triletsky, a retired colonel, reliving his army days throughout the play — a predecessor to the dotty old sea captain in Chekhov's vaudeville, *The Wedding.* There is Petrin, son of a serf, who is everyone's creditor, and, as his successor Lopakhin does in *The Cherry Orchard,* buys up property all around.

Even at this early age, from the pen of a neophyte dramatist, we marvel at how free the character portrayals are, how flamboyant, how extreme, compared with the later plays. There is Anna Petrovna, the merry, impoverished widow whose estate is about to be sold — a predecessor of Lyubov Andreevna of *The Cherry Orchard.* And yet, how much wilder and bolder she is in this youthful work! Her sexuality is right on the surface, even more so than her other descendant, Arkadina in *The Seagull.* She drinks freely (straight from the bottle!), she rides horseback, she flirts openly with numerous men, and aggressively seduces Platonov; and yet, at the same time, she exudes a clarity, a straightforwardness, an honesty and strength of character that is fresh and marvelous. In short, she is magnificent! One of her admirers, Nikolai Ivanovich Triletsky, is Chekhov's first doctor, to be followed by the other great portraits — Lvov, Khrushchov, Dorn, Astrov,

Chebutykhin. Unlike his successors, he is not the voice of reason, nor is he the *porte parole* of the author. On the contrary, he is irresponsible, indolent, and indulgent; he eats and drinks, ignores his patients, and scoffs at the practice of medicine. His is a bold portrait — that of a doctor who suffers from the disease of the times. His sister, Sasha, is one of the most beautiful female characters in the Chekhovian canon. Her religious devotion, her selflessness, and her ability, above all, to love, make her a predecessor to Chekhov's spiritual women — Anna Petrovna in *Ivanov* and Sonya in *Uncle Vanya*. And the melodrama of *Platonov* tests her faith in a more active and extreme way than any of the later works — we see her throw herself under a train and take poison for love!

The true phenomenon of the play is its central character. In creating Platonov, Chekhov reveals both a reverence for literary tradition and a remarkable ambition. For Platonov is a bold and deliberate composite of numerous classical portraits from both Russian and European literature. Foremost, in my view, he is drawn in the tradition of Don Juan — that compulsive, reckless womanizer who repels and attracts us at the same time with his seductive charm and his passion for life, and who is punished in the end. Equally, he is Hamlet in Russian translation — ineffective, brooding, erratic, sometimes cruel. Platonov is also a descendant of the romantic, Byronic antihero celebrated in nineteenth-century Russian novels — the "superfluous men" like Pechorin of Lermontov's *A Hero of Our Times* (1840), beautiful, moody, damned, unstable, aloof, disenchanted, acting out only to relieve the tedium of life or to avenge himself on the society he despises. There is also a little of Pushkin's Eugene Onegin (1823–31) in him — that proud young nobleman, so self-centered and so cruel in love. Then there is the influence of Chatsky from Griboedov's social satire *Wit Works Woe* (1822–24), the social conscience of the nineteenth-century Russian intellectual, railing at society's injustices, knowing he can do nothing to change them.

Platonov…legacy of many literary personae, six portraits combined… The neophyte dramatist was so passionately intent on creating a "literary type of significance" for the Russian stage and improving on the tradition of the "superfluous man" that he attempted them all in one. From Platonov come so many Chekhovian characters. His *ennui* is inherited by Ivanov and Treplev *(The Seagull);* his subtlety and indifferent cruelty pass on to Trigorin *(The Seagull);* his demonic side lives again in Solyony *(The Three Sisters)*. Platonov had hopes of being a Byron or a Christopher Columbus; Vanya had hopes of being a Schopenhauer or a Dostoevsky. Ivanov and Vanya, like Platonov, wish to run away to a new life. The schoolteachers Medvedenko *(The Seagull)* and Kulygin *(The Three Sisters)* are foolish, meek, and penitent — living the hopeless provincial life against which their predecessor, Platonov, railed in vain.

In the final analysis, we don't fully understand what makes Platonov "Platonov" — and this is, in my view, an achievement of the young dramatist. For unexplained behavior is what makes the characters of the later plays so real, so human, so true to life. At only twenty years of age, the young Dr. Chekhov already showed an intuitive understanding of the human psyche that was to distinguish the mature Dr. Chekhov as one of the most astute observers of human behavior in dramatic literature.

Two rare portrayals shine forth from the throng of characters who crowd this chaotic young play. They are unique in the Chekhovian canon and are therefore especially notable. First and foremost is the peasant Osip, local horse thief and criminal — an exotic creature with a bizarre blend of violence and benevolence, menace and kindness, crime and compassion, brutality and spirituality — with a capacity, above all, to love. As Chekhov's only peasant-mystic of the stage, he is unique...and funny, as well. An incarnation of Osip named Merik appears only briefly again in Chekhov's one-act play *On the High Road* in a seedy waystation bar. Apart from Osip and Merik, "low-life" criminal-saint types never appear on the Chekhovian stage and live only in his short stories. The fact that Chekhov never brings him back in a full-length play makes him all the more precious here.

Another unique character is Grekova, the little student of chemistry — fiercely intelligent and dedicated, and at the same time extremely emotional. Her gullibility reappears in the character of Varya in *The Cherry Orchard*, but by Chekhov's own description, Varya is not at all bright, so she can hardly count as a reincarnation of Grekova. No — here, Chekhov was painting a feminist portrait of the period in response to the burgeoning issue of women's emancipation in the 1880s. Grekova's portrait is interesting for another reason: It is complex. She is both intelligent and at the same time naive and impressionable, rendering her somewhat foolish — a clever and ironic blend of traits that again suggests a subtle parody of feminism. Already, at such a young age, Chekhov was creating complex characters with fascinating dualities.

Yet another value of *Platonov* is that it is gives us a view of the times. *Platonov* is the young Chekhov's first and flamboyant attempt to paint a large canvas of social and economic evolution in Russia at the end of the nineteenth century — as well as a prophecy of the future. The decay of the old social order, the rise of the new bourgeoisie, the naive attempts at social reform, the gentry's ineffectuality, erosion, and gradual extinction — this is Russia in the 1880s, and this is the canvas that the ambitious young Chekhov boldly painted in *Platonov*.

Important Chekhovian themes of the later plays are defined and explored in *Platonov*. One is the loss of the estate. Anna Petrovna is in jeopardy of losing the estate of her late husband, and she seeks to play off one suitor against another while she determines the best offer. This plot line is one of so many in this sprawling work that it ultimately gets confused and obscured. When Chekhov finally mastered the craft of playwriting, he made the loss of the estate the all-encompassing metaphor for the decline of Russia, in his final play, *The Cherry Orchard*.

Above all, it is important to note that the tone of *Platonov* is supremely comedic. In fact, Chekhov is experimenting with many tonalities here: romantic comedy, vaudevillian comedy, and comedy of manners and morals. And yet there is the ending, with its sudden, melodramatic shift in tone. This coexistence of comedy and tragedy in one work sets a precedent for all the plays to come. It was in the later work that he was able to do away with the sharp edges, the dramatic lurches, and to create an effective blend of the comedic and the tragic.

How did he accomplish so much in one play? Reading the original manuscript, one speculates that he may have written it over a period of time, perhaps bringing forward some characters and themes from the lost *Fatherless*. We shall never know the process whereby this sprawling play was written. What seems evident is the determination that drove him to write it. Somehow, during his second year of medical school, under the most adverse of circumstances, Chekhov was able to sit down and write this play. Imagine the adversities, the frustrations, the distractions! This play stands as a loving testimony of Chekhov's passion for the theatre, and of his fierce ambition to make his mark.

Marvelous and messy, unwieldy and incomparable, immature and uncontrollable, *Platonov* remains as our richest resource for appreciating the youthful genesis of the later, greater plays. And adaptations of it, including, hopefully, the one in this collection, will provide the audience with a vital impression of the young, exuberant Chekhov.

Ivanov

I have created a type of literary significance.
to Aleksandr, 10/10–12/87

I wanted to be original…
to Aleksandr, 10/23/87

It is too early for me to begin writing plays…
to Suvorin, 12/30/88

Chekhov's medical school years were significant in other ways, in terms of his development as a serious dramatist. We know that during the second year (1881), he was asked to write a review of *Hamlet,* which was being performed in Moscow in a Russian translation by Polevoy. The play had been the passion of his boyhood — translations of *Hamlet* and *Macbeth* were the first books Chekhov ever owned. Now he was able to write about it, sanctifying *Hamlet* and bemoaning the lack of well-educated, well-trained Russian actors to perform it, as well as the dearth of new Russian plays. One can almost sense a determination to write the Russian *Hamlet* from this early passion for the play.

Chekhov had to create *Platonov* before he created *Ivanov.* After all, the youthful Chekhov was gifted with the muse of comedy, not tragedy. And yet tragedy was what he longed to make his mark with on the Russian stage. The viewing of *Hamlet* confirmed it.

Knowing he wasn't ready to write a tragedy, and at the same time, desperately eager to write for the theatre, he turned to the writing of vaudevilles — short comedic parodies of the French genre that were the theatrical rage of the decade, with which he had been experimenting since his Taganrog days. The two he wrote in 1886 and early 1887 were *On the Harmful Effect of Tobacco* and *Swan Song* respectively. In their first incarnations, they were light and farcical, and yet, in their second draft version, he began adding darker tones, as he had already begun to do in his short stories. Clearly, by 1887, Chekhov was in a period of growth and change, but he hadn't found the literary and theatrical form with which to express it.

No wonder, then, that he jumped at the invitation from the Korsh Theatre for a full-length, commissioned work. Finally, a point of dramatic focus had presented itself, and a prestigious Moscow theatre had given him *carte blanche!* Here, at last, was the opportunity to make his mark as a serious dramatist, to accomplish on the stage what Pushkin, Lermontov, and Turgenev before him had accomplished in novels, to create a type "of literary significance," but in his own fashion. In a burst of excitement and inspiration, he sat down and within ten days time delivered to Korsh a full-length play entitled *Ivanov.* To his brother Aleksandr, he wrote brashly:

> I wrote this play off the top of my head, almost, after one conversation with Korsh. Went to bed, thought of a theme, wrote it down…and in ten days time, too… As for the merits of the play, I cannot be the judge. It came out to be suspiciously short in length. Everyone likes it. Korsh hasn't found a single flaw or any mistakes in the stage directions, for that matter, which proves how sharp and discerning my critics are. It is the first

time I've ever written a play, *ergo* mistakes are unavoidable. The plot is fairly complicated and not at all crude. I end each act like a short story. All the acts run on peacefully and quietly, but at the end I give the audience a punch in the nose.

to Aleksandr, 10/10–12/87

Clearly, he was giddy from the apparent ease with which he had written *Ivanov* and naive as to the process of writing for the theatre. No wonder, then, with this youthful sense of over-confidence, preparation for the production proved to be traumatic to him. The euphoria of having written the play quickly evaporated. Things went badly from the first day of rehearsal.

To begin with, Korsh promised me ten rehearsals and gave me only four, of which only two can be called rehearsals, because the other two were more like tournaments for the actors to display their skill in argument and verbal abuse. Only Davydov and Glama knew their parts; the rest of them relied on the prompter and inner conviction.

to Aleksandr, 11/20/87

In vain, Chekhov went to Korsh, the producer, to ask if he would withdraw the play. Chekhov's publisher advised him to stop interfering with the rehearsal process, but he refused.

November 19, 1887: The story of the premiere of *Ivanov* is legendary. The dramatist described it in a letter to his brother Aleksandr, providing one of the most colorful accounts of any theatrical event in his career. It reads like a tragicomedy in and of itself. Moreover, it certainly explains Chekhov's highly erratic behavior in the months to follow:

Act One. I'm backstage in a little box, that looks like a prisoner's cell. The family is in an orchestra box: they're all trembling. Contrary to all expectations, I feel calm and collected. The actors are deeply agitated; they're tense and keep crossing themselves. Curtain up. Enter the leading man, unsure of himself, unfamiliar with the lines…from the very first moment I don't even recognize my own play. Kiselevsky, whom I was counting on most, didn't get one of his lines right. Not a single one. He simply made it all up. That and the directorial blunders aside, the first act was a huge success. Many curtain calls.

Act Two: There's a crowd of people onstage. Guests. Not knowing their lines, they get all muddled and talk nonsense. Every word is like a knife in my back. But — O Muse! — this act is a great hit, too! The entire cast gets a curtain call, and they call me out, too…twice. Everyone congratulates me on my success.

Act Three: The acting isn't too bad. Again, it's a huge success. I get called out three times. Talent and virtue reign supreme.

Act Four: Scene I. Again, it's not going too badly. There are curtain calls. Then comes an interminable, exhausting intermission. The audience, unaccustomed to a break and a visit to the buffet between scenes, starts complaining. The curtain goes up on scene two. It's a beautiful set — the table is laid for the wedding scene. The orchestra plays a flourish; enter the groomsmen; they're drunk, you see, so therefore they feel obliged to cut up and clown around… It's a brawl, it's a disgrace, and I'm horrified. Whereupon Kiselevsky enters; it's his most poetic passage, he's supposed to be acting his heart out, but since my Kiselevsky doesn't know his lines — he's as drunk as a cobbler, you see — the brief poetic dialogue is painfully drawn out and awful. The audience is at a loss. The hero dies at the end of the play from a mortal insult. Meanwhile, the audience is so tired and bored that they couldn't care less; and they can't figure out why he died, anyway. (This ending was the actors' idea, not mine; I have another version.) During one of the curtain calls, I could hear distinct hissing, although it was drowned out by applause and stamping feet. In general, I'm exhausted and irritated. In fact, I'm disgusted, even though the play was a solid hit… Theatre lovers say that they've never seen such a disturbance in a theatre, ever, nor as much general applauding and hissing and brawling as they heard at my play. And there's never been a playwright at the Korsh who took a curtain call after the second act.

The play will be performed for the second time on the 23rd, with the alternate ending and several other changes — and I *am* getting rid of those groomsmen.

to Aleksandr, 11/20/87

His brother Mikhail, present at the theatre on opening night, corroborates this report, explaining that the public expectations for Chekhovian comedy only compounded the trauma of *Ivanov's* premiere.

> Many expected *Ivanov* to be a gay farce in the style of [Anton's] stories which were appearing at that time in *Oskolki,* a humorous publication… At that time, too, the Korsh Theatre produced only light comedies and farces… I was present at the first performance and remember what took place in the theatre. It was unbelievable. The audience leapt from their seats, some applauded, some hissed loudly and whistled, others stamped their feet. The chairs in the pit were moved around and mixed up to the point that nobody could find his seat; people in the boxes became alarmed and did not know whether to stay or to leave the theatre. It is difficult to imagine what happened in the gallery. A fight broke out between those who hissed and those who applauded.
>
> *from Mikhail Chekhov,* Chekhov and the Theatre

To this account, Chekhov himself added, in a letter to brother Aleksandr (11/24/87):

> …the premiere caused more excitement in the audience and backstage than the prompter had seen in all his thirty-two years in the theatre. People were screaming and yelling and clapping and hissing, there was almost a brawl in the buffet, some students in the gallery tried to throw someone out and two people were ejected by the police. It was general pandemonium. Our sister [Masha] almost fainted. The actors were in a state of shock… Am I boring you with all this?…
>
> Yours, Schiller Shakespearovich Goethe
> *to Aleksandr, 11/24/87*

The traumatic opening set off in Chekhov an emotional turmoil that was to last two full years. At first, he did not know what to think! The radically divergent response to his play threw him into a state of high anxiety. "I've felt like a psychopath all November," Chekhov wrote to Aleksandr *(11/24/87)* during the month of the play's opening. At first, he was euphoric from all the excitement, as was apparent from his signature on the above letter: "Schiller Shakespearovich Goethe." Within a week of the opening, Chekhov journeyed to St. Petersburg to secure a production, where he was met with a warm and enthusiastic response from his editor, Suvorin, and other literary colleagues. At the same time, however, he doubted whether the public really "understood" his play. Thus began the deeply unsatisfying process of rewriting *Ivanov* in preparation for the St. Petersburg production — a process that took Chekhov thirteen months and that turned him off "serious" playwriting for almost seven years.

What frustrated Chekhov most was the public's misunderstanding of his central character. He had sought to create a tragic hero — and yet he was told that Ivanov came across either as an unsympathetic scoundrel or as a "superfluous man," the popular novelistic nineteenth-century type. This confounded Chekhov. Clearly, he said, he must be a failure as a dramatist — because that was not at all what he had intended. In an eight-page letter to his publisher, Suvorin, Chekhov explains his central character's behavior in scrupulous detail, very much as if he were justifying the behavior of a friend, relative, or famous personage for whom he was responsible. In this letter, Chekhov painted a portrait of his protagonist as a young man of promise and privilege, who heroically commits to every cause imaginable after graduating university — schools, peasant life, farming, liberalism, social reform — only to burn out at thirty-five and to yearn for an undistinguished, "boring" life. Physically and morally depleted, he is filled with an indefinable feeling of guilt — an exclusively "Russian feeling," as Chekhov puts it — guilt for everything that is wrong in the world around him. To weariness, disappointment, apathy, boredom, and guilt, he adds loneliness, isolated on his estate in the provinces, numbed by long winter evenings, surrounded by the same dreary people, burdened with responsibilities and problems. He becomes irritable, excitable. (Chekhov, the doctor, even draws a graph in the letter, charting the emotional mood swings of such a man! It could have been a graph of Chekhov's own moods during this highly charged period of theatrical activity!)

Chekhov's instincts were on the mark: The problem of the play lay in his depiction of the central character. He knew who he wanted to portray — his letter states it, and yet, even with the revision and the second St. Petersburg production (which garnered him excellent reviews), Chekhov knew he hadn't gotten the character of Ivanov "right." "I failed in my attempt... It's a pity," he wrote Suvorin.

> Ivanov and Lvov seemed so alive in my imagination [...] They are still there in my mind, and I feel I haven't distorted or exaggerated them one iota. And if they came out lifeless and unclear on paper, the fault lies not in them, but in my inability to

express myself. Apparently it's too early for me to begin writing plays.

It was not until many years later, when he looked beyond the times and the conditions of society for the "cause" of Ivanov's *ennui,* when he saw life on earth and the state of the soul in much broader terms, when he stopped trying so desperately to write a character "of literary significance," when he wrote from the heart and not from the head — that Chekhov was able to depict life and human suffering "as it really is" on the stage. But, in 1887, by his own admission, he wasn't ready yet.

I still lack a political, religious and philosophical world view — it keeps changing every month, so I'll have to limit myself to the description of how my heroes love, marry, give birth, die and how they speak.

to Grigorovich 10/9/88

Cognizant of this, he threw himself with a vengeance into what came naturally to him — comedy. The opening of *Ivanov* unleashed a whirlwind of theatre activity. Even while rewriting *Ivanov,* he managed to write the two most delightful, lively, and outrageous vaudevilles of his career, *The Bear* and *The Proposal,* which became the favorites of Tolstoy, the czar, and the Russian public, and which remain today the most well-known of all of Chekhov's short plays. They brought Chekhov renewed acclaim and even unexpected financial remuneration. They also brought him some relief from the frustration of rewriting *Ivanov.*

I give you my word that I shall write no more of such intellectual and sickly plays as *Ivanov.*

to Suvorin, 12/19/88

Despite the positive reviews of the rewritten version (the play opened in St. Petersburg on January 31, 1889), Chekhov was dissatisfied, and he grew increasingly insecure about his own abilities as a serious dramatist. He sought refuge and release in writing more vaudevilles. In March, 1889, as a practical joke, he parodied a tragedy written by his publisher, Suvorin, with the outrageous *Tatyana Repina.* That was followed by *The Tragedian in Spite of Himself* in May, 1889, and next *The Wedding* in October, 1889.

> As far as my design goes [for *Ivanov*], I was on the right track,
> but the execution is good for nothing. I ought to have waited!
>
> *to Suvorin, 1/7/89*

His dreams to create the Russian *Hamlet* had been thwarted, but Chekhov refused to give them up. He only put them aside. And instead of returning to *Ivanov* for a yet another revision, he took a respite from playwriting. What he learned from *Ivanov*, he put to practice almost seven years later, revisiting the Hamlet themes in *The Seagull*, where he learned to end his plays "not with a bang, but a whimper."

Despite the imperfections that caused its author such despair and self-deprecation, *Ivanov* is still powerful on the contemporary stage when cast properly. In recent productions on the English-speaking stage with Ralph Fiennes (at London's Almeida Theatre, 1997) and Kevin Kline (at New York's Lincoln Center Theatre, 1998), theatres rely upon charismatic actors to overcome the flaws in the basic character portrayal, and to reach the audiences through the actors' humanity and broad appeal. At the same time, these productions also show that there is enough strength in Chekhov's complex characterization to bring Ivanov to life — as both an alienated and alluring martyr and a surprisingly empathetic and compelling portrait of Russia's ineffectual intelligentsia. The tragedy that emerges today is not Ivanov's; it is the Russian aristocracy's of the *fin de siècle*. Perhaps Chekhov would have been satisfied with today's reception of his problem-hero, after all.

The Wood Demon

> …it is difficult to write a good play and twice as difficult —
> and terrifying, too — to write a bad play. I would like to see
> the entire public merge into one person and write a play. Then
> you and I would sit in the very first box in the theatre and hiss
> it off the stage.
>
> *to Suvorin, 5/4/89*

The story of *The Wood Demon* — its conception, failure, and ultimate metamorphosis — is one of the most unlikely phenomena in theatre literature. There is a fascinating dramaturgical lesson to be learned in this transformation of a light romantic comedy into one of the great masterpieces of modern drama, *Uncle*

Vanya, both in terms of Chekhov's own work, and in writing for the theatre in general.

Let us begin at the inception of *The Wood Demon* — at least, at what we believe to be its inception. Evidently, during the summer of 1888, while staying with the Suvorins in the Crimea, Chekhov had discussed with his publisher and mentor the possibility of collaborating on a play. Later that year, Suvorin sent him a draft of the first act, whereupon, on October 18, Chekhov sent a detailed dramaturgical response, outlining the cast and the contents of the remaining acts. Scholars disagree as to why Suvorin withdrew from the project — perhaps he was daunted by Chekhov's extensive letter or else he was too busy, but withdraw he did, leaving Chekhov to work on it by himself in May of 1889. Chekhov called it a comedy, "lyrical" in tone, with a happy ending. Clearly, this was something new for him; it seemed almost as if he had chosen this tone to appease the public, giving it what he thought it wanted after *Ivanov.*

The letters between May and October, 1889, while he was writing the play, fluctuate in tone between euphoria and mild depression. He spent the spring in the Ukraine in the best of spirits, reveling in the out of doors, fishing, and working on the play. And yet Chekhov seemed ambivalent about it, and about playwriting, too. He worked on the play intermittently. At times he was wildly confident about it:

> If the censor does not knock me on the head, you are going
> to feel such a thrill in the autumn as you never felt standing
> on the top of the Eiffel Tower looking down on Paris.
>
> *to Suvorin, 5/14/89*

At the same time, he was peculiarly bored and disenchanted.

> …over the past two years, and for no particular reason, I've
> grown tired of seeing my works in print; I've become indif-
> ferent to reviews, to talk about literature, to gossip, success, fail-
> ure, big fees — in short, I've turned into an utter fool. There
> is a sort of stagnation in my soul… I'll have to light a fire
> underneath myself…
>
> *to Suvorin, 5/4/89*

During this whole period, in fact, Chekhov seemed to lack creative focus. There appears to have been a self-consciousness about the writing of this play, as if it did not spring organically from within him, but rather as if he were standing outside himself, watching himself writing it in fits and starts.

The play will be ready by the beginning of June. Watch out, theatre management! Five thousand goes to me! It's an awfully strange play; I'm amazed to see such strange things emerging from my own pen. My only fear is that the censors won't pass it. I'm also writing a novel that appeals to me more and lies closer to my heart than *The Wood Demon*, where I have to pretend and play the fool.

to Suvorin, 5/4/89

"Pretend…play the fool…" How ambivalent he must have been, writing this play that did not come from the heart, writing a "safe" play to appease his critics! How could he feel ownership of it?! And yet, at the same time, he was so confident about it that in May he even asked the Society of Russian Dramatists to include *The Wood Demon* as a comedy in their catalogue of plays.

There were many interruptions to his writing. That summer, his brother Nikolai, the most volatile and disturbed of all the Chekhov offspring, died a harrowing death from consumption. The family was thrown into an emotional turmoil, and, in July, Anton fled south from this exhausting experience to Yalta. In August, he returned to Sumy in the Ukraine, to the estate of the Lintvaryov family where he was a frequent guest, to finish his work on a serious tale, *A Dreary Story.*

He took up work again on *The Wood Demon* in September. By that time, the actor Pavel Svobodin had become the play's biggest champion and was counting on it for his star vehicle at the Aleksandrinsky Theatre in St. Petersburg that season. Similarly the well-known actor Lensky was committed to perform *The Wood Demon* at the prestigious Maly Theatre in Moscow. Svobodin wrote frantically to Chekhov, begging him to finish the play, or else he threatened to hang himself! Accordingly, Chekhov completed it by the end of October and submitted it to the unofficial theatre literary committee in St. Petersburg, to review it for the Aleksandrinksy production. It was unanimously rejected. The committee, led by its Chairman, the venerable novelist Grigorovich — a mentor, admirer, and close friend of Chekhov — judged the play as a dramatized novel unsuitable for the stage.

As with *Ivanov*, another melodrama unfolded. Stung by all this criticism, Chekhov felt personally betrayed.

A St. Petersburg newspaper announces that my play has been considered a "wonderfully dramatized novel." How nice. So it's one of two things: either I am a failure as a dramatist, which I willingly admit, or these gentlemen are hypocrites who pretend to love me as they do their own sons, imploring me to avoid *cliché* and present some complicated problem on the stage.

to Pleshcheyev, 10/21/89

Then came word from the actor Lensky in Moscow, declining to perform in the play at the Maly, telling Chekhov that he did not know how to write in the dramatic form, accusing him of being too spoiled by success, and advising him to stick to short story writing. Nemirovich Danchenko followed suit and wrote that he agreed with Lensky — that Chekhov simply didn't know the craft of play-writing yet. Horrified, Chekhov refused offers to have the play published.

Meanwhile, the famous actor Solovtsov, also a close friend of Chekhov, loved the play, and came forward to convince the new Abramov Theatre in Moscow to produce it. Consistent with his mood changes of this period, Chekhov was suddenly euphoric, and he accepted the theatre's invitation. He busied himself with revisions, working feverishly up until the final days of rehearsal.

December 27, 1889: The play premiered in Moscow at the Abramov. It was a resounding failure. The critics were unanimous in condemning the play, accusing Chekhov of lack of dramaturgical technique, and criticizing his depiction of the trivialities of life on the stage. Critics called the play boring, flat, and novelistic. Crushed, Chekhov wrote to his publisher:

> And now, my request: Don't print *The Wood Demon!*... If you grant my request, I shall be eternally grateful to you, and shall write for you as many stories as you wish, as many as 1,200,000. I ask it seriously... Your refusal will really hurt me to the very heart, and will cause me not a little distress, for it will keep me from working longer over *The Wood Demon.* If you have already begun to set it up, I will gladly pay for the type-setting, throw myself into the river, hang myself... whatever...!

to Kumanin, 1/8/90

The most significant aspect of this letter lies in Chekhov's desire to work on it "longer." While he was deeply dissatisfied with the play, still at the same time he sensed that he was moving in a new direction as a dramatist. It took a long sabbatical — seven years, and a major life change, including an advancing illness, before he felt ready to go back to work on this play. And the result was *Uncle Vanya*, written quietly, seven years later, with no letters, no *explication du texte*, nothing but a writer's inner conviction.

Transformation: *The Wood Demon* into *Uncle Vanya*

True — there is much in *The Wood Demon* that is weak dramaturgically. But without it, there would be no *Uncle Vanya*. And the transformation of *The Wood Demon* into *Uncle Vanya*, more than any literary criticism, tells the story of Chekhov's metamorphosis into a mature and great dramatist.

As with *Platonov,* a tantalizing mystery surrounds *Uncle Vanya* — but of a different nature. In the case of *Uncle Vanya*, we do not know when it was actually written. I agree with the recent research of British biographer Donald Rayfield that has shed some light on this unsolved mystery. Here are the facts available to us: We know from Chekhov's letters that *The Seagull* was completed in October, 1895. Rayfield points out that there are entries in Chekhov's notebook and diary made in the summer and autumn of 1896 that ultimately appear in the dialogue of *Uncle Vanya*. On October 17, 1896, *The Seagull* had its disastrous premiere at the Aleksandrinsky Theatre in St. Petersburg, following which Chekhov retreated to Melikhovo to continue writing. Finally, in December, 1896, we have the very first mention of the title *Uncle Vanya* in a letter from Chekhov to his publisher, referring to it cryptically as a "play known to no one." Indications are, therefore, that *Uncle Vanya* must have been written in the fall of 1896.

Why was Chekhov so unusually secretive about the writing of *Uncle Vanya?* Why did he not refer to the process in his letters, as he did with all the other plays? We can only guess that this secrecy reflects his sensitivity over *The Wood Demon,* an earlier work about which he was painfully insecure. Why would he call attention to the fact that his new play was based on an old one that had been so thoroughly denounced by the critics, the *literati,* and the public?

The second question is: What is the impetus behind this transformation? Why did Chekhov choose to transform the earlier play into the later one? An answer, I believe, may be found in the subtitle of *Uncle Vanya:* "Scenes from Country Life." Between the writing of *The Wood Demon* in 1889 and *Uncle Vanya* in 1896, the major event in Chekhov's life was his move to Melikhovo, the charming little "estate" that he purchased in 1892 as a retreat from the hectic Moscow life and as a quiet place to write. *The Wood Demon* was a romantic notion of scenes from country life, based on Chekhov's idyllic summers in the Ukraine as a guest of his patrons and admirers. By the fall of 1896, however, Chekhov had experienced firsthand the realities of the life of a country doctor and the manager of an "estate." He now had *real* scenes from country life to write about…

There are many features worthy of note in the transformation from *The Wood Demon* to *Uncle Vanya*, and each one is significant in appreciating the maturation of Chekhov's artistry. The drastic reduction in cast size and length, the new choice of setting, the musical orchestration of structure, the "non-plot," the crafting of characters, the creation of the ensemble, the economy of dialogue, the extraordinary vision of the passage of time, the distinctively ironic ending, the unique blend of comedy and tragedy, the new tone of absurdity — these are the main features of the dramaturgical transformation from *The Wood Demon* into *Uncle Vanya*. When a work in the theatre today is described as "Chekhovian," it is a blend of these qualities that earn it this description.

Let us examine each feature and appreciate the transformation. First, Chekhov has reduced the length of *The Wood Demon* by almost one-third. *Uncle Vanya*, the shortest of his plays — his "chamber play," as I like to refer to it — is a jewel of simplicity and economy. He has redrafted most of Act I, preserving only Vanya's long speech about the professor. He has preserved most of the magical Act II. In Act III, he has rewritten the first part, adding the remarkable map scene, and at the same time has preserved the second part, central to which is Serebraykov's climactic "sell-the-estate" speech. Most radical is the *complete* rewriting of Act IV, a phenomenon to be addressed later in this discussion. Not only did he cut, but also, and more significantly, he *refined* the text. This elegant, masterful self-editing is a trademark of the mature, consummate craftsman.

Secondly, Chekhov has introduced the unity of place in *Uncle Vanya;* instead of three settings on three different estates in *The Wood Demon*, we have all the action unified on one estate. At the same time, Chekhov has moved the estate hundreds of miles northeast — from the pastoral setting on the banks of the Psyol in the Ukraine in the south of Russia with its romantic charm, its water mill, its winding river (at Luka, near Sumy, where he summered in 1888 at the Lintvaryovs), to a colder, more northerly, forested, less idyllic environment on the edge of the wilderness. Nature in *Uncle Vanya*, instead of a fairy-tale place of romance and frolic in *The Wood Demon*, becomes a place of duality — of beauty and mystery, of allurement and entrapment, of impenetrability and danger.

Thirdly, Chekhov has reduced the cast from thirteen to eight, adding only one new character (Marina, the old nurse). Eliminated are the ancillary figures: Zheltukhin; Yulya, his sister; Orlovsky, a landowner; his son, Fyodor Ivanovich; and several servants. These are characters who seemed to serve as doubles or foils of the principal ones in *The Wood Demon*. Remarkably, Chekhov has combined their attributes and speeches with those who remain. Most significant is the absence of a central character. Whereas Chekhov's three early plays centered around a "hero" or "anti-hero," with *Uncle Vanya* we have a focus on a true ensemble, the trademark of Chekhov's later plays.

There is also the transformation of three characters of *The Wood Demon* into the rich, complex portrayals of *Uncle Vanya*. Chekhov accomplished this with delicacy and subtlety, and the secret of his technique lies in his use of detail. With a simple change of name and costume, for example, Chekhov evokes a whole new persona for a character. Thus, Uncle George (a "fancier" French name) becomes Uncle Vanya (a common Russian name similar to "Johnny"). He enters in Act I of *The Wood Demon* with no reference to his appearance; in *Uncle Vanya*, he enters in Act I, crumpled from sleep and "adjusting his dapper tie." In that one detail, a complete portrait is indicated — of a cultured, well-educated man who dreamed "of being a Schopenhauer, a Dostoevsky," thereby accentuating the pathos of his predicament in an economical, effective way.

A simple detail like "plain" transforms Sonya from a frivolous, lighthearted girl in *The Wood Demon* into one of Chekhov's most poignant and spiritual creations, the Sonya of *Uncle Vanya*. Whereas the pretty, well-educated Sonya of *The Wood Demon* gets the doctor in the end, the simple country girl Sonya of *Uncle Vanya* does not — and the results are heartbreaking. Yelena plays the piano at the top of Act III in *The Wood Demon;* at the same place in *Uncle Vanya*, she does not. This small adjustment in detail speaks volumes for Yelena's repressed, stifled sexuality. These are only a few among the many small, detailed adjustments that change the picture significantly. Working like a impressionist painter, Chekhov made changes that were subtle, often imperceptible, but their cumulative effect is evocative and powerful. When asked by the original cast of *Uncle Vanya* to describe their characters during rehearsals, Chekhov simply laughed and replied: "It's all there in the play. Read it." He was right.

Special attention must be paid to the transformation of the portrayal of the wood demon himself. This was a character embedded deep in Chekhov's heart and soul even before he began to write the earlier play, embodying his love of nature and his evolving vision of Russia. In his initial letter to Suvorin in October 1888 outlining their collaboration, his description of the wood demon's character is closer to Astrov than it is even to Khrushchov! Indeed, passages from this initial letter, quoted below, are found today in the speeches of Astrov and Sonya in Act I of *Uncle Vanya*.

> The wood demon: Poet, landscape artist, with a passionate sensitivity for nature. Once, when he was still a schoolboy, he planted a birch tree in his back garden; when it turned green and started to sway in the wind, to rustle and cast a little shade, his soul filled with pride; he had helped God create a new birch tree, he had seen to it that there was one more tree on earth! This is the source of his peculiar creativity. He realizes his ideas not on canvas or paper, but on earth, not in dead paints but

with living things… The tree is beautiful, but more than that, it has a right to live, it is as necessary as water, the sun, the stars. Life on earth is unthinkable without trees. Trees condition the climate, the climate affects the character of people etc. etc. There is no civilization, no happiness if a tree falls under the axe, if the climate is harsh and rugged, if people are also harsh and rugged… The future is terrible! Nastia [Sonya] likes him not for his ideas which are strange to her but for his talent, his passion, the broad range of his ideas… She likes the way his vision sweeps over all Russia and ten centuries ahead.

to Suvorin, 10/18/88

And yet, what a profound change there is in the soul of this character from the earlier to the later play! The simple change in name from Khrushchov (meaning "beetle") to Astrov (meaning "star") reflects the magnitude of the transformation. In Dr. Khrushchov of *The Wood Demon*, Chekhov gave the portrayal of a saintly, loving, moralizing individual dedicated to preserving the natural beauty of the forests (a theme taken from Chekhov's early stories such as "Panpipes" "Fortune" and "Steppe," celebrating the beauties of nature ultimately destroyed by man). In Dr. Astrov of *Uncle Vanya*, he gives us a complex, powerful portrayal of a man of depth, vision, and conviction, but at the same time a man who is no saint — in fact, just the opposite. He is a sensualist who is unable to love, a worshipper of beauty who cannot recognize the true inner beauty before him (in the "plain" Sonya), a doctor who is unable to heal, a visionary who drinks, an environmentalist who lives in isolation, a humanist whose feelings have grown numb. In short, he is an eccentric. It is almost as if Chekhov had to change the whole natural environment of the play from the romantic woods of the south to a darker region of Russia, in order to provide a deeper, more complex spiritual context that Astrov could inhabit.

The transformation from Khrushchov to Astrov was inspired in great part by Chekhov's residence at Melikhovo, the charming "estate" with its house and land about ninety miles southeast of Moscow, which he bought in 1892. There he practiced medicine, planted trees, and managed the estate, even as his health gradually began to decline. By the time he sat down to rewrite *The Wood Demon* in the fall of 1896, the life of a country doctor was already very much in Chekhov's soul. This profound change is reflected in the new material he added to *Uncle Vanya*. An example is the new opening scene of Act I, when Astrov and Marina, the old nurse, are sitting in the garden, waiting for the ensemble to return from their walk. In this seemingly innocuous scene, Astrov expresses the heart of the play and also poses its central question. Speaking of the recent typhus epidemic, he complains that he cannot feel anything for the mass of humanity under his care. What brings his feelings to life again, however, is the one patient who dies on his surgery table while under chloroform. That lamentation for the loss of *one* life — and for the recognition of life's intrinsic value — expresses the profound humanism that is at the core of *Uncle Vanya*. Then comes Astrov's question to the nurse:

> …those who will live after us, one hundred to two hundred years from now, those for whom we show the way, will they remember us kindly? Will they? No, nanny, they won't!
>
> Uncle Vanya, *Act I*

Another significant addition to *Uncle Vanya* is the map scene in Act III. Astrov's reverence for the Russian forests and the environment reflects Chekhov's own far-reaching vision of time and natural change, informed by his own work planting forests as well as his gradual physical decline.

Time…change…the value of a life… This is the *weltanschauung* of the mature Chekhov. To express this vision, Chekhov completely transforms the ending of the play. In The *Wood Demon*, the world of Act IV is the forest by Dyadin's water mill. In *Uncle Vanya*, the world of Act IV is completely reimagined. Instead of a lovely, wooded setting with its romantic resolution, Uncle Vanya's final act is one of suspended animation in a claustrophobic room, where lost souls huddle by fading candlelight, where life implodes, where hopeless, loveless characters sit and wait to the sound of the clicking of knitting needles and the counting of the abacus. As the lights dim on this tiny drawing-sitting-bedroom, with the remains of humanity preparing for the long Russian winter, the departing doctor remarks: "If something happens, of course, let me know — I'll come…" ominously foreshadowing the ultimate end they are all awaiting. The magic and miracle of the transformation into *Uncle Vanya* is nowhere more eloquent, nowhere more powerful, then in this stunning ending.

Finally, there is the issue of genre. *The Wood Demon* was Chekhov's "romantic comedy" — his attempt to please, to be all things to all people, having felt he failed with tragedy in *Ivanov,* and having dismissed his own genius at vaudeville. By altering one significant action in *Uncle Vanya*, Chekhov changes the entire tone of the play. In *The Wood Demon,* Uncle George commits suicide offstage at the end of Act III, following Serebryakov's sell-the-estate scene. This jarring action throws the play off-kilter. The suicide of a principal character, midway through a romantic comedy with a subsequent happy ending, seems incongruous. In *Uncle*

Vanya, however, Chekhov has Uncle Vanya shoot at the professor onstage, and miss — twice! This one economical plot adjustment transforms the play into a tragicomedy, in which the title character can't even successfully kill himself, but instead is sentenced, ironically, to live.

> Those who will live after us in one hundred, two hundred years, who will despise us because we've lived our lives so stupidly, so unspeakably — perhaps they will find their way to happiness, but you and I…We have only one hope and here it is: the hope that, while we are sleeping in our graves, we are visited by dreams, perhaps even pleasant ones.
>
> · Uncle Vanya, *Act IV*

These are Astrov's final words of consolation to Uncle Vanya in Act IV. Time, the inexorable continuum of life, the Africa never to be visited, only imagined: these are the dimensions of *Uncle Vanya* to which this fanciful, charming, light-weight romantic comedy called *The Wood Demon* has deepened, so gently, so gracefully, so subtly…and a whole new world unfolds before us…the world of the later, mature Chekhov…

The Value of *The Wood Demon*

So much of this discussion has been devoted to the transformation; it remains now to speak of the merits of the earlier work. *The Wood Demon* is alive for us today to enjoy and appreciate on its own terms. It has a unique charm, a youthful effervescence and a frivolity all its own, setting the tone for many of the ensemble scenes of the later plays — the garden scene in *The Seagull,* the name-day party in *The Three Sisters,* and the homecoming scene in *The Cherry Orchard,* for example. Several of the characters, whom Chekhov omitted when he transformed the play into *Uncle Vanya* , are very special — Orlovsky, the landowner, for example, is a delightful portrait, and his pungent banter constitutes some of Chekhov's best dialogue in the play. We see his successor in Sorin, the charming brother of Arkadina in *The Seagull.* The earlier play also offers one of Chekhov's most enchanting eccentrics: Dyadin, the owner of the mill, who is transformed into Telegin, the impoverished landowner in *Uncle Vanya.* Dyadin's scene with Yelena in Act IV of *The Wood Demon* by the water mill will capture the hearts and imaginations of actors who know those roles in both plays. His dialogue, too, is among the most colorful and charming of the entire play. It is almost a pity that Telegin, Dyadin's equally charming successor, has a far less prominent role in *Uncle Vanya*.

The light and airy charm of *The Wood Demon* has never quite been replicated again in the Chekhovian canon and is therefore to be treasured in its own right. The ultimate value of *The Wood Demon,* however, lies in uncovering for us the spiritual journey of its author, from the garden of Eden of his youth into the deeper forests of maturity.

Conclusion: Metamorphosis

> I should like to be a free artist, and I only regret that God hasn't given me the strength to become one... My holiest of holies is the human body, health, intelligence, talent, inspiration, love and the most absolute freedom — freedom from violence and lying, in whatever forms they may take. That is the program I would follow, if I were a great artist.
>
> *to Pleshcheyev, 10/89*

Chekhov's journey in the 1880s was a journey to freedom — as an individual and as an artist — freedom from the shackles of family responsibility, freedom from the allure of Moscow and its glamorous theatre life, freedom from the trappings of success, freedom from an overpowering literary tradition.

As a young writer, above all, Chekhov sought to create something of "literary significance," while at the same time trying to satisfy his own youthful ambitions and impulses to "be original." All these plays were, in his own eyes, artistic failures. This was only partly due to his inexperience as a dramatist. The truth is that none of these plays was truly organic — they came, not from within, but from external pressures: to write the Russian Don Juan, to write the Russian Hamlet, to write a romantic comedy with a moral and a message that would entertain the public and placate his critics.

Chekhov needed to free himself from the sense of obligation to create a Russian hero in the grand European and Russian tradition. It took the writing of these three early plays for him to discover that it was *humanity* he wanted to write about, not heroism — and that required an ensemble, not a central character. It was ultimately with Vanya and Astrov and Sonya *together* that he achieved empathy and understanding for his characters and their human condition — and that was because he wasn't asking for it. First he had to create Platonov, Ivanov, and Khrushchov, "ideas" of characters; then he could learn to create Vanya and Astrov and Sonya, human characters of flesh and blood.

Chekhov also needed to free himself from the classical and popular conventions of the day, to seek a new style and new forms. With the writing of *The Wood Demon*, Chekhov had already begun to move away from the old conventions of the theatre, in a direction he did not fully understand himself. Critics scornfully described the action of *The Wood Demon* featuring a name-day party in Act I as trivial and unstageworthy. Imagine how shocking and incomprehensible it was to see "life as it is" on the Russian stage in the 1880s! It was only later that Chekhov could articulate what he was trying to accomplish:

> In life, one does not shoot oneself in the head, hang oneself, or declare one's passion at every fencepost, and one does not pour out profound thoughts in a constant flow. No, mostly one eats, drinks, flirts, makes stupid remarks: that is what should be seen on the stage. One must write plays in which people come and go, have dinner, talk about the rain and the sunshine, play cards — not because this is the author's whim but because this is what happens in real life... Nothing must be fitted into a pattern.
>
> *from Gilles's* Chekhov, Observer Without Illusion, p.294

The young Chekhov knew that he had to develop a craft to render this revolutionary new "life as it is" on the stage. He had to rethink the notion of action and plot, the "punch in the nose" that he was so proud to give to the end of each act in *Ivanov*, and the melodramatic ending of the plays themselves. Ultimately, Chekhov discovered that it was far crueler to let Uncle Vanya live than to let Uncle George kill himself off at the end of Act III.

The larger discovery for Chekhov was that he no longer had to alternate from genre to genre, from vaudeville to tragedy to melodrama to romantic comedy — that he could combine them all artfully into one genre, called tragicomedy. It took him three big, bold, exciting, flawed experiments — the young plays of the 1880s — plus significant life experience and a hiatus of seven years, to find his mature voice in that special co-existence of comedy and tragedy of the later, great plays...that brilliant, magical, elusive blend known the world over as Chekhovian.

> Write a story about this, will you...how a young man, the son of a serf, a former shopkeeper, choir boy, school boy and student, taught to respect rank, to kiss the priests' hands, to worship

the ideas of others, to be grateful for his daily bread, to appreciate a beating, who went to school without galoshes, who got into fist fights, who tortured little animals, who loved to dine at the home of rich relatives, who played the hypocrite before God and men for no reason at all other than the recognition of his own insignificance — write how that young man is squeezing the slave out of himself drop by drop, and how he wakes up one fine morning and feels that in his veins there flows no longer the blood of a slave, but true human blood...

to Suvorin, 1/7/89

All letters quoted have been newly translated for this introduction.

The sources for this introduction are listed in the bibliography at the end of this collection. I wish especially to acknowledge the scholarship of Michael Frayn and Donald Rayfield, whose works are included therein.

CAST OF CHARACTERS

ANNA PETROVNA VOYNITSEVA, the young widow of a general
SERGEY PAVLOVICH VOYNITSEV, the general's son from a first marriage
SOFYA YEGOROVNA, his wife
PORFIRY SEMYONOVICH GLAGOLYEV, a landowner
GERASIM KUZMICH PETRIN, an entrepreneur and a landowner
MARYA YEFIMOVNA GREKOVA, a young chemistry student
IVAN IVANOVICH TRILETSKY, a retired colonel
NIKOLAI IVANOVICH TRILETSKY, his son, a young doctor
MIKHAIL VASILEVICH PLATONOV, a village schoolmaster
ALEKSANDRA IVANOVNA (SASHA), his wife, daughter of Colonel Triletsky
OSIP, a horse thief
YAKOV, a servant

The action takes place in the Russian provinces — on the country estate of the late general, and in the home of the schoolmaster.

Platonov

ACT ONE

The garden. In the foreground is a lawn with flowerbeds. There are benches, chairs, and a small table. Upstage is the facade of the house, with steps leading up to a verandah. To the side of the house and garden are trees, suggesting the setting of the house and the surrounding woods beyond. Through the windows of the house, a dining room is visible, where a luncheon table is being set. It is midday.

ANNA PETROVNA and TRILETSKY are seated at a small table in the garden, playing chess. IVAN IVANOVICH lies dozing upstage on the verandah, unnoticed. YAKOV clears the tea things off another table.

ANNA PETROVNA: Your move...Oh, I see, you moved already...Think before you move, why don't you...Ah ha...And I'm moving here...

TRILETSKY: What time is it?

ANNA PETROVNA: A quarter past twelve...Our guests should be arriving soon...

TRILETSKY: I'm absolutely starving...

ANNA PETROVNA: You're always hungry, there isn't a moment that you're not eating something...

TRILETSKY: So *that's* your move...Watch out for your horse, won't you?!

YAKOV: Shall I set the table now, your ladyship?

ANNA PETROVNA: Yes, do, Yakov. They'll be here any minute. Tell cook to sober up.

YAKOV: Yes, your ladyship. *(Starts into the house, passes the chess table. TRILETSKY snatches a sweet from the tray he is carrying. Exit YAKOV into the house.)*

ANNA PETROVNA: Really, Nikolai Ivanich! Eat, eat, eat, that's all you ever do! It's terrible!

TRILETSKY: Yes! Amazing, isn't it?! *(Chews.)*

ANNA PETROVNA: Last year at my homecoming, you stole into my house before lunch and devoured half a pie without even asking! Glutton! Your move...

TRILETSKY: What are you talking about? It would have gone moldy if I hadn't

eaten it. Ah-ha, so that's your move, is it? All right then …And this is mine…
(Sings.) "Let me tell you, tell you…"

ANNA PETROVNA: Quiet…I can't concentrate…In honor of our arrival last evening, cook was kind enough to get drunk. Don't worry, though, lunch will be served soon enough…

TRILETSKY: Who's been invited?

ANNA PETROVNA: The usual! Same as last year, same as always! Porfiry Semyonich, Gerasim Kuzmich, Platonov…

TRILETSKY: Your coterie of creditors, neighbors, and admirers, gathering to welcome you home…It's summer solstice time again… *(He takes her hand.)*

ANNA PETROVNA: What are you doing, doctor? Feeling my pulse? I'm fine, thank you…

TRILETSKY: I'm not feeling your pulse…I'm kissing your pulse *(kisses her hand)*…Hmm… Soft as a cushion, that's what your hands are…They're lovely! Let me kiss them again! *(Kisses her hand again.)*

ANNA PETROVNA: Concentrate, you rogue…Your move! *(She whistles.)*

TRILETSKY: She whistles like a peasant! What a woman!…

Enter VOYNITSEV and GLAGOLYEV.

GLAGOLYEV SR.: And that's how it was, dear Sergey Pavlovich. In the old days, we loved women like the truest of cavaliers, we believed in them, we worshiped them, we saw them as superior human beings… It's true, isn't it, Sergey Pavlovich, that women are superior human beings?!

ANNA PETROVNA: You're cheating!

TRILETSKY: Who's cheating?

ANNA PETROVNA: Who moved this pawn here, then?

TRILETSKY: You did!

ANNA PETROVNA: So I did, didn't I…*Pardon.*

TRILETSKY: *Pardon* is right!

GLAGOLYEV: Yes, in the old days we cherished women…We'd walk through fire for our women.

TRILETSKY: Whereas nowadays we send firemen through fire for our women.

ANNA PETROVNA: Don't be foolish, Kolya! Pay attention. Your move.

GLAGOLYEV: Last winter in Moscow, at the symphony, I saw a man weeping, he was so moved by the music. Now isn't that wonderful!

VOYNITSEV: I suppose so.

GLAGOLYEV: Well, *I* think it is. So then why were all the others sitting next to him in the audience smiling? Hmm? And he was so embarrassed that he fled from the theatre…

ANNA PETROVNA: *(To TRILETSKY.)* Pay attention!

GLAGOLYEV: In our day, a man who loved music would never flee from a theatre, he'd stay at the opera and weep till the bitter end…

VOYNITSEV: So what's your conclusion, Porfiry Semyonich?

GLAGOLYEV: There is no true love, no true passion any more in our day and age…

ANNA PETROVNA: Enough, I'm tired of this! I want to listen to Porfiry Semyonich. We'll finish our game another time.

TRILETSKY: When I'm losing, she's glued to her seat, but as soon as I start winning, she feels like listening to Porfiry Semyonich! Sit down and let's keep playing. If you don't, I'll consider it a forfeit!

ANNA PETROVNA: Whatever…

TRILETSKY: We're going to make a note of this. *(Takes a notebook from his pocket.)* We're going to make a note of this, dear lady! *(Makes a note.)* The general's widow: a grand total of…ten rubles! Oh-ho! And when shall I have the honor of seeing such a sum?

ANNA PETROVNA: You know I don't have any money! Serge, give this fool ten rubles! *(To TRILETSKY.)* My darling stepson will give it to you.

VOYNITSEV: But *maman*, I hardly have any money myself!

ANNA PETROVNA: Never mind, find some… *(VOYNITSEV reaches into his pocket, and gives TRILETSKY ten rubles.)* I have enough creditors as it is. I don't need another one.

TRILETSKY: *Merci.*

ANNA PETROVNA: *(To GLAGOLYEV, flirtatiously.)* So tell me, Porfiry Semyonich: Is a woman really a superior being to a man?

GLAGOLYEV: That's right!

ANNA PETROVNA: You're quite the feminist, Porfiry Semyonich, aren't you!

GLAGOLYEV: That's right! I love women. In fact, I worship them, Anna Petrovna. In them I see perfection…

TRILETSKY picks up a violin and begins sawing away on it.

ANNA PETROVNA: You're sure of it? Really?

GLAGOLYEV: Of course I'm sure of it. I only have to take you as an example…

ANNA PETROVNA: Seriously? Well, you certainly have an advantage, then, haven't you!

VOYNITSEV: He's a romantic.

ANNA PETROVNA: Will you stop that sawing, Nikolai Ivanich? Put that violin away! Where is everyone? Sergey, did you send for Platonov?

VOYNITSEV: Twice already.

TRILETSKY: Speaking of romantics and Platonov in the same breath…now, that's funny!

ANNA PETROVNA: He should have been here ages ago, the devil. *(Looks at her watch.)* How rude of him!

TRILETSKY: On my way over here this morning, I passed by his schoolhouse. The windows were shuttered tight. He must still be asleep. What a rogue! Haven't seen him in a while, either.

VOYNITSEV: He'll be here any minute. I can't wait for him to meet Sofya!

TRILETSKY: Where is your bride, Sergey?

VOYNITSEV: In the garden with Marya Yefimovna. She loves the garden — can't get enough of it.

TRILETSKY: I invited poor little Marya Yefimovna. She loves our summer solstices…

ANNA PETROVNA: Good God! Marya Yefimovna won't stay a minute if she knows Platonov's coming! She'll die of fright! Remember last summer? She's vowed never to see him again…

GLAGOLYEV: Why?

TRILETSKY: Platonov thinks it's his sacred duty to torture innocent women, and to amuse himself at their expense…

ANNA PETROVNA: And amuse you, too — either that, or else you're inviting her for yourself! Never mind, we'll keep an eye on Platonov, don't worry…

TRILETSKY: Papa, wake up! Wake up! Lunch will be served soon! Your daughter and son-in-law are arriving! *(Goes upstage to the verandah, where IVAN IVANOVICH has been concealed from view, dozing in a rocking chair.)*

IVAN IVANOVICH: *(Stirs, startled)* Hah? Wha—?

VOYNITSEV: Ivan Ivanovich! You're here!

IVAN IVANOVICH: Indeed, indeed…

VOYNITSEV: And how are you this morning?

IVAN IVANOVICH: Never better, never better…

VOYNITSEV: Had a couple of drops already, colonel?!

IVAN IVANOVICH: Why certainly! Got here at eight this morning, my friend. Didn't want to be late for lunch. Everyone was still asleep, so I walked in here, stamped my feet a bit, and her ladyship came in, laughing, of course. I wanted to be the first to toast her return, so we polished off a bottle of Madeira. Her ladyship had three glasses, and I had the rest!

ANNA PETROVNA: Ivan Ivanich is such a dear! I'm going to go shooting with him for quail on St. Peter's day.

IVAN IVANOVICH: We'll go sniping together, Anna Petrovna! We'll plan a polar expedition to Devil's swamp —

ANNA PETROVNA: — and try out your double-barreled shotgun!

IVAN IVANOVICH: We shall, we shall, my divine Diana! *(Kisses her hand.)* Remember last year, my dear? Ha-ha! I like your type, so help me God! Can't stand the fainthearted ones! Now here before you stands a true, emancipated woman! Smell her shoulder and you get a whiff of gunpowder! She's a commander, a commander of the brigade! Put a pair of epaulettes on her, and she'll conquer the world!

TRILETSKY: Shall I see if Yakov's finished setting the table?

IVAN IVANOVICH: I'll do it, I'll do it! *(Exits into the house.)*

ANNA PETROVNA: He probably went in to taste the caviar. Like father, like son.

TRILETSKY: Hot as hell today, isn't it, Porfiry Semyonich?

GLAGOLYEV: And that it is. As hot as on the top shelf of the bathhouse. Ninety degrees, I suppose.

TRILETSKY: But what does that mean? Why is it so hot, Porfiry Semyonich?

GLAGOLYEV: You know better than I do, doctor.

TRILETSKY: Well, in my opinion, it's this hot, because we would have died laughing, you and I, if it had been cold in the month of June!

GLAGOLYEV: I believe you've made a joke, doctor!

General laughter. GREKOVA peeks her head tentatively out from behind a tree. Hearing the laughter, she hastily withdraws.

TRILETSKY: Marya Yefimovna! Come back, come back! *(She hesitates.)* We're not laughing at you!

GREKOVA: *(Emerges uncertainly.)* Hello, Nikolai Ivanich! Greetings… everyone! *(Looks around fearfully.)*

TRILETSKY: Don't worry, don't worry! You're safe among us!

IVAN IVANOVICH: Is that Marya Yefimovna? The little student of chemistry? I wouldn't have recognized her!

TRILETSKY: Let me take your cloak. Come on, don't be shy…

GREKOVA: Hello, Anna Petrovna!

ANNA PETROVNA: Marya Yefimovna! How glad I am to see you! *(Presses GREKOVA's hand.)* So glad…I'm grateful to Nikolai Ivanich — he went to great lengths to lure you away from your village. How are you?

GREKOVA: I'm fine, thank you.

ANNA PETROVNA: You look tired! A trip of thirteen miles must be difficult…

GREKOVA: Not at all. I wanted to be the first to welcome you back before…you know…before the others get here…

ANNA PETROVNA: What others? *(Laughs.)* Ah…

TRILETSKY: Shhhhh…

ANNA PETROVNA: Platonov, Platonov, always Platonov…

GREKOVA: But Nikolai Ivanich, I thought —

GLAGOLYEV: Marya Yefimovna! *(Goes to GREKOVA and tries to kiss her hand.)* Lovely to see you…

GREKOVA: Thank you, but that will be unnecessary …

IVAN IVANOVICH: What do you mean?

TRILETSKY: It is considered humiliating to an emancipated woman, Porfiry Semyonich. You don't kiss a man's hand. Marya Yefimovna is against any form of inequality. You understand…

IVAN IVANOVICH: Let *me* try!

Enter PETRIN, upstage, carrying a newspaper.

TRILETSKY: Look, Porfiry Semyonich, one of your rivals has arrived! Greetings, Gerasim Kuzmich!

PETRIN: Good morning, everyone…your ladyship… *(He nods his head in greeting, sits and reads, apart from the others.)*

ANNA PETROVNA: Gerasim Kuzmich is not my suitor, he's my creditor. And he's been here all morning, sitting in the garden, reading the paper.

TRILETSKY: We're all here now, except for Platonov!

GREKOVA: Platonov? Coming here? Today? *(To TRILETSKY.)* But Nikolai Ivanich, you promised…How could you?! *(Tearful, she runs into the house.)*

TRILETSKY: She'll come back, don't worry, she always does…So tell us something new, Gerasim Kuzmich!

PETRIN: It says here in the paper that there has been an epidemic of anthrax this winter…Many cattle have perished… *(Continues to read.)*

Enter YAKOV, with an armful of fireworks balanced precariously.

ANNA PETROVNA: Not now, you fool, they're for tonight. You can't set off fireworks in broad daylight!

YAKOV: Yes, your ladyship.

ANNA PETROVNA: Put them in the shed. Is lunch ready?

YAKOV: Yes, your ladyship! I've set the buffet out just as you like it...

ANNA PETROVNA: We'll see about that!... *(YAKOV exits.)*

TRILETSKY: Read to us some more, Gerasim Kuzmich! It's very exciting! Makes the time pass...

PETRIN: It says here that at the summer solstice there are more hours of daylight than on any other day in the year...The sun's rays are vertical...

TRILETSKY: Does it say in the paper that people go mad as a result?

ANNA PETROVNA: We'll require your services, won't we, doctor!

VOYNITSEV: I see them coming up the walk!

GLAGOLYEV: Delightful!

ANNA PETROVNA: It's about time!

TRILETSKY: Now we can eat!

VOYNITSEV: Here they are! Here they are!

Enter PLATONOV and SASHA. There follows the general commotion of greetings.

PLATONOV: Well, what do you know, we finally got out of the house at last! Good afternoon, your ladyship! *(Goes to ANNA PETROVNA, kisses first one hand and then the next.)*

ANNA PETROVNA: Platonov! You're late! And you know how impatient I am! Dearest Aleksandra Ivanovna! *(Kisses SASHA.)*

PLATONOV: Out of the house at last! Thank God! Six months, and we haven't seen a square of parquet floor, or a drawing room, or high ceilings, or a living *soul!* We've been hibernating away in our lair all winter long like bears, and we've only just crawled out into the light of day!

VOYNITSEV: Aleksandra Ivanovna! You're plumper and prettier than ever! *(Kisses her hand.)*

PLATONOV: Well of course she is! What else is there to do all winter but sit indoors and eat sour cream? She keeps a stash of it in the cellar! *(Shakes GLAGOLYEV's hand.)* Porfiry Semyonich! So glad to see you!

ANNA PETROVNA: How are you, Aleksandra Ivanovna?! *(Embraces SASHA.)*

PLATONOV: Sergey Pavlovich! Is it really you? Good Lord! *(They embrace.)* It's been so long since I've heard that sweet tenor voice! Come on, man, let me hear you sing something!

VOYNITSEV: *(In a bass voice.)* "I'm a silly fool." *(Laughs.)*

PLATONOV: My God! He's a bass!

TRILETSKY: Greetings, brother-in-law! *(Embraces PLATONOV.)*

PLATONOV: Ah! Our ladyship's physician-in-waiting! Happy to see you, dear
fellow! You're the picture of health!

TRILETSKY: *(Embraces SASHA.)* Hello, sister dear! How's my little dumpling!

SASHA: God, you reek of scent! Are you well?

TRILETSKY: Never been better! *(Embraces PLATONOV.)* So how are things,
Misha?

PLATONOV: What things?

TRILETSKY: You know…Things!

PLATONOV: Who knows how they are! It's a long story, my friend, and not a
very interesting one. Let's sit down, then, shall we, ladies and gentlemen? God,
it's stifling! *(They sit.)* Ah…the heavenly aroma of humanity! How wonderful!
If feels as though we haven't seen each other in hundreds of years.

ANNA PETROVNA: So how is life, Mikhail Vasilich?

PLATONOV: Awful, as usual. Slept through the whole winter, never saw the light
of day for six months. Drank, ate, slept, read stories aloud to my wife…
Terrible!

SASHA: It wasn't so bad, really…

PLATONOV: It was worse than bad, it was *boring,* my darling. *(To ANNA
PETROVNA.)* And we missed you terribly. You're a sight for sore eyes! To
see you, Anna Petrovna, after an eternity of seeing either *no* people at all or,
worse, awful people, is an absolute luxury! You're more beautiful than ever!

SASHA: When did you arrive? Last evening?

ANNA PETROVNA: Yes. At ten o'clock.

PLATONOV: I saw your lights on at eleven, but I was afraid to drop by. I thought
you might be exhausted.

ANNA PETROVNA: Oh, but you should have! We were up talking until two!

SASHA whispers something in PLATONOV's ear.

PLATONOV: Oh, for God's sake! *(Slaps himself on the forehead.)* What a memory! Why didn't you remind me? Sergey Pavlovich!

VOYNITSEV: What?

PLATONOV: Here he gets married and he doesn't say a word!

SASHA: And I forgot, too! Congratulations, Sergey Pavlovich!

General commotion, and a round of embraces all over again.

PLATONOV: And may you live happily ever after, dear fellow! *(Embraces*

VOYNITSEV.) You've performed a miracle, Sergey Pavlovich! So soon, and so swiftly!

VOYNITSEV: *(Bursts out laughing.)* I even surprised myself. It all happened so fast. I fell in love, I got married!

PLATONOV: You fall in love every winter, it's just that this winter you also got married. Have you found yourself a job yet?

VOYNITSEV: They offered me a court position but I haven't decided whether to take it or not. The law doesn't really appeal to me…

PLATONOV: So? Are you going to take it?

VOYNITSEV: At this point I'm not sure of anything…

PLATONOV: So we're going to remain unemployed, are we, just as before? It's been seven years since you've graduated from the university, hasn't it? And with a law degree!

VOYNITSEV: Yes.

PLATONOV: I see… *(Sighs.)* Unemployed for seven whole years! Imagine that!

ANNA PETROVNA: It's too hot to discuss such serious subjects — makes me feel like yawning. What took you so long to get here, Aleksandra Ivanovna?

SASHA: We were so pressed for time! Misha was busy mending the birdcage, and I went to church…The cage was broken, you know, and we couldn't keep the nightingale inside.

GLAGOLYEV: But why go to church today? Is it a holiday?

SASHA: No. I asked Father Konstantin to say a requiem mass. Today is Misha's father's name day, and I wouldn't feel right if I didn't go to church.

IVAN IVANOVICH appears on the verandah, carrying a rifle.

IVAN IVANOVICH: Ta-da! My dear daughter and son-in-law! The stars of the Triletsky constellation! I salute you with a Krup gun! *(Fires the rifle.)* God, it's hot! Hello, my sweet ones! Mishenka, my dear fellow…

PLATONOV: Greetings, colonel! *(Embraces him.)* Are you well?

IVAN IVANOVICH: I'm always well! The good lord puts up with me — hasn't punished me yet. Sashenka, my child! *(Kisses SASHA on the head.)* Haven't set eyes on you in ages! Are you well?

SASHA: Yes, Papa, very well… Are *you* well?

IVAN IVANOVICH: Never been sick a day in my life! Yes… Haven't seen you in such a long time! Every day I intend to come visit you, to see my little grandson and my dear son-in-law, but I never seem to get there. It's always something, isn't it, my angels?! Day before yesterday, I was going to come over, Misha, to show you my new double-barreled shotgun, but the constable chief dropped by to play a hand of Preference. Splendid shotgun! English, hits a target dead at a hundred and seventy feet! Is my grandson well?

SASHA: Petya's very well, Papa, he sends his regards…

IVAN IVANOVICH: Now how can he possibly do that? He's five months old.

VOYNITSEV: You must take it symbolically.

IVAN IVANOVICH: I see, I see, symbolically…Tell him, Sasha, to grow up quickly. I want to take him hunting! I've got a little double-barreled shotgun especially for him! I want to make him a hunter, so that after I'm gone I can leave him all my gear.

ANNA PETROVNA: We're going to go shooting together, Ivan Ivanovich and I…

TRILETSKY: So! Everyone's here now, right? Gerasim Kuzmich, you're an intelligent fellow!! Tell us: What's the magic trick that would make our Anna Petrovna serve us something to eat?!

PETRIN: Why ask me, Nikolai Ivanich? I'm barely an invited guest, and no one pays attention to me, anyway…

TRILETSKY: There's so much splendid food and drink, Gerasim Kuzmich! You can't imagine! Caviar, sturgeon, salmon, sardines… And a six or seven layer pie — "so" high! Stuffed with all sorts of delicacies of flora and fauna —

ANNA PETROVNA: How do you know?

IVAN IVANOVICH: *(Laughs.)* He already peeked!

SASHA: Kolya!

TRILETSKY: I'm going to spy on the cook, see that he doesn't get drunk! *(Tiptoes out.)*

ANNA PETROVNA: He's after the caviar again! Outrageous!

VOYNITSEV: And where is my wife, everyone? Platonov hasn't even seen her yet! I'll go find her. She loves the garden, she can't get enough of it.

PLATONOV: Actually, Sergey Pavlovich, I'd rather you didn't introduce me to your wife. I'm curious to see whether she recognizes me. I was somewhat acquainted with her a long long time ago…

VOYNITSEV: Sofya? You knew Sofya?

PLATONOV: Once upon a time, when we were still students. Don't tell her I'm here, please…

VOYNITSEV: This man knows everybody! How does he manage it?! *(Exits into the garden.)*

Enter TRILETSKY, dragging behind him the reluctant GREKOVA.

ANNA PETROVNA: Ah, look who's here! Marya Yefimovna! Where was she hiding?

TRILETSKY: In the dining room, behind the cupboard!

ANNA PETROVNA: Come join us, dear! *(To GREKOVA.)* He won't bite you!

IVAN IVANOVICH: Marya Yefimovna, do sit down!

GREKOVA: No, really, I just stopped by to welcome you back. I absolutely must go now —

ANNA PETROVNA: Go? You only just got here! And you traveled thirteen miles!

IVAN IVANOVICH: Look who's here — Marya Yefimovna!

PLATONOV: *(Goes up to GREKOVA and bows.)* Marie Curie! May I have the honor! *(Goes to kiss her hand.)*

GREKOVA: *(Withdraws her hand.)* No, thank you. I don't like it…

PLATONOV: Why not? Am I not worthy?

GREKOVA: It's not a question of being worthy or unworthy — I just don't like it. And you don't want to anyway, do you?

PLATONOV: Don't want to? How do you know I don't want to?

GREKOVA: You wouldn't have tried to kiss my hand, if I hadn't said I didn't want you to. You only want to do it because you know I don't like it!

TRILETSKY: Not the same business as last year, Misha, please!

PLATONOV: What do you mean?!

ANNA PETROVNA: Stop it, Platonov!

PLATONOV: In a minute…How are your experiments coming, Madame —*pardon,* Mademoiselle Curie?

GREKOVA: What are you talking about?

PLATONOV: You're a student of chemistry, aren't you? I heard that you were extracting ether from beetles, to advance scientific knowledge. Sounds like a worthy endeavor! Except for the beetles, of course…

GREKOVA: *(Tearfully.)* You're always joking…

TRILETSKY: He is, isn't he, he's always joking…

PLATONOV: How rosy your cheeks are! Is that your natural coloring? You must be hot!

TRILETSKY: Stop it!

PLATONOV: Why? What have I done?

GREKOVA: I don't quite know what I do to provoke you. I go out of my way to avoid you! If Nikolai Ivanich hadn't promised that you wouldn't be here, I never would have come today. *(To TRILETSKY.)* Shame on you to lie like that!

PLATONOV: Yes, shame on you, Nikolai!

GREKOVA: It's all my fault. *(Tearfully.)* I'm so gullible! Why can't I be more like you, Anna Petrovna?

ANNA PETROVNA: Forgive me, my dear, I forgot to have a word with him.

PLATONOV: *(To GREKOVA.)* You're going to cry now, aren't you? Good idea! Cry, then! Crying makes you feel much better. Ask the doctor, he'll tell you it's good for you…

GREKOVA rushes out in tears.

ANNA PETROVNA: You've done it again, Platonov!

TRILETSKY: *(To PLATONOV.)* This is going too far!

GLAGOLYEV: You ought to apologize, Mikhail Vasilich!

PLATONOV: What for?

GLAGOLYEV: You were discourteous! To a defenseless young woman!

SASHA: *(To PLATONOV.)* Say you're sorry, or else I'm leaving!

TRILETSKY: Come on, I insist! It was cruel! I won't let you get away with it!

PLATONOV: Enough! I did a stupid thing, and there's no point wasting more words on stupidity…

GLAGOLYEV: I admire sensitivity in women! You hardly said anything to her! What a delicate creature she is…

PLATONOV: A weeping scientist, for God's sake, how absurd!

ANNA PETROVNA: For shame, Mikhail Vasilich, for shame!

PLATONOV: I've apologized, haven't I? This is getting tedious…

Enter VOYNITSEV, running, from the garden.

VOYNITSEV: *(Sings.)* She's coming, she's coming!

ANNA PETROVNA: Our Sofi's had enough of this horrible heat at last!

Enter SOFYA YEGOROVNA from the garden, carrying an armful of flowers.

SOFYA YEGOROVNA: I was talking and talking with Marya Yefimovna, and forgot all about the heat! Your garden is a paradise, Sergey! I could roam about for hours!

VOYNITSEV: Here she is! Isn't she lovely, my Sofya?!

GLAGOLYEV: Lovely, lovely as a summer's day!

SOFYA YEGOROVNA: Hello, everyone!

VOYNITSEV: Permit me to introduce my wife, Sofya Yegorovna! Ivan Ivanovich, our esteemed neighbor…

IVAN IVANOVICH: Used to carry your husband about in my arms, madame, when he was still small enough to walk under the table. He left a mark on me, a mark I shall carry with me to the grave. *(Opens his mouth.) Voilà!* No tooth! See? —

SASHA: Papa, please!

IVAN IVANOVICH: Let me finish! I was holding him in my arms and he went and knocked out one of my teeth with a pistol he happened to be playing with, the little monster! And now he's a lawyer! I'd keep an eye on him if I were you, dear lady, whose name, I regret to say, I've already forgotten. Your beauty reminds me of a certain famous painting. The same pure, porcelain complexion. Only your nose isn't exactly the same. Won't you do me the honor of permitting me to kiss your little hand?

SOFYA YEGOROVNA: *(Holding out her hand.)* Pleased to meet you!

VOYNITSEV: Porfiry Semyonich, our esteemed neighbor...

GLAGOLYEV: You are invited to call on me on Thursday, dear lady, you and Sergey Pavlovich.

VOYNITSEV: We'd be delighted!

GLAGOLYEV: You'll like my estate. Our garden is lovely, the river is deep, and we have fine, fine horses. It's a mile or so from Platonovka.

SOFYA YEGOROVNA: I know Platonovka! Is it still there?

GLAGOLYEV: Of course...

SOFYA YEGOROVNA: I used to know the owner, Platonov. Do you know what's become of him, Sergey?

VOYNITSEV: *(Stifling laughter.)* I think so. Do you happen to remember his first name?

PLATONOV: I used to know him, too. His name, I believe, is Mikhail Vasilich...

There is muffled laughter.

SOFYA YEGOROVNA: Yes, yes...Mikhail Vasilich. I knew him when he was a student, a boy, almost... You're laughing, everyone... I don't see anything to laugh about...

ANNA PETROVNA: *(Points to PLATONOV.)* For God's sake, recognize him already, or else he'll burst with suspense!

SOFYA YEGOROVNA: *(Looks at PLATONOV in astonishment.)* Mikhail Vasilich... Is it really you?

PLATONOV: No wonder you don't recognize me, Sofya Yegorovna! Years have gone by! Not even rats can ravage a face as much as these past years have done.

SOFYA YEGOROVNA: *(Gives him her hand.)* How you've changed!

VOYNITSEV: And may I introduce his wife, Aleksandra Ivanovna, sister of the wittiest of men, doctor Nikolai Ivanich!

SOFYA YEGOROVNA: *(Gives SASHA her hand.)* Very pleased to meet you. *(TO PLATONOV.)* So you're married, too! Yes, years have gone by...

PLATONOV: With such a splendid introduction, I suppose I may inquire how you are, Sofya Yegorovna. Are you well?

SOFYA YEGOROVNA: I'm fine, fine. And how are you? What are you doing now?

PLATONOV: Fate has played a cruel trick on me, one I never could have foreseen since the time when you saw me as the second Byron, or when I saw myself as the next Prime Minister, or Christopher Columbus, even...I am a schoolmaster, Sofya Yegorovna. That is all.

SOFYA YEGOROVNA: You? A schoolmaster?

PLATONOV: Yes. Strange, isn't it...

SOFYA YEGOROVNA: Incredible! But...why not something more?

PLATONOV: It's a long story, Sofya Yegorovna.

SOFYA YEGOROVNA: But certainly you graduated from the university?

PLATONOV: No. I dropped out.

SOFYA YEGOROVNA: Dropped out? But...that doesn't prevent you from being an individual, does it?

PLATONOV: Forgive me, I don't understand your question...

SOFYA YEGOROVNA: I mean, that doesn't prevent you from having a calling, of serving a cause, for example, such as women's emancipation, educating the peasants...That doesn't prevent you from serving an ideal — does it?

PLATONOV: Well no, it doesn't, but then again, it couldn't prevent me. *(Laughs.)* I'm deadweight. Deadweight exists for the sole purpose of standing in its own way...

SOFYA YEGOROVNA: Surely you're not deadweight! Not you, Mikhail Vasilich!

PLATONOV: Surely not! We all keep very busy here. We're working all the time. Women's emancipation and all that. Triletsky heals the sick, in between mealtimes. And Porfiry Semyonich here has taken up farming. Watches his estate grow. We get the city papers, two weeks late of course, but still we get them, and Gerasim Kuzmich reads them aloud, when he's not buying up everyone else's property, that is. So you see, we're all toiling. And this is my wife, Aleksandra. A wife is one's civic duty. Propagation of the race. We're multiplying. I now have a son to inherit my ideas. We have no money, you see, so we bequeath our ideas.*(Pause.)* What's the matter, everyone? You'd think this was a funeral. We're putting on a vaudeville, and we're not even getting a single laugh!

General laughter.

GLAGOLYEV: I try not to laugh, Mikhail Vasilich. I have a weak heart!

PLATONOV: *(Points to TRILETSKY.)* Who told you that, him? If you believe that charlatan, you'll soon be six feet under.

PETRIN: He once tried to cure my lumbago. Said: "Don't eat this, don't eat that, don't sleep on the floor" — and in the end, he never cured it. So I ask him: "Why did you take my money if you didn't cure me?" And he says: "I was professionally obliged to do one of two things," he says, "either cure you or take your money."

TRILETSKY: Let me refresh your memory. All I ever got from you for six house calls was a ruble, and a torn ruble at that. I tried to give it to a beggar, and even *he* wouldn't take it. "It's torn," the beggar said, "and the serial number's missing."

PLATONOV: That's because it's peasant money...

ANNA PETROVNA: That's enough, Platonov. Sofya Yegorovna, I apologize — no one's introduced Gerasim Kuzmich...

PLATONOV: Why should we? Look at him! He's always reading!

PETRIN: It says here in this paper that the Russian winter gets longer and longer each year...

PLATONOV: What would we know if Gerasim Kuzmich himself did not tell us! We're deeply indebted, Gerasim Kuzmich Petrin!

PETRIN: You can say whatever you like about me: Petrin this, Petrin that, Petrin the son of a peasant...Well, what about Petrin? *(Puts his newspaper into his pocket.)* Perhaps Petrin even went to the university, perhaps Petrin even has a degree! *(To PLATONOV.)* That's more than you can say.

PLATONOV: And what has it taught you?

PETRIN: It's taught me a lot...about life!

PLATONOV: Such as —

PETRIN: I'll tell you what it's taught me! When a man is born, he can choose one of three roads before him, that's all. And no other choices are possible. If he travels down the one to the right, the wolves will eat him. If he travels down the road to the left, he will eat the wolves. And if he travels down the one before him, he will eat himself.

TRILETSKY: *(Pause.)* What does *that* mean?

PLATONOV: And have you really come to this staggering conclusion about life by way of education?

PETRIN: Education — and experience...

PLATONOV: Ah, yes, experience! And do you know what his experience has earned him? Sixty taverns. That's right, ladies and gentlemen. This man owns sixty taverns, while you, your ladyship, haven't got sixty kopeks!

PETRIN: Sixty-three taverns, actually.

PLATONOV: He's charitable, he's well-respected, and everyone bows down to him —

VOYNITSEV: Calm down, Mikhail Vasilich!

ANNA PETROVNA: Platonov, will you please!

SASHA: Misha, it isn't nice! *(Softly.)* You're embarrassing me!

PETRIN: If someone's going to lecture, young man, it's not going to be you. I'm a citizen, and, truth be told, an upright one, too. And who are you? Who are you indeed, young man? Forgive me, I like you very much, Mikhail Vasilich, you're a very intelligent man, but you've squandered your education, your land, your fortune… You're a teacher, and your calling is sacred, and yet you don't even care. Frankly, you don't deserve your calling, you're depraved…

PLATONOV: In other words I'm a Russian…

PETRIN: What's that supposed to mean?

ANNA PETROVNA: He just won't stop! Why spoil our summer solstice with your moralizing, Platonov?

VOYNITSEV: Hush!

TRILETSKY: Oh, let them quarrel their heads off. It's entertainment.

PLATONOV: Just look around you, seriously, look what's happening to us, take it all in, it's enough to send you into oblivion! And what's worst of all is that anyone who's in the slightest degree honest just keeps silent, dead silent, and only looks on! *(Indicates PETRIN.)* Everyone looks at him with terror, they all bow down before this vulgarian because they're in debt to him up to their ears!

ANNA PETROVNA: Calm down, Platonov! It's the same business as last summer, and I just won't stand for it!

GLAGOLYEV: Mikhail Vasilich, really!

TRILETSKY: Stop it, Platonov!

PLATONOV: Look who's talking! Have you visited your patients today?

TRILETSKY: I can't — it's almost lunchtime!

VOYNITSEV: Enough, Mikhail Vasilich!

SASHA: Misha, please!

ANNA PETROVNA: Take no offense please, Gerasim Kuzmich!

PETRIN: I never do, your ladyship, I never do…

YAKOV: *(Enters.)* Lunch is served!

ANNA PETROVNA: Good! In that case, ladies and gentlemen, let's sit down and eat!

TRILETSKY: Hoorah! You could starve to death around here! *(Grabs SASHA by the hand and runs into the house. PETRIN folds his newspaper and follows.)*

VOYNITSEV: *(Nudges IVAN IVANOVICH, who has nodded off.)* Ivan Ivanich! Ivan Ivanich! Wake up! Time for lunch!

IVAN IVANOVICH: *(Jumps up.)* Eh? Who?

VOYNITSEV: Lunchtime!

IVAN IVANOVICH: Very good, my dear fellow!

GLAGOLYEV: A word, Anna Petrovna!

ANNA PETROVNA: Later, Porfiry Semyonich! The food's getting cold. It's always better to talk after lunch!

GLAGOLYEV exits with VOYNITSEV and IVAN IVANOVICH.

PLATONOV: Don't look so astonished! This world is unknown to you! *(Lowers his voice.)* It's a world of fools, Sofya Yegorovna, complete, utter, hopeless fools… *(She stares at him, turns, and runs into the house.)*

ANNA PETROVNA: Have you got hold of yourself?

PLATONOV: I have, indeed. Let's not be cross now, shall we? *(Kisses her hand.)* My dear lady, each and every one of them should be thrown out of the house, really.

ANNA PETROVNA: With what pleasure, my insufferable Mikhail Vasilich, I would drive these guests away! The problem is, you see, that the honor, which you so kindly defended on my behalf, is irrelevant. Neither you nor I can ever drive them away. For they are all, I'm afraid, our benefactors and creditors. One look at them sideways and tomorrow we'll be thrown out of this estate. It's either honor or the estate, as you see. Well, I choose the estate. You can take it however you like, my dear philosopher, but if you don't want me to leave this beautiful place, then don't talk to me of honor, and "don't disturb the geese, my dear," as the poet says…

OSIP appears from behind the trees.

PLATONOV: Well well well, if it isn't the Prince of Darkness!

ANNA PETROVNA: *(Seeing OSIP)* God, no! Not him!

PLATONOV: Come here, Osip! Don't worry! We're not going to arrest you!

OSIP: May I? *(Removes cap, and enters with hesitation.)*

ANNA PETROVNA: No, you may not! How dare you! Why did you come here?

OSIP: To congratulate your ladyship on her safe return —

ANNA PETROVNA: Well, I don't need your congratulations! *(To PLATONOV.)* Get him out of here, Platonov! I'm angry with him.

TRILETSKY and VOYNITSEV appear on the verandah, holding glasses of champagne.

ANNA PETROVNA: *(To OSIP.)* Tell them in the kitchen to give you some dinner. Look at those eyes! The eyes of a wild beast! How many trees have you stolen from us this winter?!

OSIP: Only three or four, your ladyship…

ANNA PETROVNA: Liar!

OSIP: May I kiss your hand?

ANNA PETROVNA: *(Reluctantly offers him her hand.)* Oh, go ahead…

OSIP: I'm much obliged, your ladyship, for your kindness.

PLATONOV: *(To TRILETSKY and VOYNITSEV.)* Gentlemen, I have the honor of introducing one of the most fascinating carnivores in the contemporary human zoo. Known to all as Osip, local horse thief, parasite, and murderer.

OSIP: Thanks for the introduction, Mikhail Vasilich!

ANNA PETROVNA: Don't provoke him, Platonov. You don't know what he's capable of…

TRILETSKY: And what *is* your profession, my good fellow?

OSIP: Theft, sir.

TRILETSKY: An intriguing occupation…

PLATONOV: Where have you been lurking all these months? In prison?

OSIP: Maybe… It's cold in the forest in wintertime!

PLATONOV: Good God, he's smiling! What a face! You could even smash a stone on it! You're not one of this world, Osip. You live above the law, beyond the boundaries of time and space…

OSIP: I have something for your ladyship.

ANNA PETROVNA: Really? And what might that be?

PLATONOV: Something stolen, undoubtedly.

OSIP: Yes, sir. *(Reaches under his coat and reveals a live baby rabbit.)* Stolen from nature, sir.

ANNA PETROVNA: Good God, Osip! Now what!

OSIP: He's soft and silky, your ladyship. Thought you'd want to hold him…

ANNA PETROVNA: Take it 'round to the kitchen…No, never mind, cook will want to serve him up.

TRILETSKY: *Lapin au vin blanc*…delicious!

OSIP: I'll build a little home for him with twigs…

ANNA PETROVNA: All right, enough! Now, go!

OSIP: *(Bows.)* I remain your ladyship's humble servant. Good day, gentlemen…
(Exits.)

ANNA PETROVNA: Keep him away from me, Platonov! I shudder when he's
near, as if someone's walking over my grave…

YAKOV: *(Appears at the door.)* Your guests are waiting, your ladyship…

TRILETSKY: Come inside! Let's drink to the health of the newlyweds!

ANNA PETROVNA: They're calling for me. Don't you dare leave, Platonov. Let's
go for a drive after lunch. We'll finish this conversation later. *(Exits into the
house with TRILETSKY.)*

*The sound of toasting, glasses clinking, and laughter is heard inside. An accor-
dion plays.*

VOYNITSEV: Why are you hiding, Mikhail Vasilich? Do come inside! Let's drink
to my Sofya's health!

PLATONOV: I can't take my eyes off your wife. What a lovely lady she is! You're
a lucky man!

VOYNITSEV: *(Laughs.)* Yes, I know, very lucky, in fact!

PLATONOV: I've known her for a long long time, Sergey Pavlovich! She's lovely
now, and she was lovely then!

VOYNITSEV: So lucky, so lucky! And what about your wife?

PLATONOV: My foolish little Sasha? You can hardly tell her apart from all the
other peasant girls! Look at her sitting there, hiding behind the decanter of
vodka! All upset and anxious from my behavior! How she suffers, poor thing,
at the thought that everyone hates me!

VOYNITSEV: Forgive me, but aren't you happy with her?

PLATONOV: Happy? Who knows? I only know that she's my family. Take her
away from me, and I'm lost, believe me. We're meant for each other — she's
a fool and I'm an outcast…

VOYNITSEV: You must spend time with my Sofya, Mikhail Vasilich, make her
feel welcome. I want you to be close, close friends. Yes, so lucky! So lucky —

TRILETSKY: *(At the door, with a plate of food.)* Platonov! We're waiting!

OSIP reappears from behind the trees.

ANNA PETROVNA: *(At the door.)* Come, parasites, eat! It's getting cold!

(VOYNITSEV exits into the house.) Osip, I told you, go round to the kitchen. They'll give you something to eat there.

PLATONOV: I'm coming! *(To OSIP.)* I'd rather be dining with you, Osip. I prefer your company to the company of fools. You're not dangerous at all!

OSIP: I might not agree with you there, sir. But thank you anyway.

PLATONOV: And now, go in I must. I haven't been drunk in ages. It's time! *(Exits into the house.*

OSIP remains onstage gazing at the house. From within comes laughter and the clinking of glasses, as an accordion strikes a chord.

END OF ACT ONE

ACT TWO

Evening. The garden. The same scene as before. From the windows float the sounds of laughter, conversation, a piano and violin playing quadrilles, waltzes, and so on. Upstage of the garden is a gazebo, decorated with hanging lanterns. The garden and the house are illuminated. Guests and servants wander through the garden. Upstage, YAKOV stands on a ladder and hangs lanterns.

IVAN IVANOVICH and SASHA enter from the house. As they descend the stairs, SASHA supports IVAN IVANOVICH, who is slightly inebriated and singing.

SASHA: My God, when will it all end! Nikolai's drunk, Misha's drunk, and now you're drunk, too! It's disgraceful!

IVAN IVANOVICH: *(Singing.)*
    "We shall never blink an eye
    Till we hear the battle cry" —

SASHA: You shouldn't be permitted in a respectable household! *(Tries to budge him.)* Come on, Papa, let's go home!

IVAN IVANOVICH: Wait…what was I saying? Ah, yes! Another five years of service and I'd have been a general! Served on a general's staff once, thinking up ways to kill the Turks! Never used a bayonet, though, still don't know how to…

SASHA: Generals don't drink like that.

IVAN IVANOVICH: Oh yes, they do!

SASHA: You're old — you ought to be setting an example!

IVAN IVANOVICH: Blah blah blah… Just like your mother… Same eyes, same hair…and you walk like her, too, like a funny little goose… *(Kisses her.)* Just like your poor dear mother… *(Tearfully.)* How I loved her!

Enter TRILETSKY from the garden, slightly inebriated.

TRILETSKY: Here you are, your honor, ten kopeks! *(Gives him money).*

SASHA: What are you doing?

TRILETSKY: I won it off of Anna Petrovna at cards this morning!

IVAN IVANOVICH: I'll take it, my boy, I'll take it! *Merci.* I wouldn't accept it from a stranger, but if it's my own son, why of course, with pleasure! Your father is an honest man, children! Never ever have I robbed my fellow man or my country! And believe you me, all I ever had to do was to reach out my hand, and I'd have been rich and famous today!

TRILETSKY: That's admirable, Father, admirable indeed. Where are you going?

IVAN IVANOVICH: Home. I'm taking this little creature home…

TRILETSKY: Where's Platonov?

SASHA: I don't know. He's drunk. And I'm worried about Petya!

IVAN IVANOVICH: She's too afraid to go home alone. I'll take her, and I'll come right back.

TRILETSKY: You must come back! We're having fireworks! *(To SASHA.)* Here's three rubles, Sashenka!

SASHA: Add two more. I'll buy Misha another pair of summer trousers. He only has one. When I wash them, he has to wear his winter pair…

TRILETSKY: If it were up to me, I wouldn't buy him any trousers. Let him walk around with no trousers at all!

IVAN IVANOVICH: You're a smart man, Kolya! And you'll be a great doctor one day, too! I met the great Pirogov once, in Kiev…brilliant physician…nice man, too. Never cured anybody, though —

SASHA: Come on, Papa, it's time to go. Good-bye, Kolya!

TRILETSKY: He hasn't budged an inch. *(Takes off his cap and puts it on his father's head.)* Forward march, old fellow! Left, right, left, right…!

IVAN IVANOVICH: Abou-u-ut face! Are you ready, Sasha? Come, let me carry you!

SASHA: Don't be silly!

IVAN IVANOVICH: I always used to carry your mother. I would stagger a lot doing it, but still I would carry her. Once we fell and came crashing down a hill. She simply laughed, the little goose, she never got angry. Come on! *(Tries to lift her.)*

SASHA: Don't be ridiculous! And your cap isn't on straight. *(Straightens his cap.)* You're a dear, Papa!

IVAN IVANOVICH: Yes, yes. *(Tearfully.)* How I loved your poor mother! *(Starts offstage.)* Lord, how we've sinned! Never said my prayers as a youth! Now I serve Mammon! Terrible… *(They exit.)*

ANNA PETROVNA: *(Calling from the house.)* Triletsky, where's Yakov?

TRILETSKY: Out in the garden, hanging lanterns.

ANNA PETROVNA: Tell him to hurry. He's got to prepare the fireworks!

YAKOV speeds up his activity. PETRIN and GLAGOLYEV enter from the garden.

TRILETSKY: Ah! Pasha! Gerasya! Here you are! Another game, gentlemen?

PETRIN: Haven't you won enough tonight?

TRILETSKY: Once more! And make the stakes higher!

GLAGOLYEV: Whoever wins, proposes to Anna Petrovna!

TRILETSKY: Bravo! *(They gather around the downstage table.)* He who draws the queen of hearts proposes to Anna Petrovna! *(Draws a deck of cards from his pocket, shuffles it, and lays it fanlike out on the table.)* Un, deux, trois! Ready, gentlemen?

PETRIN: *(Draws a card.)* …The king of spades…

GLAGOLYEV: *(Draws a card.)* …Never mind…

TRILETSKY: Well?

GLAGOLYEV: *(Reluctantly.)* Jack of clubs.

TRILETSKY: *(Draws a card.)* …Ah-ha!

PETRIN: Again? Nikolai Ivanich, you fixed the cards!

GLAGOLYEV: Nikolai Ivanich, Nikolai Ivanich! How much do you want for the queen of hearts? Please! I'll pay! *(Reaches in his pocket for a fistful of ruble notes. ANNA PETROVNA appears at the window.)*

ANNA PETROVNA: Triletsky, where are you? Come dance with me! *(She disappears.)*

TRILETSKY: *(Gives the card to GLAGOLYEV. Grabs the rubles.)* For the widow of a major general, five rubles! *Tout de suite! (Runs into the house.)*

PETRIN: What a waste of money! You won't propose. You'll just sit there like a toadstool in one place, you won't say a word, you'll just gaze at her! Is that a way to woo a lady?

GLAGOLYEV: She'll never marry me. I'm an old man, and she's a European, she's young and educated and passionate…

PETRIN: Tonight is the night, Porfiry Semyonich! Fireworks! Our merry little widow has been laughing and singing and kissing everyone in sight!

GLAGOLYEV: You sound as if you'd like to marry her yourself…

PETRIN: She wouldn't have me. I'm a peasant…

GLAGOLYEV: And anyway, if she marries me, you'll claim all the promissory notes on the loans you made to her late husband. She won't let her stepson go bankrupt, so she'll pay up! With my money!

PETRIN: What can I do? Everyone owes me!

A waltz strikes up. ANNA PETROVNA appears at the window.

ANNA PETROVNA: Who wants to dance with me next? Platonov, where are you?

GLAGOLYEV: I do, Anna Petrovna! I do! *(Rushes to the house. PETRIN follows after.)*

VOYNITSEV and SOFYA YEGOROVNA enter from the garden.

VOYNITSEV: You're so quiet tonight, Sofya! What's the matter?

SOFYA YEGOROVNA: Nothing…

VOYNITSEV: You mustn't keep secrets from your husband!
    (They sit.)

SOFYA YEGOROVNA: Don't pay any attention to my mood. I don't understand it myself, really… *(Pause.)* Let's get away from here, Sergey.

VOYNITSEV: Away?

SOFYA YEGOROVNA: Yes.

VOYNITSEV: But the summer season's only just starting!

SOFYA YEGOROVNA: We'll go abroad. Shall we?

VOYNITSEV: If you really want to… But why?

SOFYA YEGOROVNA: I don't know, I just feel like it! No, really, it's lovely here, it's lively and gay, but we must go away. Just the two of us. Alone.

VOYNITSEV: Sofya! My Sofya! You do love me, don't you?!

SOFYA YEGOROVNA: Don't ask me any more questions, please.

VOYNITSEV: We'll go away tomorrow — we'll leave here right away! *(Kisses her hand.)* I understand how you feel! It's tedious for you here! So many new faces —

SOFYA YEGOROVNA: They're not to blame…

VOYNITSEV: Just give them a chance, Sofya! Get to know them! Why do you avoid Platonov, for example? Have a heart-to-heart talk with him, he's an excellent fellow! And talk with *maman* and Triletsky! *(Laughs.)* They're my favorite people. I love them. And you'll love them too, when you know them better.

ANNA PETROVNA: *(From the window.)* Sergey! A-oo! Is that you, Sergey? Come inside for a minute! It's time to prepare the fireworks!

VOYNITSEV: Right away, *maman!* *(To SOFYA YEGOROVNA.)* We'll leave tomorrow, if you haven't changed your mind. *(Exits into the house.)* Sofya! My wife! She loves me! I'm so happy, so happy!

Pause. The music plays. Enter PLATONOV.

PLATONOV: So you're here, Sofya Yegorovna. Are you alone?

SOFYA YEGOROVNA: Yes…

PLATONOV: Do you shun us, mere mortals that we are?

SOFYA YEGOROVNA: I'm not shunning you…

PLATONOV: May I? *(Sits down next to her.)* Why are you avoiding me, Sofya

Yegorovna? You won't even look at me! When I'm in one room, you run to the other, when I come into the garden, you leave it —

SOFYA YEGOROVNA: I don't know what you mean —

PLATONOV: Do I offend you?

SOFYA YEGOROVNA: No. It was *I* who offended *you!* That stupid interrogation — forgive me, please... Are you angry with me?

PLATONOV: No, of course not... *(Pause.)* Do you remember, Sofya? That summer, by the lake?...

SOFYA YEGOROVNA: Please, don't...

PLATONOV: Do you remember?

SOFYA YEGOROVNA: I don't want to remember. Our past was beautiful, but try to understand. You're Mikhail Vasilich, the school teacher... You're married, and so am I... Let's leave the past alone. Once upon a time, a boy loved a schoolgirl, a schoolgirl loved a boy. It's an old, old story, too trite to attach any meaning to...

PLATONOV: You're a coward, Sofya Yegorovna!

SOFYA YEGOROVNA: What?

PLATONOV: You're being pursued, aren't you?! Snatched from the arms of your loving husband?! Platonov is in love with you, that eccentric Platonov! Here's a delicacy for our little egotist no other gourmet has ever tasted before!

VOYNITSEV: *(From the house.)* Sofya! A-oo!

SOFYA YEGOROVNA: Why are you saying this? To shock me?... I won't listen... *(Attempts to go.)*

PLATONOV: Wait! Don't go, Sofya Yegorovna! Stay, please! Listen to me... I'm an ordinary school teacher. That's all I've done since we parted. But that is not my calling. What have I done for myself? What seed have I sown and nurtured to fruition? And now? My God, it's shocking! I open my eyes and I see mediocrity all around me, sullying the earth, swallowing up my fellow man, and yet I sit here, arms akimbo, I sit and watch in silence and do nothing... And one day I'll be forty, and nothing will change... And at fifty I'll be just as I am today — no change in sight! — and meanwhile I grow fat and idle and dull and indifferent to all but the pleasures of the flesh... And what lies ahead?! Death!! A life is lost! Wasted! My hair stands on end when I think of such a death! How can I rise above it all, Sofya Yegorovna? *(Pause.)* You are silent. You don't know, how could you? No, Sofya Yegorovna, don't feel sorry for me! To hell with me, anyway! But what about *you?* Where is your youth, your purity, your courage? What has become of it? To spend years in idleness, while others toil for you, to watch their suffering and look them straight in the face — it's depravity!

SOFYA YEGOROVNA: I can't bear to hear this —

PLATONOV: Wait! One more word. How is it you've become so spoiled and opinionated and affected? Who taught you to lie? Oh, how different you were before! Please, let me finish, then I'll let you go! How lovely you were then, how magnificent! Darling Sofya Yegorovna, you can still rise above it! Gather all your strength and rise above it, for the love of God, before it's too late!

VOYNITSEV: *(Calling from the house.)* Sofya! A-oo!

SOFYA YEGOROVNA: Leave me alone! I can't bear it! I'm going away! *(Runs into the garden.)*

Enter ANNA PETROVNA from the house, followed by GLAGOLYEV. PLATONOV sees them coming, and hides behind some trees.

ANNA PETROVNA: Yakov! It's enough, now. I told you to come in! It's time to prepare the fireworks!

YAKOV takes the ladder, bows, and goes into the house. Carrying the ladder up the stairs in one hand, and a lantern in the other, he stumbles and bumps the ladder against his head.

ANNA PETROVNA: Fool! Let me carry it. *(Takes the ladder. YAKOV exits into the house.)*

GLAGOLYEV: Wait, Anna Petrovna! I need to talk to you about something…

ANNA PETROVNA: Yes? *(Stands the ladder against the railing.)*

GLAGOLYEV: I…

ANNA PETROVNA: What can I do for you, Porfiry Semyonich?

GLAGOLYEV: Well, you see, Anna Petrovna… What I want to say is…I am in need…

ANNA PETROVNA: Yes?

GLAGOLYEV: I am in need of… a mistress of my household…

ANNA PETROVNA: So?

GLAGOLYEV: What I mean is, I don't expect you to love me… It's just that I own a paradise…but there are no angels in it.

ANNA PETROVNA: I've often wondered, Porfiry Semyonich, what I would do in paradise, if I ever end up there, that is, for you see, I'm no angel. God knows, I'm only human! *(Laughs.)*

GLAGOLYEV: A good person will find something to do anywhere, on earth or in paradise…

ANNA PETROVNA: A good person?! Really, Porfiry Semyonich!

GLAGOLYEV: God did not bestow upon me many attributes. I was born to do great deeds and ended up doing lots and lots of little worthless ones... But to love! —

ANNA PETROVNA: No. And not another word about it... And please, Porfiry Semyonich, don't attach too much importance to my refusal. If we could possess everything we love, there would be no room left for our possessions! There's a tasty morsel of philosophy for you!

GLAGOLYEV: *(In despair.)* Anna Petrovna! I can't bear it! Anna Petrovna! *(Runs off into the woods.)*

ANNA PETROVNA sits on the bench, humming to the music coming from the house. PLATONOV emerges from the trees.

ANNA PETROVNA: So there you are! I've been looking for you! Good God! *(Laughs.)*

PLATONOV: What's the matter?

ANNA PETROVNA: Imagine! Porfiry Semyonich just proposed to me. He wants to marry me. He'll save the estate from being auctioned. He'll pay back all my husband's debts to Gerasim Kuzmich. I'll be rich. I'll learn to till the soil on his land, I'll help you in your school. What do you think?

PLATONOV: Why not?

ANNA PETROVNA: A loveless match? You advise it?

PLATONOV: What do you want me to say?

ANNA PETROVNA: Anything! I don't know, I'm in such a funny mood tonight! Cool, fresh air, a starry sky! Pity that a lady can't sleep out of doors under this sky. When I was a girl, I always slept in the garden on the summer solstice...

PLATONOV: How lovely you look tonight... But then again you always look lovely!

ANNA PETROVNA: What about us, Mikhail Vasilich? We haven't seen each other all winter! Are we still friends?

PLATONOV: Of course, why wouldn't we be?

ANNA PETROVNA: We *are* friends then, aren't we? Great friends!

PLATONOV: What are you getting at?

ANNA PETROVNA: Well, you know very well, don't you, that between a man and a woman there is only one step between friendship and love?...

PLATONOV: So that's it! You're a lovely, intelligent, passionate woman, Anna Petrovna. Please, let's forget the past, shall we! Let's simply stay friends. And don't forget I am just a wee bit married...

OSIP emerges from behind the trees. He is carrying a nest.

ANNA PETROVNA: Not now, Osip.

OSIP: Your ladyship, please —

ANNA PETROVNA: What is it, you fool?

OSIP: A nest, Anna Petrovna. Of baby starlings. For you, your ladyship. You love starlings. "Never cage a starling, Osip," you always say: "A starling needs his freedom."

VOYNITSEV: *(Calls from the house.)* Anna Petrovna! The fireworks! We're waiting for you!

ANNA PETROVNA: Save it for later, Osip. Go down to the riverbank. We're setting off the fireworks there. Hurry! And get that ladder out of here! Don't steal it, either! *(To PLATONOV.)* We'll finish this conversation later...You'll perish without me, Platonov! *(Runs into the house. OSIP exits with the ladder.)*

GLAGOLYEV: *(Dashes in.)* Anna Petrovna! Where has she gone? *(PLATONOV points wordlessly to the house.)* Anna Petrovna! My queen of hearts! Wait! *(Dashes into the house.)*

PLATONOV: Summer solstice...the longest night of the year! Will it never end?...

Enter GREKOVA from the garden, unaware of PLATONOV.

PLATONOV: Boo! *(GREKOVA shrieks.)*

GREKOVA: Oh, no! Not you, Mikhail Vasilich! *(Turns to go.)*

PLATONOV: Wait, please, Marya Yefimovna, don't go. I won't disturb you, I promise. I'm disturbing everyone tonight.

GREKOVA: You were so cruel to me at lunch today, Mikhail Vasilich.

PLATONOV: Forgive me, my little Marie Curie, forgive me...you must! I publicly apologize! I burn with the shame of fifty bonfires! *(Bows low to her.)*

GREKOVA: *(Uncertainly.)* How do I know that?

PLATONOV: This time I mean it, I swear... *(Takes her hand.)* Peace? *(Goes to kiss her hand.)* Oh, sorry, I forgot, really, forgive me. Give me one more chance... Come dance with me. You look so lovely this evening!

GREKOVA: How cruel you are, Platonov! You *know* I'm not lovely! And you don't really want to dance with me! You ask me just to torture me! Just like this afternoon... *(Weeps.)*

PLATONOV: Don't cry, my little chemist. Let me console you with a lovely little waltz! *(He embraces her gently and sways with her to the music.)* One two three one two three — Ma-rie! Ma-rie! Ma-rie! Cu-rie!

GREKOVA: What are you doing?!

PLATONOV: I haven't the faintest idea! *(He kisses her.)*

GREKOVA: Why are you kissing me?!

PLATONOV: Who else is there to kiss?! *(Kisses her again.)*

GREKOVA: Do you…love me?

PLATONOV: *(Laughs.)* Love!

GREKOVA: You do love me, don't you? Or else you wouldn't have kissed me! Tell me! Say it! Do you love me?

PLATONOV: Not a drop, my darling! I love only one little fool, and that's out of having nothing better to do…

GREKOVA: What?… You're a scoundrel, Mikhail Vasilich, do you know that? I despise you! *(She goes toward the house.)* Why does this always happen! It's all my fault! *(In tears.)*

Enter TRILETSKY.

TRILETSKY: Ah, Marya Yefimovna! Want a ruble?

GREKOVA: Nikolai Ivanich, if you have any regard for me, have nothing whatsoever to do with this man! I've never been so insulted in my entire life! Never!

TRILETSKY: Not again!

GREKOVA: I am offended, and meanwhile you're joking… No, I mustn't cry, I mustn't — I'm a scientist! Go on, be his friend, love him, bow down to him, fear him! You all think he's the second Hamlet, so admire him, then! The scoundrel!

TRILETSKY: But what can I do?

GREKOVA: Nothing! You're a coward! Get away from me, go back to your wretched buffet!

TRILETSKY: Marya Yefimova, please! —

GREKOVA: I shall have him dismissed! He shall no longer teach here! He has no right to be a schoolmaster. Tomorrow I shall go to the director of the school!

TRILETSKY: What do you have to say for yourself, Platonov?

PLATONOV: The same as always… *(Shrugs.)*

GREKOVA: You see? *(Bursts into tears again. She runs off, almost colliding with SOFYA YEGOROVNA.)*

TRILETSKY: Sofya Yegorovna! What are you doing here?

SOFYA YEGOROVNA: Where's Sergey? I must find him!

ANNA PETROVNA: *(Offstage.)* Nikolai Ivanich! Where are you?

TRILETSKY: Her ladyship calls. I'm being summoned. It's time to light the fireworks. Excuse me, please... *(Bows, and exits.)*

SOFYA YEGOROVNA: *(Sees PLATONOV.)* Not you! *(Attempts to leave.)*

PLATONOV: Wait! *(He grabs her hand.)*

SOFYA YEGOROVNA: Leave me alone! They're coming —

PLATONOV: To hell with them! Let them come!

SOFYA: You're torturing me!

VOYNITSEV: *(From the house.)* Sofya! A-oo!

SOFYA YEGOROVNA: That's Sergey! I must go to him!

PLATONOV: Why, Sofya Yegorovna? You'll only sink deeper and deeper into the mire —

SOFYA YEGOROVNA: I'm not listening!

PLATONOV: Tell me truly, my darling, in the name of our past, what could possibly have driven you to marry such a man?

SOFYA YEGOROVNA: He's fine, he's noble —

PLATONOV: Why say it? You don't believe it!

SOFYA YEGOROVNA: He's my husband! I've told him we must go away from here...

PLATONOV: Do whatever you want. But I'm going to tell you the truth! Why didn't you choose a man who struggles and suffers for what he believes in? Anyone else but this pygmy, who is up to his neck in debt and idleness!

VOYNITSEV: *(Calling from the house.)* Sofya! Where are you?

PLATONOV: I loved you so! *(Softly.)* I loved you more than anything else on earth! These hands, these eyes... Poor Sofya! If only I could find the strength, wretch that I am, I'd tear you up by the roots and take you away from this swamp, and myself along with you...

More voices offstage coming from the house. VOYNITSEV rushes onstage, carrying sticks of fireworks.

VOYNITSEV: Ah, here they are, just whom we're looking for! Come, let's light the fireworks! *(Shouts.)* Yakov! To the river! Forward march! *(To SOFYA YEGOROVNA.)* Have you changed your mind, Sofi? Are you staying?... Sofya! Answer me! *(SOFYA nods her head.)* You're staying! Hoorah! Your hand, Mikhail Vasilich! You've convinced her! I knew I could count on you! *(Presses PLATONOV's hand.)* We've all fallen under your spell! Come, let's light the fireworks! To the river! *(Dashes off.)*

PLATONOV: It's up to you, Sofya! Up to you!...

VOYNITSEV: *(Offstage.)* Platonov, are you coming?!

PLATONOV: To hell with it, I'd better be off! *(Shouts.)* Sergey Pavlovich, wait, don't light the fireworks without me! Tell Yakov to hurry — I need him to get the boat ready. Sofya, come! Let's go for a ride on the river! *(Rushes off upstage right.)*

ANNA PETROVNA rushes out of the house with YAKOV, who is carrying lighted sparklers.

ANNA PETROVNA: Wait! Sergey, wait for me! Keep on firing the cannon! *(To SOFYA.)* Sofya, why do you look so strange?

PLATONOV: *(Offstage.)* Fireworks!

ANNA PETROVNA: Coming! *(Runs off with YAKOV.)*

TRILETSKY, PETRIN, and GLAGOLYEV enter from the house.

GLAGOLYEV: *(To SOFYA YEGOROVNA.)* Where is she?

SOFYA YEGOROVNA: Who?

GLAGOLYEV: Anna Petrovna?

SOFYA points toward the river.

GLAGOLYEV: Anna Petrovna! Wait for me!

PETRIN: Steady, man, steady! You're a suitor! Prepare yourself!

TRILETSKY: A love song before we go! Let's practice!

GLAGOLYEV: We haven't got time!

TRILETSKY: *(Sings. PETRIN joins in.)* "Tell her my flowers..."

GLAGOLYEV: Stop it!, please! I'm a sensitive man! *(Shouts, in the direction of the river.)* Anna Petrovna, wait for me! *(PETRIN and GLAGOLYEV rush offstage.)*

TRILETSKY: Sofya Yegorovna!

SOFYA YEGOROVNA: Leave me alone, I beg of you!

TRILETSKY: Want a ruble?

SOFYA YEGOROVNA: You're not a doctor, you're a clown!

TRILETSKY: Right! I'm the widow's court jester — that's how I earn my keep! I get pocket money, too. They'll tire of me one day... Aren't you coming?

SOFYA YEGOROVNA: *(In anguish.)* I don't know, I don't know...

TRILETSKY: For some strange reason I suddenly have the urge to run my fingertips over your perfectly porcelain forehead — just to see what it's made of. God, what an overpowering urge! Not to offend you, mind, but simply —

SOFYA YEGOROVNA: Fool!

ANNA PETROVNA: *(Offstage.)* Nikolai Ivanich! Where are you?

TRILETSKY: Alas, I must bid you farewell! Sorry! *(Takes her hand and kisses it.)* Why are we all acting this way? Must be the summer solstice! Till we meet again! I'd love to talk more, but —

VOYNITSEV: *(Offstage.)* Hurry!

TRILETSKY: *Adieu! (Rushes offstage.)*

Commotion from the direction of the river, offstage upstage right.

VOYNITSEV: *(Offstage.)* Ready or not!! Where are the matches?

ANNA PETROVNA: *(Offstage.)* Here they are, idiot!

PLATONOV: *(Offstage.)* Who's coming out on the river with me? Sofya, a-oo! Are you coming?

SOFYA YEGOROVNA: I can't bear it! I can't! It's too much! *(She clutches at her bosom.)* My ruin…or my happiness! He'll ruin me, or else he'll save me, he'll offer me a new life! My new life — how I welcome you, how I bless you!

VOYNITSEV: *(Offstage.)* Ready?

SOFYA YEGORVNA: Yes!

TRILETSKY: *(Offstage.)* Look out!

VOYNITSEV: *(Offstage.)* Fire!

Huge explosion of multicolored fireworks fills the dark sky. The crowd cheers offstage. SOFYA YEGOROVNA watches the fireworks, enraptured.

END OF ACT TWO

ACT THREE

Later that night. A clearing in the forest. At the edge of the clearing, stage left, there is a schoolhouse. Along the clearing, vanishing into the distance, are railway tracks, which turn right near the schoolhouse. A bright moon shines above. There is a row of telegraph poles. An occasional train whistle sounds in the distance. A guitar strums softly, somewhere.

SASHA sits by the open window. OSIP stands before the window, a rifle slung across his back. A bench stands close by.

OSIP: How could it have happened? Simple... I'm walking along a path in the forest, not far from here, I look, and there she is, standing in the river bed, her dress all tucked up like this, and she's scooping water from the stream with a burdock leaf. Scoop it up and drink it, scoop it up and drink it, then she wets her whole head with it... So I walk down to the stream, up close to her, and I look... She pays no attention to me at all, it's as if she's saying: "Fool! Why should I pay any attention to a peasant like you?" "Your ladyship," says I, "I see you're having a drink of cold, fresh water, right?" "What business is it of yours?" she says. "Go on, get out of here, go back to where you came from." Never even looked at me twice. Well, I must say I was frightened, and hurt, and ashamed of being a peasant. "What are you staring at me for, fool? Never seen a woman before, have you?" Then she gives me this knowing look. "Or perhaps you've taken a liking to me!" says she. "I like you, I like you a lot!" says I. "You're a noble, sensitive, warmhearted individual, you're beautiful. Never in my life have I seen a more beautiful lady. Manka, our local beauty, the constable's daughter," says I, "next to you? — why she's nothing but a horse, a camel! You're so delicate! If I kissed you right now," says I, "You'd drop dead on the spot!" So, she bursts out laughing. "Go ahead," she says, "Kiss me, if you want to!" Well, when she says that, I start feeling hot all over. I go up to her, take her gently by the shoulder, and kiss her right then and there, right on the spot, first on the cheek and then on the neck...

SASHA: *(Laughs.)* And what did she do?

OSIP: "All right now," she says, "Off with you! And don't forget to wash more often," she says, "and clean your nails." So off I go.

SASHA: The nerve she has! *(Gives OSIP a plate of cabbage soup.)* Here, eat up! Go, sit down somewhere.

OSIP: I'm not a gentleman, I don't mind standing. Thank you for your kindness, Aleksandra Ivanovna! I'll repay you one day...

SASHA: Take off your cap. It's a sin to eat with your cap on. And say Grace, too!

OSIP: *(Removes his cap.)* It's been a long time since I've said Grace... *(Eats.)* Anyway, since then I seem to have gone mad. Can you believe it? Can't eat, can't sleep. She's always there before me. I've only to close my eyes, and there she is. I'm in such a state, I feel like hanging myself! I even thought of drowning myself, or shooting her husband, the general. And then, when she became a widow, I started running all kinds of errands for her. I shot a partridge for her, I caught quail, I painted her gazebo all sorts of different colors. I even brought her a live wolf once. I tried to satisfy her every whim. Everything she told me to do, I did. If she told me to eat myself up, I'd have done it... Love...What can you do about it...

SASHA: Yes...When I fell in love with my husband, Mikhail Vasilich, I didn't know if he loved me too, and how I suffered over it. Sometimes I even prayed to God to let me die, sinner that I am...

OSIP: You see? What feelings! *(Drinks the soup straight from the plate.)* You wouldn't have any more soup, would you?

(Hands her the plate.)

SASHA: *(Leaves, and a moment later appears at the window with a saucepan.)* There's no more soup, but would you like some potatoes? They're roasted in goose drippings...

OSIP: *Merci... (Takes the saucepan and eats.)* God, I'm full! Anyway, as I was saying, Aleksandra Ivanovna, I kept going to her house, like a madman. Last year after Easter I brought her a rabbit. "Here you are, your ladyship," says I. "Look at this little cross-eyed rabbit I brought you!" She took it in her hands, looked at it, and says to me: "Is it true what they say about you, Osip, that you're a thief?" "The absolute truth," says I. "They wouldn't be saying it if it wasn't true!" So I told her everything. "We must reform you," she says. "Off you go on a pilgrimage to Kiev. Go, and in a year you'll come home a different person." So I dress up like a beggar, sling a sack over my shoulder, and off I go to Kiev. But nothing happened! Yes, I was reformed, but not entirely...Wonderful potatoes these are!... Near Kharkov I fell in with questionable company, spent all my money on drink, got into a fight, and came home. Even lost my passport... She won't take anything from me now. She's angry with me...

SASHA: Why don't you go to church, Osip?

OSIP: I'm afraid to go to church in daylight. I've caused a lot of trouble, you know...

SASHA: Why do you harm people?

OSIP: You don't know about the rough life, Aleksandra Ivanovna. You couldn't comprehend such things. And what about Mikhail Vasilich, hasn't he harmed anyone?

SASHA: If he has, it's unintentional! He's a good man!

OSIP: An intelligent fellow, your husband is... He's got many fine qualities. Except that there's very little human kindness in him. According to him, everyone's either a fool or a lackey. And that's not right, is it? I mean, if I were a good man, I wouldn't behave like that. I'd comfort the lackeys and the fools and the thieves. After all, they're the unhappiest souls on earth! One must pity them. No, there's very little kindness in him, very little. Hates himself, I suppose, that's why. Can't be kind to others if you're not kind to yourself... *(Sighs.)* I could eat potatoes like yours for a hundred years! *(Hands her the saucepan.)* I humbly thank you...

SASHA: You're welcome.

OSIP: *(Sighs.)* You're a fine lady, Aleksandra Ivanovna! You're one of a kind.

SASHA: Mikhail Vasilich should be coming any minute! The fireworks were over hours ago...

OSIP: Don't count on it. At this very moment, he's discussing the affairs of the heart with her ladyship. He's a good-looking fellow, your husband! If he wanted to, he could have the entire female sex after him, he's got such a silver tongue. He's fawning over the widow all the time. But she won't let him get away with it. He might be eager, but she —

SASHA: That's enough. I don't like what you're saying now. Go, God bless.

OSIP: I'm going. You should have been in bed long ago. Waiting up for your husband, most likely?

SASHA: Yes...

OSIP: What a good woman you are! Platonov must have searched ten years for such a wife, with candles and a search party. And he found her, too... *(Bows.)* Farewell, Aleksandra Ivanovna! Good night! Sweet dreams!

SASHA: Go safely!

OSIP: I'm off. Going home... My home is where the earth is the floor and the ceiling is the sky, and who knows where the walls and roof are... He whom God has cursed makes his home in this house. There's plenty of room, though there's nowhere to lay your head. And the best thing is, you don't pay taxes... *(Starts offstage.)*

SASHA: I think I hear him coming now!

OSIP: Good night, Aleksandra Ivanovna! Come visit me, please, in the forest! Ask for Osip — every bird or lizard knows where to find me. *(He exits, and can be heard whistling moments later.)*

SASHA: *(Comes out of the schoolhouse with a candle.)* Misha's footsteps...I hear them: left, right, left right... *(Extinguishes the candle.)* At last...!

Enter PLATONOV.

PLATONOV: Correction, my darling! A drunkard has neither right nor left! He only has backwards, sideways, and downward...

SASHA: Come, my drunken sweetheart, sit here! Please!

PLATONOV: Yes, let's sit... *(They sit down on the bench.)* Why aren't you asleep, my little protozoan?

SASHA: I was waiting for you. They kept you out so late!

PLATONOV: Yes, late... Has the express come through yet?

SASHA: Not yet. A freight train came by about an hour ago.

PLATONOV: That means it's not two o'clock yet. How long have you been back?

SASHA: I was home by ten. Petya was crying for all the world to hear. I left without saying good-bye — I hope they'll forgive me. Was there dancing after I left?

PLATONOV: There was dancing, and supper, and fireworks, and all sort of goings on...

SASHA: Fireworks! I love fireworks! Were they wonderful?

PLATONOV: Oh, yes...

SASHA: How Sofya Yegorovna must have danced and danced! She's so lovely! I've never seen a more beautiful lady. There's something so special about her...

Pause.

PLATONOV: Oh! How stupid, how loathsome...

SASHA: What's the matter?

PLATONOV: What have I done! *(Covers his face in his hands.)* It's disgraceful! Hide me, Sasha! Hide me!

SASHA: What *have* you done?

PLATONOV: The things I said to Sofya Yegorovna!

SASHA: What things?

PLATONOV: I've been vile, vile as never before!

SASHA: You're drunk, poor thing! Come, let's go to bed!

PLATONOV: When have I ever *not* been vile? Oh, where can I hide from the shame? And here you are, you love me, you shelter me...I can't understand why! Why? Why do you love me?

SASHA: What a question! How could I *not* love you? You're my husband!

PLATONOV: Is that the only reason?! Oh, my little firefly, my funny little fool!

(Kisses her on the forehead.) What would happen if you weren't so blissfully ignorant? Would you still be happy if it dawned on you, little innocent that you are, that there is nothing in me worth loving? *(Kisses her hands.)* My own, my very own! Because of your ignorance, I'm blissful, too! I have a family, like everyone else! A family…

SASHA: You're talking nonsense tonight!

PLATONOV: You're a treasure, that's what you are! You should be kept in a glass case on the table! How did we ever manage, you and I, to bring little Petya into God's world? You should be making little gingerbread men, not little Petyas, my soul!

SASHA: I don't understand you!

PLATONOV: God forbid you should ever understand me! May the earth be balanced on the spouts of whales, and whales on pitchforks, before you ever understand me! Where could we find faithful wives, if there were no women like you, Sasha! *(Tries to kiss her.)*

SASHA: *(Angrily.)* Go away! Why did you marry me, then, if I'm so stupid? You should have found yourself a clever wife! Go to bed! You're drunk! And a schoolmaster, too! Shame on you! *(Goes into the schoolhouse.)*

PLATONOV: *(Alone.)* Inside, outside, what difference does it make? How stupid it all is, how abominable, how absurd! I'm disgusted by it all… Hide for shame! But where? I can't hide from myself! *(The sound of a train whistle, mournful, in the distance.)* Oh, to run away — to leap onto the next train and ride far far away! The light of the last car will recede in the distance, and the darkness swallow me up forever…

The sound of horses' hooves are heard. Enter ANNA PETROVNA, wearing a riding habit, with a whip in her hand.

ANNA PETROVNA: It's you! How perfect! I thought you might still be up! How can anyone sleep on such a night? God gave us winter for sleeping! …What's the matter? Are you drunk?

PLATONOV: Sober, drunk, what's the difference… And you? Walking alone in the moonlight, my somnabula?

ANNA PETROVNA: I didn't walk, my darling, I rode!

PLATONOV: What brought you all the way out here?

ANNA PETROVNA: You! I couldn't find you after the fireworks. You disappeared without a trace!

PLATONOV: It's late, Anna Petrovna, you ought to go home…

ANNA PETROVNA: Come, come, there's nothing to be afraid of! Why not take in the lovely night air together?

PLATONOV: Shhh! Someone will hear us…You'd better go, Anna Petrovna. I can see your head's full of all kinds of nonsense…

ANNA PETROVNA: Nonsense, at my age?

PLATONOV: What do you mean, "at your age"?! You're as young as the summer in June. You have your whole life before you!

ANNA PETROVNA: I don't want my whole life before me, I want it now! I *am* young, Platonov, I feel it! Like a wind, blowing right through me!

PLATONOV: Why do you look at me like that? You proud, magnificent woman — think what you're doing!

ANNA PETROVNA: I already have!

PLATONOV: A woman with such a mind, with such stature and beauty, to come to me?! I don't understand it!

ANNA PETROVNA: Oh, yes you do! Liar! Aren't you ashamed? On such a night, beneath such a sky, to tell such a lie! Lie in autumn, if you like, in the mud, in the slush, but not here, not now! Look up, you fool! Up there, the stars are twinkling, a thousand eyes are watching you, watching and listening, they know that you're lying! You understand very well! *(Puts her arms around him.)* There's no other man I could love as much as I love you! And there's no other woman you could love as much as me! Come, let's seize this love, seize it for our own!

PLATONOV: But I'll do to you what I've done to countless other women. I can't help it!

ANNA PETROVNA: *(Laughs.)* How dazzling you look in the moonlight! Your eyes are shining like bits of green glass! Drive away those demons, my poor Don Juan, don't let them disturb all this loveliness…You see before you a woman who loves you and whom you love, the weather is wonderful — what could be more simple? Enough talking! I want to forget myself! If only you knew how hard my life is! I want to live! Everything around us is alive and moving! Tomorrow we'll solve all our problems, but tonight, let us live, Michel, live, live! *(Kisses him.)*

PLATONOV: This is all so very trite! For God's sake, go, before it's too late!

ANNA PETROVNA: Fool! I'll never let you get away! *(Throws her arms around his neck.)* I'll have you, even if it destroys us both! You're mine! I claim you! *(Kisses him again.)*

PLATONOV: Wait! … Someone's coming…

ANNA PETROVNA: Quickly… Over here! *(They hide behind the trees.)*

Enter TRILETSKY, wearing tails, disheveled, unsteady on his feet.

TRILETSKY: *(Goes up to the school house and knocks on the window.)* Psssst! Sasha! Little sister! Sasha!

SASHA: *(Opens the window.)* Who's there? Is that you, Kolya? What do you want?

TRILETSKY: You're not asleep yet? Good. Let me spend the night here, my sweet!

SASHA: Of course…

TRILETSKY: I'll sleep in the schoolroom. Only please, don't let Misha know that I'm here: I won't get a moment's rest from his moralizing! My head is spinning, terribly, I'm seeing double… I'm standing in front of one window, but it seems like there are two! Which one should I climb in? Good thing I'm not married! If I were, I'd be a bigamist… *(Starts to climb in the window.)*

SASHA: Hush, Kolya, you'll wake the baby!

TRILETSKY: Meanwhile, my precious, I blew my nose down there by the felled oak tree — you know, the one near the stream — and I dropped forty rubles out of my handkerchief. Go find them, darling, tomorrow morning early, would you? Find them and keep them for yourself…

SASHA: How careless you are, Kolya! Oh, yes! I almost forgot — the shopkeeper's wife came over and asked that you come as soon as possible, she says it's urgent. Her husband has taken ill suddenly — a stroke, it seems. Go, quickly!

TRILETSKY: To hell with him! I can't be bothered. I have a splitting headache, and my stomach's killing me…

SASHA: But the shopkeeper, Kolya — shouldn't you go to him?

TRILETSKY: Rest. I need rest. We'll see about it in the morning. Out of my way… *(Climbs in through the window.)*

SASHA: Hurry up, climb in! You're standing on my dress… *(Closes the window.)*

PLATONOV: The scoundrel! What about his patient?

ANNA PETROVNA: Sshhh… Someone else is coming! *(They stay hidden behind the trees.)*

Enter GLAGOLYEV and PETRIN, reeling. PETRIN is singing "Tell her, my flowers…"

PETRIN: *Vive* Petrin, bachelor of law! Show me the way! Where are we? What's this? *(Bursts into laughter.)* Here, my dear Porfiry Semyonich, is the citadel of public education! Here's where they teach fools to forget God and cheat their fellow man! That's what we've come to… And here, my friend, is where that fellow — what the hell's his name? — Platonov lives. A civilized

Russian…Where is Platonov now, Pasha? Tell me, don't be ashamed! Blowing sweet nothings in the widow's ear?

GLAGOLYEV: I couldn't find the widow after the fireworks. Searched for her everywhere…

PETRIN: Maybe she's inside with the schoolmaster! Shall we look?

GLAGOLYEV: I want to go home, Gerasya…

PETRIN: Let's rest a moment. We'll stand watch for her… *(Sits down on the rail-road tracks.)*

GLAGOLYEV: I'm awfully tired! To hell with them all!

PETRIN: Ah, Porfiry, Porfiry…Did you drink champagne? I suppose you're drunk by now! And whose champagne have you been drinking? Mine! You drank my champagne, and you ate all my food. The widow's dress is mine, and Seryozha's stockings are mine, too. Everything's mine! I've given them everything! And yet the heels on my own shoes are worn. My father was a peasant, he never dared to come near their house. And now I own everything in it. I've given them everything I own, squandered everything, and what have I gotten in return? Go on, ask me, what have I gotten in return? Insult and injury…That's right…Their lackey skips over me at the table, and still manages to poke me with his elbow…

GLAGOLYEV: She's a countess, a baroness! An aristocrat! She needs money, she deserves it… *(Sits down next to him.)*

PETRIN: That's it! Not another kopek! Do you hear? Not one more kopek! Let her husband turn angrily in his grave! No more! I'll present the promissory notes tomorrow! *(Starts to doze off.)*

GLAGOLYEV: Please, give me a chance —

PETRIN: Tomorrow!

GLAGOLYEV: Gerasya, wake up…Please…How painful this all is… *(Resting, they both doze off.)*

ANNA PETROVNA: *(Emerges from behind the trees.)* Are they gone? No, look… They dozed off!…

PLATONOV: *(Stands over them.)* And here you have them, our aristocracy: the landowner, the new barbarian… *(Raising his voice, toward the house.)* And a doctor who refuses to heal the sick… Poor Russia!

ANNA PETROVNA: *(Takes his arm.)* Shhh… Shall we go?

PLATONOV: Yes, let's go. Why not? We'll all be despicable! Let's all go to hell…and as soon as possible!

SASHA: *(Calls from the window.)* Misha, is that you?

PLATONOV: Curse it all!

SASHA: *(At the window.)* Ah-ha! I see you! Who are you with? *(Peers out.)* Anna Petrovna! It's you! What a surprise! I hardly recognized you! You're all in black!

ANNA PETROVNA: *(Laughs)* Hello, Aleksandra Ivanovna!

SASHA: And you're wearing a riding habit! Going for a ride? How wonderful! It's such a lovely night! The summer solstice! Let's go too, Misha!

ANNA PETROVNA: I've had enough, Aleksandra Ivanovna. I'm going home…

SASHA: Of course. In that case, Misha, come inside. Really, I don't know what to do! My brother doesn't feel well. He's had too much to drink, I'm afraid. Please, come inside! You come in, too, Anna Petrovna! I'll go down to the cellar and fetch some cream. We'll all have a glass together! It's lovely when it's cold!

ANNA PETROVNA: I thank you, but I must go home now… *(Lowers her voice. To PLATONOV.)* Go — I'll wait for you at the gazebo…

SASHA: I'll run down to the cellar — I'll only be a minute. Come inside, Misha! *(She vanishes.)*

PLATONOV: *(Whispers.)* I'd forgotten she even existed…

ANNA PETROVNA: It wouldn't be the first time…

PLATONOV: She trusts me! How can she trust me? Go, I'll settle her into bed, then I'll come. She loves it when I rub her back gently…

ANNA PETROVNA: Come quickly…

PLATONOV: We almost caused a scandal! Good-bye for now… *(Goes into the schoolhouse.)*

ANNA PETROVNA: Surprise, surprise! I'd forgotten she existed, too…How cruel…Ah well, if we must sin, then we must! Only God will know, anyway! And it won't be the first time…Meanwhile, I'll stand watch over my sleeping suitors…Poor Russia, indeed…

OSIP emerges from behind the trees.

ANNA PETROVNA: Good God! Osip? Is that you? You frightened me!

OSIP: Good evening, your ladyship. *(Bows.)* What brings you to our parts?

ANNA PETROVNA: What are you doing here?

OSIP: Taking in the wonders of the moonlit night, your ladyship. My mother always said there's a sinner buried under every stump in the forest, and they shine so that people will pray for them…Are you shining tonight, your ladyship?

ANNA PETROVNA: You impertinent devil, you've been spying! *(Takes him by the chin.)* Did you see everything?

OSIP: Everything.

ANNA PETROVNA: Why are you so pale, eh? *(Laughs.)* Are you in love with me, Osip?

OSIP: I am whatever you want me to be, madam...

ANNA PETROVNA: So you *are* in love, then!

OSIP: I don't understand you... *(In tears.)* I worshiped the ground you walked on. You were the most sacred being on earth to me. If you commanded me to jump into flames, I'd jump...

ANNA PETROVNA: Enough, you fool! Go hunt some more rabbits and bring them to me — I'll take them. Only promise me this: Don't you dare touch Platonov! Do you hear me?

OSIP: I'll take no more orders from you, your ladyship!

ANNA PETROVNA: Is that so, really? Do you want to end up in prison? Or worse, in a monastery?...There, there, don't cry. What are you, a child? Enough. I'm going home. When he comes for me, fire a shot!

OSIP: When who comes?

ANNA PETROVNA: Platonov, you fool!

OSIP: But he won't come to you — he's with his wife now!

ANNA PETROVNA: We'll see. Farewell! Don't forget! One shot! *(Runs offstage.)*

OSIP: *(Bangs his cap on the ground and weeps.)* All is lost! Lost forever! I'll tear him to shreds! *(Retreats through the trees.)* I'll kill him...

PLATONOV shoves TRILETSKY out of the schoolhouse door.

PLATONOV: Out! Go to the shopkeeper's immediately! March!

TRILETSKY: Prod me with a stick tomorrow, if you have to. I won't go tonight!

PLATONOV: You're a scoundrel, Nikolai, a scoundrel! Do you understand? What if the shopkeeper is already dead?

TRILETSKY: If he's already dead, then may his soul rest in peace. Meanwhile, I'm not going there tonight! I'm going to bed!

PLATONOV: You're going, you swine! You're going! *(Shoves him.)* I will not let you sleep! What is the matter with you, anyway? You're supposed to be a doctor! Why do you spend your time idle and indolent, stuffing yourself, wasting the best years of your life?!

TRILETSKY: Stop it, Misha. Really! —

PLATONOV: Why don't you practice medicine? Why don't you do research? You're a scientist, not an animal!

TRILETSKY: To hell with my profession!

PLATONOV: What kind of man are you, anyway? Why are you alive? What God do you worship, you twisted soul? Nothing will ever come of us! Nothing, I tell you!

TRILETSKY: Listen, Mikhail Vasilich, who gave you the right to intrude on other people's lives? Tend to you own!

PLATONOV: We'll never amount to anything, none of us! We're hopeless! We aren't worth a kopek! *(Weeps.)* We live on earth and we occupy space. That's all. And we'll die and no one will remember us…A great fog will descend upon us, and swallow us up! We shall never be remembered! Ever! We're fools!

TRILETSKY: You *do* take me for a fool, don't you? All of you do! But what do you know about me, really? Tell me, please! Yes, I'm hopeless. I'm bored senseless, living in this wilderness. Awakened by dogs in the dead of the night. Fearing a call to a patient's bedside. Always dreading typhus. Not giving a damn about it, or those who have it. I'm ashamed of living and drinking like this, knowing that no matter what I do, no matter what, nothing will change…

PLATONOV: How vulgar, tawdry and sullied it all is…

TRILETSKY: *(Pause.)* I'll go to the shopkeeper's. All right? I'll go!

PLATONOV: What difference does it make… Maybe you'll save him, and maybe you won't…And tomorrow another shopkeeper will have a stroke…

TRILETSKY: I'm going…now…

PLATONOV: Whatever…

TRILETSKY: *(He goes and then stops.)* A parting word…Practice what you preach. If you can't stand the sight of yourself, how can you stand the sight of others?… *(Exits.)*

PLATONOV: *(Looks at PETRIN and GLAGOLYEV, sleeping on the embankment of the railroad tracks.)* Look at them all. It's not just me, it's everyone, they're all vile, all of them! Where are all the decent people in Russia? Good God! Are there any? Don't go to her, you fool! Stay with your wife!…No! No! I want to live! I *shall* go *(points in the direction where ANNA PETROVNA exited)*, I *shall* keep on drinking and debauching and defiling!…

OSIP emerges from the trees.

PLATONOV: Eavesdropping again, you outlaw? Get away from here!

OSIP: Good evening, Mikhail Vasilich.

PLATONOV: What are you doing here, you menace?

OSIP: Taking in the night air… See how that stump is shining in the moonlight! Like a dead man rising from his grave…There's another! There must be many sinners in this world, Mikhail Vasilich! Where are you off to now, may I ask?

PLATONOV: That's none of your affair!

OSIP: Are you going to the widow's?

PLATONOV: Away, you scoundrel!

OSIP: I'll go, but I'll be back, Mikhail Vasilich... *(Exits.)*

PLATONOV: *(After a pause.)* To go, or not to go... *(Sighs.)* A woman utters a word, and unleashes a storm within me...

SASHA: *(At the window.)* Misha, are you there?

PLATONOV: Yes, my poor treasure!

SASHA: Come inside!

PLATONOV: No, Sasha! I need to be out in the air for a while. My head is throbbing. Sleep, my angel!

SASHA: Good night, then! Come to bed soon! *(Closes the window.)*

PLATONOV: How easy it is to deceive one who believes in you so blindly! I blush to think of it...I'm going! *(Starts offstage.)*

Enter SOFYA YEGOROVNA.

PLATONOV: Omigod! You! What are *you* doing here, Sofya Yegorovna?!

SOYFA YEGOROVNA: Mikhail Vasilich...

PLATONOV: Are you out of your mind?

SOFYA YEGOROVNA: Mikhail Vasilich...

PLATONOV: Please, Sofya, I was just going inside...

SOFYA YEGOROVNA: Where did you go after the fireworks?! I've been searching for you everywhere! I came all the way out here to find you!

PLATONOV: Go away, please!

SOFYA YEGOROVNA: Mikhail Vasilich! I heard every word you said to me. Every single word. "It's up to you," that's what you said. And now, I'm taking the first step. Come, let us take the next one together. I am reborn.

PLATONOV: You are?

SOFYA YEGOROVNA: Take me. I am yours.

PLATONOV: Right now?

SOFYA YEGOROVNA: Right now!

PLATONOV: What about Sergey?

SOFYA YEGOROVNA: Sergey is drunk; I sent him off to go hunting. I'll wait for you at the gazebo with the four pillars.

SASHA: *(Calls from inside the house.)* Misha! Come inside!

PLATONOV: *(Looks around.)* What is this?! A public square?

SOFYA YEGOROVNA: At the gazebo with the four pillars! You've rekindled the flame of life in me, Michel! I am reborn! *(Runs offstage.)*

PLATONOV: Wait! Not the gazebo!!!... *(After a pause.)* So now you've done it, you've really done it! You've ruined a defenseless creature, an innocent woman who belongs to another! You've destroyed her forever!…Away to the four corners of the earth, banish me to a life of hard labor and poverty! I must never show my face again till Judgment Day! *(Pause.)* Strange…How can a beautiful woman, with skin like marble, with glorious hair, how can such a woman love a crank, a crackpot, a worthless wretch like me?…Does she really love me? It's unbelievable! Me! *(Laughs.)* Sofya! She loves me! Such happiness! And the happiness is mine! A new life, with new faces, new scenery! I'm going! To the gazebo by the four pillars!…My God, they'll both be there!…No, wait — there are *two* gazebos! Good…I'll check them both! Wait for me there, my Sofya! You were mine, and mine you shall be once more! *(Goes and then stops.)* Omigod, what about the widow? *(Turns and cries out.)* Sasha, I'm coming inside! Open the door! Let me in! I won't go, I won't, I won't… *(Pause.)* I'm going! *(He turns to go.)* I'm sick of it all — the canary cages, the cream, the sticky caresses…What is my life worth, anyway? *(Starts offstage.)* Go on, destroy it…

Enter VOYNITSEV, who collides with PLATONOV.

VOYNITSEV: Here he is, here he is! Mikhail Vasilich! *(Embraces PLATONOV.)* So? What are you waiting for? Come, let's go hunting!

PLATONOV: Leave me alone!

VOYNITSEV: What's the matter, my friend? *(Laughs.)* I'm drunk! For the first time in my life, I'm drunk! God, how happy I am! My friend! *(Embraces PLATONOV again.)* Are you coming with us? She dispatched me! Sofya, my bride, she sent me out to shoot some game for her. Imagine!

PLATONOV: I'm not going hunting.

VOYNITSEV: *(Sees PETRIN and GLAGOLYEV sleeping. He shakes them, overjoyed.)* Gerasim Kuzmich! Porfiry Semyonich! Wake up! *À la chasse!* Never mind, Misha, never mind! *(They stir.)*

GLAGOLYEV: *(To VOYNITSEV.)* What is it, Sergey Pavlovich!

VOYNITSEV: *À la chasse, mes amis!* Hurry! *(To PLATONOV.)* Have you heard what we're planning to do? A stroke of genius, isn't it?! We're thinking of putting on *Hamlet!* Word of honor! We'll have 'em on their knees! *(Laughs.)*… How pale you are! Are you drunk, too?

PLATONOV: Leave me alone…

VOYNITSEV: It's all my idea! Tomorrow we start painting the scenery. Sofya is Ophelia, you're Claudius, Triletsky is Horatio, and Porfiry Semyonich is Polonius! Aren't you, Porfiry Semyonich! I'm so happy! So happy! Shakespeare, Sofya, you, and *maman!* What more do I need? Oh, well, yes, and Glinka. That's all! …By the way, I'm Hamlet. "O shame! Where is thy blush? Rebellious hell, if thou canst mutiny in a matron's bones,/To flaming youth let virtue be as wax/And melt in her own fire."*(Laughs.)* Not a bad Hamlet, am I?! What's your line, Porfiry Semyonich?

GLAGOLYEV: "And this above all, to thine own self, be true!"…

VOYNITSEV: Bravo! Come, quickly! *À la chasse!*

PLATONOV: *(Tears himself free.)* Fool! *(Runs offstage.)*

VOYNITSEV: *(Calls after him.)* Misha! Where are you running to?

PLATONOV: *(Calls back.)* Who knows?!

VOYNITSEV: Well, well, well! He *is* drunk, after all! Ah, so what! Who cares! "Ophelia, nymph, in thy orisons be all my sins remembered!" Come, Gerasya! Porfiry, come! *(Exits with GLAGOLYEV.)*

PETRIN: And who will pay for the scenery and the costumes, Sergey Pavlovich? Eh?! Who? *(Follows after.)*

Pause. The sound of an approaching train is heard.

OSIP: *(Runs in.)* Where is he? *(Glances around.)* Where is he? He's not here! Mikhail Vasilich? Mikhail Vasilich! *(Looks around, pauses.)* Is he gone?*(Runs to the window and knocks.)* Mikhail Vasilich! Mikhail Vasilich! *(Breaks a windowpane.)*

SASHA: *(At the window.)* Who's there?

OSIP: Call Mikhail Vasilich! Hurry!

SASHA: He's not here! What's happened?

OSIP: He's not? That means he's gone to the widow's! It's too late, Aleksandra Ivanovna, all is lost! He's gone to the widow's, curse him!

SASHA: Why would he go to the widow's!

OSIP: As God is my witness, he's gone to the widow's! She ordered him to meet her! I heard everything, I saw everything! They were embracing, they were kissing, right here —

SASHA: You're lying!

OSIP: May God strike my mother and father dead, may I never see them in heaven if I'm lying! He's gone to the widow's! He's left his wife and child! Go after him, Aleksandra Ivanovna! No, no, it's too late. *(Takes the rifle off his shoulder.)* She's given me my orders , and obey them I shall, for the very last time! *(Fires a shot in the air.)* Let them meet! I shall murder him, Aleksandra Ivanovna! Never you fear, Aleksandra Ivanova, never you fear! I'll cut his throat — don't doubt it for an instant!

The lights of the train appear. The sound crescendos.

SASHA: *(Appears in a nightdress, with her hair flowing loose.)* He's gone away… Deceived me… *(Sobs.)* I am undone…Dear Lord, kill me… *(The train whistle is heard.)* I don't want to live… *(Throws herself down on the tracks.)* He deceived me, he deceived me…Mother of God, kill me!

OSIP rushes up to SASHA. He picks her up and carries her off the tracks just as the train approaches.

OSIP: Never fear, Aleksandra Ivanovna, I'll cut his throat…Never fear!

The headlight of the train shines sharply with a blinding intensity. With a roar, the train rushes through.

END OF ACT THREE

ACT FOUR

Early the next day. A room in the schoolhouse. Morning sunlight streams through the windows. Doors to the right and left. A cupboard with dishes, a chest of drawers, an old fortepiano, chairs, a divan covered with oilcloth, a guitar, and so on. General disarray.

PLATONOV is stretched out on the divan by the window; his clothes are dishevelled. His face is covered with a blanket. Enter ANNA PETROVNA. She approaches the divan.

ANNA PETROVNA: Platonov!... *(She shakes him.)* Platonov! Wake up!

PLATONOV: Go away...

ANNA PETROVNA: Go away? What do you mean "go away"?!

PLATONOV: What time is it?

ANNA PETROVNA: After nine...in the morning! For God's sake, Platonov, where were you?

PLATONOV: *(Groans.)* What a night!

ANNA PETROVNA: Platonov, I'm asking you! Where were you? Why didn't you come? I waited for you all night at the gazebo!

PLATONOV: I did! I *did* come to the gazebo!

ANNA PETROVNA: You did *not!*

PLATONOV: I did, too...to the gazebo with the four pillars! We made love all night long! You couldn't have forgotten —

ANNA PETROVNA: Fool! Not *that* gazebo! I was at the *other* gazebo!

PLATONOV: The *other* one? My God...What are you saying?

ANNA PETROVNA: No...what are *you* saying?! Ach, Platonov, Platonov, what have you done? Whom have you seduced now? Never mind, it's impossible — there's no one else around here you *could* seduce. You must have been hallucinating. It's the summer solstice...Happens every year...

PLATONOV: Leave me alone! Summer solstice, summer solstice...I never knew what that meant, anyway...

ANNA PETROVNA: Look at this place! Bottles everywhere, place in disarray. What will Aleksandra Ivanovna say?

PLATONOV: We'll never know, will we...She's gone!

ANNA PETROVNA: Gone!

PLATONOV: She's taken Petya and left me. She's gone to her brother's. I'm alone. I'm truly punished...

ANNA PETROVNA: Ach, Platonov, Platonov...Don Juan and a coward all in one… *(Starts gathering the bottles.)* This place looks like a tavern! Aleksandra Ivanovna ought to return. You need her, you'll think of something to say… She doesn't have to fear me as a rival…I'm very fair-minded, you know…It's not my intention to come between you… *(Takes a sip straight from a bottle.)* This vodka's quite good, actually…Come on, let's have a little drink! Just one, and then after that we won't drink any more. *(She pours him a glass and hands it to him. He drinks.)* Cheers! Now I'll have one, too… *(Pours.)* Here's to all bad men! *(Drinks.)* And you're one of them! Hmmm…This vodka's excellent! You have good taste…Now, say good-bye to your delicious vodka! *(Pours the first bottle out the window, then hesitates.)* Pity to pour it out…

PLATONOV: It doesn't matter…

ANNA PETROVNA: *(Pours herself another drink.)* I know what…I'll take you away with me, Platonov, rehabilitate you…

PLATONOV: I can't go away with you…I can't go away with anyone…I'm done for …

ANNA PETROVNA: Do something, Platonov! Change your life!

PLATONOV: I can't, Anna Petrovna…I'm lost…I don't know how to love…And if you can't love, you're lost!

ANNA PETROVNA: Nonsense, Platonov! Of course you can love! I'll teach you! I'm taking you away with me! I'll tell Porfiry Semyonich I'll marry him, I'll ask for a loan, and off we'll go —

PLATONOV: Too late, Anna Petrovna, too late …

ANNA PETROVNA: Nonsense! Get dressed, I'll be back with my carriage in a matter of minutes…

PLATONOV: Please, Anna Petrovna…

ANNA PETROVNA: Stop talking and start packing! Hurry! A new life, Platonov…a new life! *(Kisses him and exits.)*

PLATONOV: *(Alone.)* A new life! Who needs a new life!…I'm lost…lost… In Europe, a man perishes because life is too cramped and too crowded. In Russia, a man perishes because life is too vast. There is so much space, there are so many paths to choose from, that a man cannot find his true way…I'm lost! *(Cries out.)* Sasha! Where are you? Come back! Help me find my way! *(A knock at the door.)* She's come back!

Enter OSIP.

PLATONOV: Not you!
OSIP: Good morning, Mikhail Vasilich!

PLATONOV: What are you doing here, Osip? Answer me, you demon! *(Looks at him.)* What's the matter with you? You look pale…Are you ill?

OSIP: I've come to say good-bye, sir.

PLATONOV: Where are you going?

OSIP: I'm not going anywhere…*You* are!

PLATONOV: Really? You're a prophet, Osip! A visionary! All right, then, tell me, where I am going?

OSIP: Do you really want to know?

PLATONOV: Please!

OSIP: To the other world!

PLATONOV: That far, eh? And are you here to send me off?

OSIP: Exactly, sir. I've ordered your carriage.

PLATONOV: So you've come to kill me, then, have you? Good. Someone's got to do the job.

OSIP: I used to respect you, Mikhail Vasilich, I held you in the highest esteem! But now…You're too bad a man to live! Why was the widow here just now? Why were you at the gazebo last night with Sofya Yegorovna? And where is your wife? Which of these women do you truly love? And you say you're not a bad man! Well, Judgment Day has come at last! *(Throws PLATONOV to the ground, gets on top of him, and draws a knife.)*

PLATONOV: Sasha, help me! Sasha!

VOYNITSEV enters and stops by the door.

VOYNITSEV: Stop it! My God! *(Cowers in the doorway.)*

OSIP stands up, puts away the knife.

VOYNITSEV: Osip, please! You're terrifying me!

OSIP: All right, sir, I won't do it — at least not now, not in front of you. *(To PLATONOV.)* But I'll be back! *(Leaps through window.)*

PLATONOV: *(To VOYNITSEV.)* Is this the epilogue, or is the comedy continuing? *(Pulls himself unsteadily to his feet.)* I'm all right, I'm all right…Just my arm…I'll lie down for a bit… *(Drops onto the divan.)*

VOYNITSEV: Mikhail Vasilich!

PLATONOV: Go away, please… *(Covers his head with the blanket.)*

VOYNITSEV: Mikhail Vasilich! I've come to tell you…that you've destroyed me. Do you realize that? Once fate bestowed upon me a precious gift, and that gift has been taken from me! You're the most brilliant man in the district, but that wasn't enough for you…You had to take my happiness, too!

PLATONOV: I'm not listening!

VOYNITSEV: I know I deserve it, I know. I'm idle, weak, foolish, sentimental, I know…And now a friend has dealt me the final blow! *(Weeps.)*

PLATONOV: Go away, please!

VOYNITSEV: I shall, right away. I was going to challenge you to a duel, but here I stand, weeping instead…I'm weak…I'm going…Have I lost her for good?

PLATONOV: Yes.

VOYNITSEV: I see. One man's misfortune is always another man's happiness! However, that story's already been told…I wish you all the best.

PLATONOV: Please, Sergey Pavlovich!

VOYNITSEV: Yes, of course. I'm going!

PLATONOV: I beg of you!

VOYNITSEV: I'm going! There's nothing more to say… *(Turns to go, but hesitates.)* Give her back, Platonov! Please! You're happy as it is! Save me, dear fellow! Won't you? Give her back to me! *(Breaks down and sobs.)* She's mine…mine! Understand?

PLATONOV: I shall shoot myself, I swear to you! A curse has been put on my head! *(Sobs.)* Everything I touch, I destroy. I bring misfortune to all. *(Goes to the door and calls out.)* Sasha, for God's sake! Come back!

Enter GLAGOLYEV, wearing a hat and carrying a walking stick.

PLATONOV: Now what?!

GLAGOLYEV: *(Removes his hat.)* Are you alone, Mikhail Vasilich?

PLATONOV: As you see… *(Indicates VOYNITSEV, weeping in the corner.)*

GLAGOLYEV: I'm sorry to call on you so early in the morning. I'll disturb you for only a moment. I only want to ask you one question. Answer me, and I'll go, right away…What's the matter with you, Mikhail Vasilich? You're pale, you're trembling…Are you ill?

PLATONOV: What's the matter with me? I'm feverish, I must be, or else I'm going mad! My head is spinning…

GLAGOLYEV: It's a strange question, perhaps even a foolish one, but for God's sake, answer me! I find myself in a terrible position! Our mutual acquaintance — I always thought of her as the model of perfection — Anna Petrovna, I mean…you know her better than anyone else. She has just consented to be my wife. But the things people have said about her…well, let us say that they have opened my eyes…Is she an honest woman, Mikhail Vasilich? Is she worthy of being the wife of an honorable man? I don't know how to phrase my question! Help me, please, for God's sake! They say that she… and you…

PLATONOV laughs.

GLAGOLYEV: I see…Mikhail Vasilich, you have ruined my life.
PLATONOV: I've ruined everyone's life.
GLAGOLYEV: You sow the seeds of depravity and destruction wherever you go. And the worst of it is that you go unpunished, that fate doesn't not strike back at you.
PLATONOV: Go away! I always thought you were a foolish old man.
GLAGOLYEV: I don't care what you think of me. I'm not afraid to tell the truth.
PLATONOV: I know why you're so honorable — you have no strength left to sin. You're not alive any more! *(Exits, laughing.)*
GLAGOLYEV: *(Turns to VOYNITSEV.)* Sergey Pavlovich! Is it true? I ask you about your stepmother's behavior, forgive me please, but I must know: Is it true? *(VOYNITSEV continues to sob.)* I see…Thank you.

Enter ANNA PETROVNA, dressed for travel, carrying a bag.

ANNA PETROVNA: Misha? *(Sees VOYNITSEV.)* Serge, where's Platonov?
VOYNITSEV: Don't ask me, *maman!*
ANNA PETROVNA: *(Sees GLAGOLYEV.)* What are you doing here?
GLAGOLYEV: Please forgive me, Anna Petrovna. I must leave.
ANNA PETROVNA: Where are you going?
GLAGOLYEV: Away from here! I shall search for happiness elsewhere. There is no honor here…
ANNA PETROVNA: Porfiry Semyonich, wait — !
GLAGOLYEV: No honor…and no love! *(Exits.)*
ANNA PETROVNA: So now he's gone, too! He's gone…and so is the estate, I'm certain of it… *(Sighs.)* Never trust your enemies in this world, nor your friends, either!
VOYNITSEV: Never trust your friends, that's for certain!
ANNA PETROVNA: Well, my heir apparent! What will you do now? Where will you go? What God gave your ancestors will be taken away from you. The estate is gone. You'll have nothing left.
VOYNITSEV: It's all the same to me, *maman.*
ANNA PETROVNA: No, it is not all the same. You can earn it back! You have

your whole life before you, a decent, purposeful life! Why grieve? You'll work! You're a scholar, a citizen, a married man! If you want to, you'll go far!

VOYNITSEV: I don't give a damn about the estate. A terrible misfortune has befallen our house, *maman.*

ANNA PETROVNA: *(Laughs.)* You're frightening me! Nothing's happened!

VOYNITSEV: Go ahead, laugh! Just you wait, you won't be laughing much longer!...She has betrayed me, *maman!*

ANNA PETROVNA: Who?

VOYNITSEV: Sofya! She's betrayed me! Permit me to introduce you to a cuckold!

ANNA PETROVNA: Don't be foolish, Sergey! What kind of a stupid notion is that!

VOYNITSEV: I swear to God it's true!

ANNA PETROVNA: It can't be! Here? In Voynitsev?

VOYNITSEV: Yes, here, in your accursed Voynitsev!

ANNA PETROVNA: And whom, in our accursed Voynitsev, might steal up behind you and plant a pair of horns on your aristocratic head, may I ask? There's no one here who could possibly equal your Sofya...oh, no...

VOYNITSEV: Oh, yes!...

Enter SOFYA YEGOROVNA, dressed for travel, carrying a bag.

SOFYA YEGOROVNA: I'm ready, Mikhail Vasilich! ... *(Sees VOYNITSEV and ANNA PETROVNA.)* Sergey, Anna Petrovna, what are you doing here?

ANNA PETROVNA: ...I don't believe it!...

VOYNITSEV: You see, *maman?*

Enter PLATONOV, his arm in a sling, in a dressing gown.

PLATONOV: Sofya, it's you!

SOFYA YEGOROVNA: Of course, it's me! I'm ready! We're going away!

ANNA PETROVNA: Who is going away?

SOFYA YEGOROVNA: We are. Platonov and I. It's all been decided. Sergey knows all about it. Don't you, Sergey?! We're going away, to start a new life! We'll work! We'll eat the fruits of our labors, from our own calloused hands, from the sweat of our brows —

PLATONOV: Where? Where will you work? Women like you are lying around idle, like sheaves of corn in the sun! You don't know how to work! And you don't know how to live! None of us do! Why delude yourself, Sofya? It's hopeless, for all of us…

SOYFA YEGOROVNA: But we're going to start a new life!

PLATONOV: I don't need a new life! I still don't know what to do with the old one!

ANNA PETROVNA: Is this true, Mikhail Vasilich?

PLATONOV: I feel feverish… My arm hurts… I need to lie down —

ANNA PETROVNA: Answer me!

PLATONOV: It's true… I don't want anything any more, neither love, nor hate, the only thing I want is peace! I beg of you… Enough is enough… *(Lies down on the divan and covers his head.)*

SOFYA YEGOROVNA: What is he saying? I don't understand…

PLATONOV: Our affair is over, that's what!

SOFYA YEGOROVNA: So you're not going away with me, is that it?

PLATONOV: No…

ANNA PETROVNA: Of course not! He's going away with *me!*

VOYNITSEV: *Maman!*

SOFYA YEGOROVNA: Villain! *(Drops the bag. Weeps.)*

PLATONOV: I'm not going away with anyone! I'm sick…

SOFYA YEGOROVNA: *(Wrings her hands.)* What will become of me? Tell me! I shall die! I can't bear this cruelty! Not one more minute! I shall kill myself! *(Collapses in an armchair in hysterics.)*

VOYNITSEV: *(Goes to SOFYA YEGOROVNA.)* Sofi!

ANNA PETROVNA: Calm down, Sofi! Give her some water, Sergey!

VOYNITSEV: Sofi! Don't, please! *(TO PLATONOV.)* What are you waiting for, Mikhail Vasilich? Go away, for God's sake! You're destroying everything!

ANNA PETROVNA: Calm down, Sergey! Don't you see! He doesn't love her! He's only seduced her, that's all! Don't you know the difference, you fool?! There, there, Sofi! Enough!

SOFYA YEGOROVNA: Get away from me! All of you!

PLATONOV: Where shall I go? I'm burning with fever…I'm numb with cold…I wish it were over…

SOFYA YEGOROVNA: You wish it were over…and what about me? I gave myself to you! I knew I was killing my husband, but I stopped at nothing! What have you done to me? *(Weeps.)*

VOYNITSEV: Sofi, please, you're killing me all over again!

PLATONOV: What a situation!

ANNA PETROVNA: Calm down, Sofi! This is not the time…He's ill!

SOFYA YEGOROVNA: Is it possible to trifle with another human life as you have? My life is now completely ruined... I'm no longer alive... Save me, Platonov! It's not too late!

ANNA PETROVNA: What are you saying, Sofi?!

SOFYA YEGOROVNA: Platonov, I'm asking you... *(PLATONOV turns away from her.)* All right, then, I'm begging you. *(Falls on her knees.)* Save me!

VOYNITSEV: Sofi!

ANNA PETROVNA: This is too much, Sofi! You can't do this! No man is worth going on your knees for. *(Tries to lift her up.)* Get up! You're a woman!

PLATONOV: I was wrong, Sofya Yegorovna, wrong... But what can I do? I can't go away with *all* of you!

Enter TRILETSKY.

TRILETSKY: Where is he? *(Sees PLATONOV.)* The tragedy is almost over, tragedian!

PLATONOV: What do *you* want?

TRILETSKY: What are you doing here, you miserable man? Aren't you ashamed of yourself, you sinner?

PLATONOV: What is it, Nikolai?

TRILETSKY: The brutality of it all! *(Sits and covers his face with his hands.)* Your punishment has come at last, Mikhail Vasilich, you villain!

PLATONOV: What happened?

TRILETSKY: What happened? Don't you know? Or don't you care, even?

ANNA PETROVNA: Nikolai Ivanich! What happened?

PLATONOV: Is it Sasha? Tell me, Nikolai! Please!

TRILETSKY: Your Day of Judgment is here!

PLATONOV: It's Sasha, isn't it? Nikolai, what has happened?!

TRILETSKY: She's poisoned herself!

PLATONOV: What are you saying?

TRILETSKY: She's poisoned herself! I've been trying to save her. Father is with her now.

PLATONOV: My Sasha! Where is she? I'm going to her! *(Rips off the arm sling.)* I shall save her! *(Tries to stand, sways.)*

TRILETSKY: Why talk of saving her? You shouldn't have murdered her in the first place!

PLATONOV: Sasha...She's poisoned herself! I'm crushed like a dog under the carriage wheel. If this is my punishment, I haven't the strength to bear it! Look at me now, all of you! I am punished at last! Aren't you happy?

TRILETSKY: Yes! Some husband you are! You murdered an innocent woman, an angel, for the pure sport of it!

PLATONOV: No more, please, no more… I'm going to her… *(Stands, then falls back on the divan.)* I'm shaking… I can't stand!

VOYNITSEV: Stop shouting, everyone! I can't bear it!

TRILETSKY: I don't know if she'll survive…

PLATONOV: Save her, Nikolai, save her… If Sasha lives, I repent… Tell her, please…Let me go to her! *(Tries to stand.)* My head is spinning… I feel terribly weak… Wait… I'll rest for a moment, then I'll go… Water!…

ANNA PETROVNA: Here…drink! *(Gives PLATONOV water.)*

PLATONOV: *(Drinks eagerly.)* Thank you, lovely lady! I'm a scoundrel, a scoundrel!… My arm hurts…I'm exhausted…Give me more water. I'm terribly ill, Nikolai! I can hardly hold my head up… It might fall off my shoulders any minute…I must be running a fever. I see little soldiers in calico uniforms with peaked caps marching before my eyes… Everything's green and yellow…Give me some quinine… I must go to her…

TRILETSKY: Don't look at me to treat you! It wouldn't hurt you at all to be ill…It would clear your conscience!

PLATONOV: There's a tiny grand piano crawling on your bosom, Anna Petrovna! How ludicrous!… I'm raving… Nikolai, save her and I'll repent…I'll repent!

ANNA PETROVNA: He's in no shape to go anywhere!

SOFYA YEGOROVNA: Somebody! Do something!

TRILETSKY: What?

SOFYA YEGOROVNA: Save Sasha!… Save *me!* *(Sobs.)*

PLATONOV: I can't save anyone! I can't even save my*self!*

ANNA PETROVNA: Come on, Sofya, let's get some fresh air! *(Takes her by the arm.)*

TRILETSKY: I'll give her a sedative! *(TRILETSKY leads SOFYA offstage.)*

ANNA PETROVNA: I wouldn't mind one myself!

VOYNITSEV: Wait, Sofi! Wait for me! *(Follows them.)*

ANNA PETROVNA: Courage, Sergey! Act sensibly! Be a man!

VOYNITSEV: I'll try, *maman!* I'll do my best.

ANNA PETROVNA: You're not the first to be deceived, and you won't be the last… *(She exits after him.)*

PLATONOV: Tell Sasha I repent, Nikolai… Tell her… A cigarette, Nikolai, and a glass of water! *(Glances about.)* Where is everyone? Have they gone? *(Waves his hands before his eyes.)* Mouches volantes… Clouds… Soon I'll be raving… Shame, I'm feverish with shame! I've ruined innocent, defenseless women, not out of passion, Spanish-style, but out of stupidity, Russian-style… I ought to kill myself! *(Stumbles to the table and rummages about.)* A full arsenal! Choose! *(Takes a revolver and puts it to his temples.)* Finita la commedia! One intelligent Russian less in this world! *(Prays.)* Gospodi pomilui, gospodi pomilui! Christ, forgive me my sins! Forgive me my sins! Save my soul, replenish me, guide my steps… Now I know: If you but once betray the one you love, you'll never escape the web of lies and deceit…

Enter GREKOVA. She sees PLATONOV holding the revolver.

GREKOVA: No, Platonov, no! Don't do it! *(Rushes over to him and takes the revolver. She places it on the table near the door.)*

PLATONOV: Sasha! Sasha! *(Sees GREKOVA.)* Wait — who is this? Ah! *(Laughs.)* My mortal enemy…

GREKOVA: Platonov! What's wrong? You look ill!

PLATONOV: Forgive me, Marya Yefimovna, forgive me!

GREKOVA: Why should I?

PLATONOV: I repent! Believe me!

GREKOVA: How can I believe you?

PLATONOV: I'm burning with shame! Here, feel my forehead! I'm feverish with shame!

GREKOVA: *(Doubtfully.)* What's the matter?

PLATONOV: I'm ill…You were right to want to get me fired. But it would be cleverer still if you'd stopped loving me…

GREKOVA: You look so pale…

PLATONOV: I wanted to shoot myself, but I couldn't. Self-preservation. Your mind tells you one thing, your instinct — another. I chose life, but I don't deserve it. You're a scientist, you understand! *(Kisses her hand.)* How cold your little hands are!

GREKOVA: *(Reluctantly.)* You're really ill, aren't you…

PLATONOV: I'm burning with shame…Sasha's left me, she's at death's door, and I'm too weak to go to her…They're throwing me out…Rest…I need rest…

GREKOVA: I've come to tell you I feel so guilty. I wrote to the school district to have you transferred, and now you're so ill! I've destroyed you. *(Tearfully.)* It's all my fault…

PLATONOV: Never mind, I'm not worthy of teaching any more…I've sinned too much as it is…

GREKOVA: Let me take you home with me! I'll care for you!

PLATONOV: *Merci,* you wonderful girl, you…Cigarettes, water, and a bed to lie down in. Is it raining outside?

GREKOVA: Yes.

PLATONOV: Good. We'll drive in the rain… I shall be purified, and Sasha will forgive me… We're not going to court, are we? I'm not on trial, am I? I repent!… Am I raving?

GREKOVA: A little. Let's go! My carriage is covered.

PLATONOV: No…Let the rain purify me…How lovely you are…Why are you blushing? I won't touch you. Just let me kiss your cold little hands again… *(Kisses her hand and draws her to him.)*

GREKOVA: *(Sits on his knees.)* No… I mustn't do this …

PLATONOV: I'm burning… *(Kisses her on the cheek.)* Your cheek is so cool… Rest, rest… *(Kisses her again.)* I love all women! You're all so soft and beautiful! I touch you and I feel alive… Forgive me! *(Kisses her again.)*

GREKOVA: I know what happened… It was Sofya, wasn't it?

PLATONOV: Sofya, Zizi, Mimi…there are so many of you! I love you all! And you love me, too, all of you, don't you? I've offended you all, and yet you still love me…I offended Grekova, for example, and still she loves me…But wait, you're Grekova, aren't you? Forgive me…

GREKOVA: What is wrong with you?

PLATONOV: Platonov is wrong with me… Tell me, Marya Yefimovna, do you love me? Honestly, I don't want anything — just tell me you love me.

GREKOVA: Yes, God help me… *(Puts her head on his chest.)* Yes…

PLATONOV: *(Kisses her head.)* They *all* love me…

GREKOVA: I'll take care of you…I will…

Enter SASHA, supported by IVAN IVANOVICH and YAKOV.

IVAN IVANOVICH: Look, my son-in-law!

YAKOV: Look who's here, sir!

IVAN IVANOVICH: Mikhail Vasilich! It's your wife! She's come to forgive you!

PLATONOV: *(Turns and sees them, GREKOVA still seated on his lap.)* Sasha! *(They all see GREKOVA, and recoil in horror.)*

SASHA: Misha!

PLATONOV: Sasha, you're alive!

IVAN IVANOVICH: Mikhail Vasilich, what's going on here?

PLATONOV: You're alive, Sasha, alive!… I repent, Sasha, forgive me please… I repent…

SASHA: How could you, Misha, how could you?…

Enter TRILETSKY, ANNA PETROVNA, VOYNITSEV and SOFYA YEGOROVNA.

TRILETSKY: What's all this commotion?...Sasha!

ANNA PETROVNA: Marya Yefimovna!

GREKOVA: Please, I can explain —

ANNA PETROVNA: Will you tell me what you are doing here?

VOYNITSEV: Mikhail Vasilich, I can't believe it!

SOFYA YEGOROVNA: Stand back, everyone! *(She stands in the door, holding a revolver that she has snatched from off the table. She points it at PLATONOV. To PLATONOV.)* This was your last chance!

VOYNITSEV: Sofya, what are you doing?!

TRILETSKY: Sofya, please!

SOFYA YEGOROVNA: He's ruined too many lives! Too many!

PLATONOV: I repent!

SOFYA YEGOROVNA: Too late! You must pay!

ANNA PETROVNA: I agree! Let me do it!

GREKOVA: Don't! He repents!

ANNA PETROVNA and GREKOVA wrestle for the gun. SOFYA manages to retrieve it and aims at PLATONOV. SASHA throws herself between SOFYA YEGOROVNA and PLATONOV.

VOYNITSEV: Sofya!

IVAN IVANOVICH: Sasha, my child!

TRILETSKY: Sofya, don't shoot!

SASHA: Everyone, please!

Everyone freezes. SOFYA stands poised, gun pointed at PLATONOV. SASHA shields PLATONOV from SOFYA with her body.

SASHA: *(Softly.)* Please!... *(Turns to PLATONOV, who is trembling. Gently.)* Misha...

PLATONOV: *(Sobs.)* Sasha... I'm lost... My life... it's too much for me...too much...

SASHA: Mishenka... Please... Let me care for you... You must have hope, Mishenka, hope... And you must love... Only with love, is life worth living... We have each other, and our family, and a beautiful, long life together... We'll be happy, so happy...Have patience, Misha, patience...

PLATONOV: Sofya, Marya, Anna — I swear to you, I never knew the difference...

SASHA: Have faith!...
PLATONOV: Forgive me, Sasha… I repent!
SOFYA: No, he doesn't! —
VOYNITSEV: *(Puts his arm around SOFYA.)* Shhh, Sofya…
PLATONOV: I repent!
IVAN IVANOVICH: *(In tears.)* He repents!

Suddenly, a shot rings out from stage left. All freeze. OSIP stands in the door with a smoking rifle. PLATONOV drops to his knees, then to the floor.

OSIP: Judgment Day, at last!
SASHA: Misha! *(Throws herself on him.)*
ANNA PETROVNA: Osip! You fool!
IVAN IVANOVICH: But he repented!
TRILETSKY: Too late!… Too late!

Freeze. Lights intensify. Blackout.

END OF PLAY

IVANOV

A Drama in Four Acts

CAST OF CHARACTERS

IVANOV, NIKOLAI ALEKSEEVICH, a government official in the office of peasant affairs

ANNA PETROVNA, his wife, née Sara Abramson

SHABELSKY, MATVEY SEMYONOVICH, a Count, Ivanov's uncle on his mother's side

LEBEDEV, PAVEL KIRILICH, president of the local district council

ZINAIDA SAVISHNA, his wife

SASHA, Lebedev's daughter, aged twenty

LVOV, YEVGENY KONSTANTINOVICH, a young doctor in the district

BABAKINA, MARFA YEGOROVNA, a young widow, landowner, daughter of a rich merchant

KOSYKH, DMITRY NIKITICH, a tax officer

BORKIN, MIKHAIL MIKHAILOVICH, a distant relative of Ivanov and the manager of his estate

AVDOTYA NAZAROVNA, an old woman of indeterminate occupation

YEGORUSHKA, a dependent of the Lebedevs

FIRST GUEST

SECOND GUEST

PYOTR, Ivanov's servant

GAVRILA, a servant of the Lebedevs

The action takes place in one of the provinces of Central Russia.

Ivanov

ACT ONE

A garden on IVANOV's estate. To the left is the facade of the house with a terrace. There is one open window. In front of the terrace is a broad, semicircular area, from which paths lead into the garden, center and right. To the right there are garden seats and tables. On one table, a lamp is burning. Evening is approaching. Behind the raised curtain, someone is practicing a duet on the piano and cello.

IVANOV is seated at a table, reading a book. BORKIN, wearing a pair of large boots and carrying a gun, appears upstage in the garden; he is slightly drunk; upon seeing IVANOV, he tiptoes up to him, and points the gun right in his face.

IVANOV: *(Seeing BORKIN, shudders and leaps up.)* Misha, for God's sake…you scared me to death…You and your foolish jokes, I'm upset enough as it is…*(Sits.)* You like it, don't you, frightening people…

BORKIN: *(Laughs loudly.)* All right, all right…sorry, sorry. *(Sits next to him.)* I won't do it again, I won't, I promise…*(Takes off his cap.)* It's hot. You won't believe it, my friend, but we covered over ten miles in three hours…I'm all worn out…My heart, feel how it's beating…

IVANOV: *(Reading.)* Good, I will, later.

BORKIN: No, feel it, now. *(Takes IVANOV's hand and puts it on his chest.)* Do you hear it? Ta-ta-ta-ta-ta-ta. Sounds like I've got heart trouble. Any minute and I might die a sudden death. Listen, will you be sorry if I drop dead?

IVANOV: I'm reading…later…

BORKIN: No, seriously, will you be sorry if I drop dead? Nikolai Alekseevich, will you or won't you be sorry if I die all of a sudden?

IVANOV: Stop bothering me!

BORKIN: Come on, man, tell me: Will you be sorry?

IVANOV: I'm sorry that you smell of vodka, that's what I'm sorry about. Really, Misha, it's disgusting.

BORKIN: *(Laughs.)* Do, I, really? Amazing…Actually, there's nothing so amazing about it. I ran into an investigator in Plesniki, and as a matter of fact, we did put away about eight glasses. To tell you the truth, drinking is very bad for you. Tell me, isn't it bad for you? Eh? Isn't it?

IVANOV: This is unbearable…Look, Misha, this is getting insulting…

BORKIN: All right, all right…sorry, sorry! God bless you! Go on, sit there, sit, don't get up…*(Gets up and starts to exit.)* People are amazing, you can't even talk to them. *(Comes back.)* Oh, yes! I almost forgot… Eighty-two rubles, please!…

IVANOV: What do you mean, eighty-two rubles?

BORKIN: To pay the workmen tomorrow.

IVANOV: I don't have it.

BORKIN: I humbly thank you! *(Mimics him.)* "I don't have it"… But we have to pay the workmen. I mean, don't we?

IVANOV: I don't know. I don't have any money today. Wait till the first of the month, when I get my salary…

BORKIN: What's the point in talking to people like you!… The workmen aren't coming to get paid on the first of the month, they're coming tomorrow morning!…

IVANOV: So what am I supposed to do about it? All right, go on, nag me, plague me…And what is this abominable habit of bothering me, whenever I'm trying to read or write?…

BORKIN: I'm asking you: Do we or do we not have to pay the workmen? Oh, why do I bother talking to you!… *(Waves his hand.)* You landowners, to hell with you…Gentlemen agriculturalists, scientific farmers…Hundreds of acres, and not a kopek in your pocket…You've got wine cellars, and not a corkscrew in sight…I'm going to take the troika tomorrow out from under you and sell it, that's what I'm going to do! Yes, indeed!…I've already sold all the oats, before they were even harvested, and tomorrow I'll sell all the rye. *(Walks about the stage.)* You don't think I'm going to stand on ceremony about it, do you? No, sir, you've got the wrong man…

The voice of SHABELSKY and ANNA PETROVNA are heard offstage, from behind the window.

SHABELSKY: *(Offstage, unseen.)* "It's impossible to play with you…A stuffed pike has a better ear for music than you do, and your touch is appalling."

ANNA PETROVNA: *(Appears at the open window.)* Who was just talking out there? Is that you, Misha? Why are you marching around like that?

BORKIN: I'm talking to your *cher Nicolas* here, what do you expect?

ANNA PETROVNA: Listen, Misha, have them put some hay down on the croquet lawn.

BORKIN: *(Waves his hand.)* Leave me alone, would you, please…

ANNA PETROVNA: My, my, what a tone of voice… It doesn't suit you, my dear.
If you want to get anywhere with women, then never get angry and never
patronize…*(To her husband.)* Nikolai, come on, let's do somersaults in the
hay!…

IVANOV: Anyuta, don't stand in front of an open window, it's bad for you.
Please…*(Shouts.)* Uncle, close the window!

The window is closed.

BORKIN: Don't forget, in two days the interest is due to Lebedev.

IVANOV: I remember. I'll go to Lebedev's today, and ask him for an extension…*(Looks at his watch.)*

BORKIN: When are you going there?

IVANOV: Soon.

BORKIN: *(Quickly.)* Wait, wait!…I think it's Shurochka's birthday today…Ta-
da!…And I'd forgotten…What a memory, eh? *(Jumps up.)* I'm going, I'm
going…*(Sings.)* I think I'll have a swim, chew a little paper, take three drops
of smelling salts to sober up — and what do you know, I'll start the day all
over again…My dear dear Nikolai Alekseevich, my sweet friend, my angel,
you are so very very irritable, all the time, you moan and groan, you're always
depressed, always, and yet think of what we couldn't do together! I'd do anything for you…Want me to marry Marfusha Babakina for you? I'll do it. And
you get half the dowry…No, wait, not half, all of it, all of it!…

IVANOV: Stop talking nonsense…

BORKIN: No, really, I'm serious! Do you want me to?…I mean, marry
Marfusha? Half the dowry…Anyway, why am I saying all this? You don't
understand, don't you? *(Mimics.)* "Stop talking nonsense." No, really,
you're a good man, an intelligent man, really, you are, but you have no…oh,
how shall I put it…no nerve, no flair. You know what I mean, no "devil-may-
care," no "do things in a big way," whatever…You're a neurotic and a cry-
baby, I mean, if you were normal, you'd be making a million this year. Now
take me, for example, if I had two thousand three hundred rubles, right now,
that is, in two weeks time I'd have twenty thousand. You don't believe me,
right? In your opinion — nonsense, right? Well, no, it's not, it's not nonsense…All right, I'll tell you what, give me two thousand three hundred, and
I'll give you back twenty thousand in a week. Look over there, on the other

bank of the river, Ovsyanov is selling that strip of land, the one right opposite us, for two thousand three hundred rubles. If we buy that strip, then both banks will be ours. And if both banks are ours, then don't you see, we have the right to dam up the river. Isn't that so? We build a mill, and as soon as we announce that we want to put up a dam for it, then everyone living below that point on the river will raise an uproar, and we say: "Kommen sie hier," — if you want us *not* to build a dam, then pay up. You follow? The Zarevsky factory will pay five thousand, Korolkov will put up three thousand, the monastery will pay five thousand...

IVANOV: All this is double-dealing and deceitful, Misha...If you want to avoid arguing with me, then keep it to yourself.

BORKIN: *(Sits in a chair.)* Of course!...I knew it!...You won't do a thing yourself, and you won't let me do anything, either...

Enter SHABELSKY [the COUNT] and LVOV.

SHABELSKY: Doctors — they're the same as lawyers, the difference being that lawyers only rob you, whereas doctors rob you and kill you...Present company not included, of course. *(Sits on the little divan.)* Charlatans, profiteers...Perhaps, in some arcadian land, there might be found an exception to this rule, but...in the course of my lifetime I've spent twenty thousand on medical treatment and haven't met one doctor, not one, who wasn't an absolute crook.

BORKIN: *(To IVANOV.)* That's right, you won't do anything yourself and you won't let me do anything, either. And that's why we don't have any money...

SHABELSKY: I repeat, present company excluded...Now then, there might be exceptions, although, however...*(Yawns.)*

IVANOV: *(Closing his book.)* What do you have to say, doctor?

LVOV: *(Glances at the window.)* Exactly what I said this morning: She must leave for the Crimea immediately. *(Walks about the stage.)*

SHABELSKY: *(Bursts out laughing.)* To the Crimea!...Misha, why aren't we doctors? It's so simple...You have a Madame "So-and-so Angeau," or an "Ophelia," let's say, and she's choking and coughing away, you know, from boredom, so you pull out a piece of paper and you write out a prescription: First, take one young doctor, then take a trip to the Crimea, and then in the Crimea, take one young Tartar...

IVANOV: *(To the COUNT.)* Don't be such a bore! *(To LVOV.)* To go to the Crimea you've got to have the means. Let us suppose that I might find them, still she would refuse to go...

LVOV: Yes, she would.

Pause.

BORKIN: Listen, Doctor, is Anna Petrovna really so seriously ill, that she absolutely must go to the Crimea?...

LVOV: *(Looks toward the window.)* Yes, consumption...

BORKIN: Ssssss!...that's bad...For a long time I've known, from that look on her face, that she won't last long.

LVOV: Please...speak softly...they can hear us in the house ...

Pause.

BORKIN: *(Sighing.)* Yes, this life of ours...Mortal life is like a flower, blooming resplendent in the field: Along comes a billy goat, he gobbles it up, and presto! — no more flower...

SHABELSKY: It's all nonsense, nonsense, and more nonsense...*(Yawns.)* Nonsense and lies.

Pause.

BORKIN: And I, ladies and gentlemen, I am teaching Nikolai Alekseevich how to acquire money. I've given him one absolutely marvelous idea, but, as usual, I've fired right into the ground. You can't reach him...look at him: melancholia, spleen, anxiety, depression, misery...

SHABELSKY: *(Stands and stretches.)* You're a man of genius, you instruct us all, you teach us all how to live, but not me, you haven't taught me a thing...So come now, O wise one, show me a way out of all this...

BORKIN: *(Stands.)* I'm going for a swim...Good-bye, ladies and gentlemen...*(To the COUNT.)* You have countless ways out...If I were in your place, I'd have twenty thousand within a week. *(Exiting.)*

SHABELSKY: *(Following after him.)* How? Come on, show me.

BORKIN: There's nothing to show. It's very simple, really...*(Returns.)* Nikolai Alekseevich, give me a ruble!

IVANOV silently hands him a ruble.

BORKIN: *Merci! (To the COUNT.)* You've got all the trump cards!

SHABELSKY: *(Following after him.)* Well, what are they?

BORKIN: If I were in your place, I'd have thirty thousand within a week, if not more. *(Exits with the COUNT.)*

IVANOV: *(After a pause.)* Useless people, useless talk, meaningless answers to foolish questions — all this, doctor, has made me ill. I've become irritable, irascible, impatient, temperamental, petty, so much so that I no longer know myself. For days at a time I suffer headaches, insomnia, ringing in my ears…And there's nowhere for me to go…Absolutely nowhere…

LVOV: Nikolai Alekseevich, We must talk seriously.

IVANOV: Talk.

LVOV: It's about Anna Petrovna. *(Sits.)* She will not agree to go to the Crimea, but she would, with you.

IVANOV: *(Thinks.)* To go together, we must have the means. They'd have to give me an extended leave. And I've had a leave once this year already…

LVOV: Let us assume that this is true. But allow me to continue. The most important treatment for consumption is absolute rest, but your wife knows not even a moment of rest. Your attitude toward her is a constant source of anxiety. Forgive me, I'm upset and I shall speak plainly. Your conduct is killing her. *(Pause.)* Nikolai Alekseevich, allow me to think better of you!…

IVANOV: It's true, it's true…I'm terribly guilty, no doubt, but my head is in such confusion, such a lethargy weighs upon on my soul, and I haven't the strength even to understand myself. I understand neither myself, nor others…*(Glances toward the window.)* They can hear us, come…*(They stand.)* My dear friend, I'd tell you everything from the very beginning, but it's such a long and complicated story, that I'd be telling it till dawn. *(They walk together.)* Anyuta is a rare and wonderful woman…Because of me she has renounced her faith, her father and mother, her inheritance, and were I to request one hundred sacrifices more, she would perform them without blinking an eye. As for me, I am neither remarkable, nor have I sacrificed a thing. However, it's a long story…The fact of the matter is, dear doctor *(considers for a moment)*, that…to put it succinctly, I married for passionate love, I vowed love eternal, but…five years have passed, she still loves me, while I…*(Spreads his hands in a gesture of helplessness.)* Here you've told me that she soon will die, and I feel neither love, nor regret, but rather a kind of emptiness, a weariness. To look upon me must be horrifying; and I myself don't understand what will become of my soul…

They exit along the path. Enter SHABELSKY, then ANNA PETROVNA.

SHABELSKY: *(Laughing as he enters.)* Word of honor, this is no scoundrel, this is a mastermind, a genius! A monument should be built in his honor. He combines all the contemporary diseases into one: lawyer, doctor, banker, and charlatan. *(Sits on the lowest step of the terrace.)* And in fact he doesn't have a single degree, that's what's so amazing…I mean, think of what a brilliant and accomplished operator he might have been, had he actually acquired some culture, or a liberal education! "In a month you can amass twenty thousand," he says. "And you have a trump card — your title of 'Count'. *(Laughs loudly.)* Any girl would come running after you with her dowry…"

ANNA PETROVNA opens the window and looks down.

SHABELSKY: "Do you want me to arrange a match between you and Marfusha?" he says. *"Qui est-ce que c'est,"* who is this Marfusha anyway? Oh, right, I know who that is, Balabalkina…Balabalkina…the one who looks like a washerwoman.
ANNA PETROVNA: Is that you, Count?
SHABELSKY: What?

ANNA PETROVNA laughs.

SHABELSKY: *(With a Jewish accent.)* Vy are you leffing?
ANNA PETROVNA: I was thinking of one of your little sayings. Do you remember, when you were talking before supper? "A repentant knave, a —" …How does it go?
SHABELSKY: "A Jew who was saved, a repentant knave, a horse who was lame, they're all the same!"
ANNA PETROVNA: *(Laughs.)* You can't recite a simple limerick without malice. What a malicious man you are. *(Seriously.)* No, seriously, Count, you really are malicious. It's depressing to live with you, depressing and unnerving. You grumble and growl, and everyone's a fraud or a scoundrel. Tell me the truth, count: Have you ever said anything good about anyone?
SHABELSKY: What is this, an interrogation?
ANNA PETROVNA: We've lived together under the same roof for five years, and not once have I ever heard you speak of people with equanimity, without rancor and derision. What harm has anyone ever done to you? And do you really, sincerely, believe, that you are better than all the rest of us?
SHABELSKY: That, above all, I do not believe. I'm as much of a villain, a swine in a skullcap, as anyone else. *Mauvais ton*, a discarded old shoe, that's what

I am. And I'm very hard on myself, always. Who am I? What am I? Once I was rich, free, happy, even, and now…I'm a hanger-on, a parasite, a sponger, I'm anybody's fool. I'm contemptuous, I rant and rave, and in return they laugh at me; I laugh back, they nod their heads sadly and say: "The old fool, he's off his rocker"…But more often than not they don't even listen or pay attention…

ANNA PETROVNA: *(Quietly.)* It's crying again…

SHABELSKY: Who? Who's crying?

ANNA PETROVNA: The owl. It cries every evening.

SHABELSKY: Let it, then. Things can't get any worse than they already are. *(Stretches.)* Ach, my darling Sara, if only I could win a hundred thousand or more, I'd show you a thing or two…Only then, you wouldn't see me any more. I'd escape from this prison, from this almshouse, and wouldn't set foot in here again till Judgment Day…

ANNA PETROVNA: And what would you do, if you win?

SHABELSKY: *(Thinks for a moment.)* First of all, I'd go to Moscow to hear the gypsies play. Then…then off I'd go to Paris. I'd rent a flat there, and go visit the Russian church.

ANNA PETROVNA: And then what?

SHABELSKY: All day long, I'd sit by my wife's grave and think. I'd sit by her grave, and I'd sit and I'd sit, till I die. My wife is buried in Paris…

Pause.

ANNA PETROVNA: How terribly depressing. Let's play another duet, shall we?

SHABELSKY: Good, get out the sheet music. *(ANNA PETROVNA exits.)*

Enter IVANOV and LVOV.

IVANOV: *(Appears on the path with LVOV.)* My dear friend, you graduated only last year, you're still young, and hale, and hearty, while I am thirty-five years old. Yes. I have the right to advise you. Never marry a Jewess, or a neurotic, or a blue stocking, pick someone ordinary, and dull, and drab, who doesn't shine, who doesn't make any unnecessary noise. In principle, set your life according to a mold, a pattern. The greyer and more monotone the background, the better. Don't battle against the multitude, my dear man, don't joust at windmills, don't knock your head against a stone wall…And God protect you from all forms of modernized farming, progressive schools, impassioned oratory…Encase yourself into a shell and do the little insignificant work that God gave you to do…It's cozier, healthier, and purer. For the life that I lead, — how wearying it is! Oh, how wearying!…How flawed, how unjust, how absurd…*(Sees the COUNT, irritated.)* Uncle, you're always underfoot, you never give anyone the chance to talk in private!

SHABELSKY: *(In a tearful tone.)* Well curse me then, where else am I to go! *(Jumps up and goes into the house.)*

IVANOV: *(Calls after him.)* Sorry, sorry! *(To LVOV.)* Why did I offend him? No really, I'm losing control. I've got to do something with myself. I've got to…

LVOV: *(Agitated.)* Nikolai Alekseevich, I've heard you out and…and forgive me, I'll speak plainly, I won't mince words. In your voice, in your intonation, never mind the content of your words, there is such heartless egotism, such cold-blooded callousness…Here is someone close to you, dying, and all because she is close to you, her days are numbered, and you…you somehow find it possible not to love her, instead, you parade around, posing, pontificating…I can't express it, I don't have the gift of speech, but…but I can say that I dislike you profoundly!…

IVANOV: Perhaps, perhaps you do…I can see it, from your point of view. But isn't it also possible that you just don't understand me…Yes, probably I am very, very guilty…*(Listens.)* I think the horses are ready. I'm going to go and get dressed…*(Goes toward the house, and stops.)* Doctor, you don't like me and you don't hide it. That does you credit…*(Exits into the house.)*

LVOV: *(Alone.)* Curse him…Another lost opportunity, and I didn't say what I should have to him…I simply can't speak to him without losing my composure! I've hardly even opened my mouth to utter a word, and suddenly I'm suffocating *(points to his chest)*, I'm churning inside, my tongue sticks in my throat. I hate this "Tartuffe," this self-righteous scoundrel, to the depths of my soul…There he goes…For this unfortunate woman, her only happiness on earth is to have him by her side, she lives and breathes him, she beseeches him to spend but one single evening with her, that's all, and he…he simply cannot…For him, you see, the house is suffocating, claustrophobic. If he would have to spend one evening at home, he'd put a bullet through his brain from the anguish of it. Well, of course, poor man…he needs the freedom, the space, to plot his vile strategies…Oh, I know why you go to the Lebedevs every evening! I know!

Enter IVANOV in a hat and coat, SHABELSKY, and ANNA PETROVNA.

SHABELSKY: *(Entering from the house with IVANOV and ANNA PETROVNA.)* Really, *cher Nicolas,* it's simply inhuman!…You go out every single evening, and we stay home alone. We retire at eight from sheer boredom. This is not life, this is scandalous! And why is it that you can go out, while we never can? Why?

ANNA PETROVNA: Leave him alone, Count! Let him go, let him go…

IVANOV: *(To his wife.)* And where can you go? You're an invalid. You're ill, you can't be out after sundown…Go on, ask the doctor. You're not a child, Anyuta, you must be reasonable…*(To the COUNT.)* And why would you want to go there?

SHABELSKY: I'd go to hell itself, or into the jaws of a crocodile, any place but stay here. I'm bored! I'm almost comatose from boredom! I'm sick of everything. You leave me home, so she won't be lonely, and I torment her, I torture her!

ANNA PETROVNA: Leave him alone, Count, really, leave him alone! Let him go, if he'll enjoy himself there.

IVANOV: Why that tone, Anyuta? You know I don't go there for pleasure! I have to discuss the loan.

ANNA PETROVNA: I don't understand why you are justifying yourself? Go! Who is keeping you here?

IVANOV: Ladies and gentlemen, let's not torment one other! Really, is this necessary?!

SHABELSKY: *(In a tearful voice.) Cher Nicolas,* please, I beg of you, take me with you! I'll meet some fools and scoundrels there, and maybe even have a good time. Really, I haven't been anywhere since Easter!

IVANOV: *(Irritated.)* Fine, let's go! How sick I am of all of you!

SHABELSKY: Really? Oh, *merci, merci…(Joyfully takes his arm and takes him aside.)* May I borrow your straw hat?

IVANOV: Yes, you may, only hurry, please!

The COUNT runs into the house.

IVANOV: Yes, how weary I am of all of you! But, my God, what am I saying! Anya, I am speaking to you in an insufferable tone of voice. I've never been like this before. So, good-bye, Anya, I'll be back by one.

ANNA PETROVNA: Kolya, darling, stay at home!

IVANOV: My own, sweet darling, my poor unhappy one, I beg of you, don't keep me from going out in the evening. It is cruel, it is unjust on my part, but, please, permit me this injustice! It is such unbearable torture for me to stay at home! From the moment the sun sets, a melancholy sinks into my soul. Such a melancholy! Don't ask me why. I don't know, myself. I swear to you, I don't! Melancholy here, and then I go to the Lebedevs, and it's even worse; I come home, and again, the melancholy, and so it goes, all night long…I simply despair!…

ANNA PETROVNA: Kolya…if only you'd stay! We'll talk, like we used to… We'll have supper together, we'll read…The old grumbler and I, we've learned so many duets for you…*(Embraces him.)* Stay!…*(Pause.)* I don't understand you. This has been going on for a year now. Why have you changed?

IVANOV: I don't know, I don't know…

ANNA PETROVNA: And why don't you want me to go out with you in the evening?

IVANOV: If you really must know, then I'll tell you. It's rather cruel to talk about it, but it's better to say it…When this depression descends upon me, then I…I no longer love you. I run from you at such times. In a word, I've got to get out of the house.

ANNA PETROVNA: Depression? Yes, I understand, I understand…Do you know what, Kolya? Try, as you did before, sing, be merry, get angry, if you want…Stay, we'll laugh, we'll drink brandy, and your depression will dispel in a minute. Would you like me to sing? Or else come, let's sit in your study, in the darkness, like we used to, and you'll tell me about your depression…You have such suffering in your eyes! I shall gaze into them and weep, and we'll both feel better…*(Laughs and weeps.)* What else, Kolya? The flowers bloom again each spring, so why not joy? Right? So, come then, come…

IVANOV: Pray to God for me, Anya! *(Starts to exit, stops, and thinks.)* No, I can't! *(Exits.)*

ANNA PETROVNA: Go. *(Sits at the table.)*

Enter LVOV.

LVOV: *(Walks about the stage.)* Anna Petrovna, live by this rule: When the clock strikes six, you must go inside and you must not come out till morning. The evening damp is very bad for you.

ANNA PETROVNA: Yes, sir.

LVOV: What do you mean, "yes, sir"! I'm serious.

ANNA PETROVNA: And I don't want to be serious. *(Coughs.)*

LVOV: You see, — you're coughing already…

Enter SHABELSKY.

SHABELSKY: *(Enters in a hat and coat from the house.)* And where is Nikolai? Have they ordered the horses? *(Quickly crosses and kisses ANNA PETROVNA's hand.)* Good night, my lovely! *(Grimaces.)* Gevalt! Hek-skuse me, pleez! *(Exits quickly.)*

LVOV: Fool!

Pause; the distant sound of a harmonica is heard.

ANNA PETROVNA: What a pity!…The coachmen and the cooks are all having a party, while I…I'm left all alone…Yevgeny Konstantinovich, why are you pacing so? Come here, sit down!…

LVOV: I can't sit down.

Pause.

ANNA PETROVNA: They're playing "Little Finch" in the kitchen. *(Sings.)* "Little finch, little finch, where have you been? Drinking vodka down on the green." Doctor, are your mother and father living?

LVOV: My father's dead, my mother's still alive.

ANNA PETROVNA: Do you miss your mother?

LVOV: I have no time to miss her.

ANNA PETROVNA: *(Laughs.)* The flowers bloom again every spring, but not happiness. Who told me that expression? God, let me think…I believe it was Nikolai, yes. *(Listens.)* The owl is crying again.

LVOV: Let it cry.

ANNA PETROVNA: I'm beginning to think, doctor, that fate has cheated me. The majority of people, who may be no better than I, still have experienced happiness and have not had to pay for it. I have paid for it all, for all of it!…And how dearly! Why must I pay such a terrible price?…My dear friend, you are so careful with me, so gentle, you're afraid to tell the truth, but don't you think I know what my illness is? I know very well. However, it's so depressing to talk about it…*(In a Jewish accent.)* Hekscuse, pleez! Can you tell me a joke?

LVOV: No, I can't.

ANNA PETROVNA: Nikolai can. And, you know, I'm also beginning to be astonished by the unfairness of others: Why don't people respond to love with love, why do they reward truth with lies? Tell me: How much longer will my parents continue to despise me? They live roughly sixty miles from here, and day and night I feel their hatred, even in my dreams. And how am I supposed to take this depression of Nikolai's? He tells me he no longer loves me, but only in the evenings, when his anxiety oppresses him. This I understand, this I can tolerate, only imagine if he were to stop loving me entirely! Of course, this is impossible — but what if it were to happen all of a sudden? No, no, I must not even think of it. *(Sings.)* "Little finch, little finch, where have you been?…" *(Shudders.)* What terrible thoughts torment me!…You're not a family man, doctor, you wouldn't understand most of this…

LVOV: You astonish me…*(Sits next to her.)* No, really…you absolutely astonish me, you do! Explain it to me, would you, help me to understand, how you, an intelligent, pure, almost saintlike creature, could delude yourself, could allow yourself to be dragged off into this den. Why on earth are you here? What do you have in common with that cold, callous…but let's leave your husband out of it! — how could you possibly exist in this vulgar, uninhabitable environment? Oh merciful God!…That bitter, crusty, crazy old count, and that villain, that fraud of frauds, Misha, with his vile face…Illuminate me, why are you here? How on earth did you ever come to this place?

ANNA PETROVNA: *(Laughs.)* That's exactly what he said once…Word for word…But his eyes are bigger, and when he talks about something passionately, they glow, like brightly burning coals…Go ahead! Talk, talk!

LVOV: *(Stands and waves his hand.)* What can I say? Come inside…

ANNA PETROVNA: You say all sorts of things about Nikolai. But how do you know him? Really, how can you know a man after half a year? He is a remarkable man, doctor, and I only wish you'd known him two or three years ago. Now he's depressed, he's silent, he does nothing, but before…What a delight!…I fell in love him the moment I saw him. *(Laughs.)* I looked, and the mousetrap snapped shut — "klop"! He said: Let us go…And I cut myself off from everything, you know, the way you cut off dead leaves from a flower, and I went… *(Pause.)* But it's not the same any more…Now he goes to the Lebedevs, to divert himself with other women…and I…I sit in the garden and listen to the owl cry…*(The watchman knocks.)* Doctor, do you have any brothers?

LVOV: No.

ANNA PETROVNA sobs.

LVOV: Now what? What's the matter?

ANNA PETROVNA: *(Stands.)* I can't bear it, doctor, I'm going there…

LVOV: Where?

ANNA PETROVNA: There, where he is…I'm going…Tell them to prepare the horses. *(Runs into the house.)*

LVOV: No, I absolutely refuse to practice medicine under these conditions! Never mind that they don't pay me a kopek, but then they turn me inside out, they torment my soul!…No, I refuse! Enough!…*(Goes into the house.)*

END OF ACT ONE

ACT TWO

The reception hall in the Lebedevs' house; upstage center is the door into the garden; to the right and left are doors. Antique, expensive furniture. A chandelier, candelabras, and paintings — all under dustcovers. ZINAIDA SAVISHNA sits on the divan; alongside her sits the FIRST GUEST. Upstage, near the entrance into the garden, a card game is in progress; the players include KOSYKH, AVDOTYA NAZAROVNA, YEGORUSHKA, and THE SECOND GUEST. GAVRILA stands by the right door with a tray of delicacies. Guests circulate from the garden through the right door and back again, during the scene. BABAKINA enters from the right door and makes her way to ZINAIDA SAVISHNA.

ZINAIDA SAVISHNA: *(Joyfully.)* Darling, Marfa Yegorovna…
BABAKINA: Hello, Zinaida Savishna! Allow me to congratulate you on your daughter's birthday…*(They kiss.)* God willing, that —
ZINAIDA SAVISHNA: Thank you, darling, I'm so delighted…And how are you?…
BABAKINA: Very well, and thank you for asking. *(Sits next to her on the divan.)* Hello, all you young people!…

The FIRST GUEST stands and bows.

FIRST GUEST: *(Laughing.)* "Young people"…are you really so old?
BABAKINA: *(Sighs.)* We can't pretend we're young any more…
FIRST GUEST: *(Laughing politely.)* Pardon…You may be a widow, but you could outstrip any young girl.

GAVRILA brings BABAKINA tea.

ZINAIDA SAVISHNA: *(To GAVRILA.)* How in the world are you serving that? Bring some preserves…why not gooseberry?…
BABAKINA: Don't bother, really, I'm fine, thank you.

Pause.

FIRST GUEST: Marfa Yegorovna, did you travel here by way of Mushkino?…
BABAKINA: No, by way of Zaimishche. The road is better that way.
FIRST GUEST: I see.
KOSYKH: Two spades.

YEGORUSHKA: Pass.

AVDOTYA NAZAROVNA: Pass.

SECOND GUEST: Pass.

BABAKINA: The price of lottery tickets, my darling Zinaida Savishna, has gone way up. Did you ever? — tickets for the first draw are already at two hundred seventy, and for the second they're almost at two hundred fifty. It's unheard of…

ZINAIDA SAVISHNA: *(Sighs.)* How nice for those who already have lots of them…

BABAKINA: Not really, darling; they may be worth something, but they're not a good investment. The insurance alone could kill you.

ZINAIDA SAVISHNA: You're quite right, my darling, but still, one lives in hope…*(Sighs.)* God willing…

FIRST GUEST: Now in my opinion, *mesdames,* it doesn't pay to have capital these days. That's what I think. Securities yield very small dividends, and investments are extremely dangerous. The way I see it, *mesdames,* people who have money today are in a more risky position, then those, *mesdames,* who…

BABAKINA: *(Sighs.)* How true!

The FIRST GUEST yawns.

BABAKINA: Really, is it proper to yawn in the presence of ladies?

FIRST GUEST: *Pardon, mesdames,* it was accidental.

ZINAIDA SAVISHNA stands and exits out the right door; a prolonged silence.

YEGORUSHKA: Two diamonds.

AVDOTYA NAZAROVNA: Pass.

SECOND GUEST: Pass.

KOSYKH: Pass.

BABAKINA: *(Aside.)* My God, what boredom, you could die from it!

Enter ZINAIDA SAVISHNA and LEBEDEV.

ZINAIDA SAVISHNA: *(Entering from the door on the right with LEBEDEV, softly.)* What are you doing, sitting out there? You're such a *prima donna!* Sit with your guests! *(Takes her former seat.)*

LEBEDEV: *(Yawns.)* Ach, our sins, our unforgivable sins! *(Sees BABAKINA.)* Well, if it isn't our little sweetheart! Our sugarplum! *(Greets her.)* How is our precious?…

BABAKINA: Very well, thank you very much.

LEBEDEV: Well, thank God, then!…Thank God! *(Sits in an armchair.)* So, now…Gavrila!

GAVRILA brings him a glass of vodka and a glass of water; he tosses off the vodka and washes it down with water.

FIRST GUEST: To your good health!…

LEBEDEV: Good health, right!…I'm glad I'm alive. *(To his wife.)* Zyuzyushka, where's our birthday girl?

KOSYKH: *(Tearfully.)* Tell me: why didn't we take any tricks? *(Jumps up.)* Come on, tell me, why did we lose, damn it?

AVDOTYA NAZAROVNA: *(Jumps up, angrily.)* Because, my dear, you don't know how to play the game, and if you don't know the game, then don't play it. How could you possibly *lead* someone else's suit? No wonder you were stuck with a worthless ace!…

Both rush downstage from behind the table.

KOSYKH: *(Tearfully.)* Allow me, ladies and gentlemen…I was holding the ace, king, queen, jack, and seven other diamonds, an ace of spades and one small heart, do you hear me, only one, and, God knows why, she couldn't even bid a small slam!…I bid "no trump"…

AVDOTYA NAZAROVNA: *(Interrupting.)* No, *I* bid no trump! You bid *two* no trump…

KOSYKH: This is outrageous!…Allow me, please, ladies and gentlemen…You had…no, I had…no you had…*(To LEBEDEV.)* You be the judge, Pavel Kirilich…I had the ace, king, queen, jack, and seven other diamonds…

LEBEDEV: *(Plugs up his ears.)* Stop it, I beg of you…stop it…

AVDOTYA NAZAROVNA: *(Shouts.)* No, *I* bid no trump!

KOSYKH: Damned if I'll ever sit down to play with that old trout again! *(Rushes out into the garden.)*

AVDOTYA NAZAROVNA: Ugh!…He makes my blood boil…Trout! Trout yourself!…

BABAKINA: You weren't exactly so sweet yourself, old girl!

AVDOTYA NAZAROVNA: *(Sees BABAKINA, clasps her hands.)* Angel, darling!…Look who's here, and blind old hen that I am, I didn't even see her…Dearest…*(Kisses her on the shoulder and sits down next to her.)* What bliss! Let me look at you, my little white swan! Tfoo, tfoo, tfoo…that's to ward off the evil eye!…

LEBEDEV: Stop gushing…Better to find her a husband…

AVDOTYA NAZAROVA: And so I shall!…I shall not sleep in my grave, sinner that I am, until I have her and my Sanyechka married off! I shall not sleep in my grave…*(Sighs.)* Where can you find husbands these days? Here they sit, the husbands of the future, all ruffled up like a bunch of wet roosters!…

SECOND GUEST: A most unfortunate comparison. From my point of view, *mesdames*, if our young people of today prefer a life of celibacy, then that is the fault of our social system…

LEBEDEV: Come on, come on!…Stop philosophizing!…I don't like it!…

Enter SASHA.

SASHA: *(Enters and goes to her father.)* Such wonderful weather we're having, and you're all sitting here in this stuffy old room, ladies and gentlemen.

ZINAIDA SAVISHNA: Sashenka, haven't you noticed, Marfa Yegorovna is here.

SASHA: Forgive me, please. *(Goes to BABAKINA and greets her.)*

BABAKINA: You've become proud, Sanyechka, proud and stuck up, you haven't been to see me even once. *(Kisses her.)* Congratulations, darling…

SASHA: Thank you. *(Sits next to her father.)*

LEBEDEV: Yes, Avdotya Nazarovna, it's difficult to find husbands these days. And not only husbands — you can't even find a best man. These young people nowadays, and no offense meant, they're so spoiled, so soured, God bless them…They don't dance, they don't make conversation, they don't even drink sensibly…

AVDOTYA NAZAROVNA: Oh, no, they're experts at drinking, provided you supply it for them…

LEBEDEV: There's no trick to drinking, — why even a horse can drink…No, it's a question of drinking *sensibly!*… Now in our time, it used to be that you'd slave over your studies all day long, but come evening, off you'd go to the first bright lights and spin like a top until dawn…Dance, and amuse yourself with the young ladies, and that sort of thing. *(Makes a gesture of drinking.)* And you'd make up stories, tell lies, and philosophize until your tongue got paralyzed…But the young men nowadays…*(Waves his hand.)* I don't understand them…They serve neither God nor the devil. There's only one man in this district who knows his way around, but he's already married, *(sighs)* and it looks like he's losing his mind…

BABAKINA: Who's that?

LEBEDEV: Nikolasha Ivanov.

BABAKINA: Yes, he's a fine man *(grimaces)*, only he's so unhappy!…

ZINAIDA SAVISHNA: And no wonder, darling! *(Sighs.)* Poor man, what a mistake he has made!…He married his little Jewess, and poor man, he expected her father and mother to give her mountains of gold, but it turned out to be quite the opposite…Ever since she converted, her father and mother don't even want to know her, they curse her…And so he never even received a kopek. He's sorry now, of course, but it's too late…

SASHA: Mama, it isn't true.

BABAKINA: *(Heatedly.)* Shurochka, what do you mean, it isn't true? Everyone knows. If there hadn't been the income, then why in the world would he have wanted to marry a Jewess? Are there really so few Russians around? He made a mistake, darling, a big mistake…*(Quickly.)* And lord, how he gives it to her! Really, it's laughable. He'll come home from somewhere or other, and right away he'll say to her: "Your father and mother have cheated me! Get out of my house!" But where can she go? Her father and mother won't take her back; she could work as a maid, but she hasn't any training…So he torments her and torments her until the count takes her side. If it weren't for the count, she'd have been dead long ago…

AVDOTYA NAZAROVNA: And sometimes he locks her up in the cellar and makes her eat garlic: "Here he says, eat it, you so and so…" And she eats and eats until it comes out her ears.

Laughter.

SASHA: Papa, that's a lie!

LEBEDEV: So what? Let them talk, let them talk, it's good for their health… *(Shouts.)* Gavrila!…

ZINAIDA SAVISHNA: And so he is ruined, poor man. His affairs are completely in shambles, darling…If Borkin weren't managing the household, he and his little Jewess would have nothing to eat. *(Sighs.)* And how we've suffered on account of him, my darling!…How we've suffered, God only knows! Believe me, my sweet, it's been three years since he's owed us nine thousand rubles!

BABAKINA: *(Horrified.)* Nine thousand!…

ZINAIDA SAVISHNA: Yes…my dear dear Pashenka managed to lend it to him. He can't tell whom he should lend money to, and whom he shouldn't. I'm not talking about the principal, — God bless it if we ever see it, but at least have the decency to pay the interest on time!…

SASHA: *(Heatedly.)* Mama, you've told this story a thousand times!

ZINAIDA SAVISHNA: What do you mean? What are you taking his side for?

SASHA: *(Stands.)* How can you possibly have the heart to talk this way about someone who has done you no harm? What has he ever done to you?

SECOND GUEST: Aleksandra Pavlovna, permit me to say a word or two? I respect Nikolai Alekseich and always have had regard for him, but, speaking *entre nous,* he seems to be somewhat of an opportunist.

SASHA: I congratulate you, if that's what you believe.

SECOND GUEST: As proof of what I say, I present to you the following fact, which was told to me by his aide, or, rather, shall I say, his sidekick, Borkin. Two years ago, at the time of the livestock epidemic, he bought cattle, insured them…

ZINAIDA SAVISHNA: Yes, yes, yes! I remember that incident. I heard it about it as well.

SECOND GUEST: He insured them, and what do you know, he infected them with the plague and collected the insurance premium.

SASHA: My God, what nonsense this all is! What nonsense! No one ever bought cattle and infected them! It was Borkin himself who fabricated this scheme and went around bragging about it. When Ivanov found out about it, Borkin begged his forgiveness for a whole two weeks after. Ivanov was only guilty of the fact that he has a gentle nature and didn't have the heart to fire this Borkin, yes, guilty because he believes in people too much! He's been robbed, he's been swindled out of everything; anyone who wanted to, could have made a fortune from his idealism.

LEBEDEV: Shura, you little hothead! Calm down!

SASHA: Why do they talk such nonsense? Oh, this is so boring, so very boring! Ivanov, Ivanov, Ivanov — it's as if they have nothing else to talk about. *(Goes to the door and returns.)* I'm astonished! I am positively astonished by your patience, gentlemen! Really, aren't you bored sitting here? The air is thick with boredom! Say something, entertain the ladies, go on! And if you don't have anything to talk about except Ivanov, why then laugh, sing, dance, anything…

LEBEDEV: *(Laughs.)* That's right, give it to them, give it to them but good!

SASHA: No really, listen, do me the favor, please! If you don't want to dance, and laugh, and sing, if all this is boring to you, then I ask you, I beg of you, for once in your lives, just for fun, astonish us, amuse us, summon up all your strength and just this once think up something witty, something brilliant, something even rude or vulgar, but at least something that's novel or new! Or else why don't all of you, all together, perform some small feat, barely noticeable but nevertheless distinctive, so that all the young ladies for once in their lives might look at us and say: "Ah"! Look, you all want to impress us, of course you do, so why not at least try? Oh, ladies and gentlemen! You're not as you should be, really, you're not!...One look at all of you and the flies die and the lamps start smoking!...I've told you a thousand times and I'll keep on telling you, you're not as you should be! You're not!

Enter IVANOV and SHABELSKY.

SHABELSKY: *(Entering with IVANOV from the right door.)* Who's been making speeches? Is it you, Shurochka? *(Laughs loudly and shakes her hand.)* Congratulations, my angel, may God grant you live longer and never be born again…

ZINAIDA SAVISHNA: *(Joyfully.)* Nikolai Alekseevich…Count!…

LEBEDEV: Well! Of all people…Count! *(He goes to greet them.)*

SHABELSKY: *(Seeing ZINAIDA SAVISHNA and BABAKINA, holds both arms out to them.)* Two treasures on one sofa!…It's a pleasure to see you! *(Greets ZINAIDA SAVISHNA.)* Hello, Zyuzyushka! *(To BABAKINA.)* Hello, my little flower!…

ZINAIDA SAVISHNA: I'm so glad. You visit us so rarely, Count! *(Shouts.)* Gavrila, tea! Sit down, please! *(Stands, goes to the right door and returns immediately, looking extremely worried.)*

SASHA sits in her former place. IVANOV greets everyone silently.

LEBEDEV: *(To SHABELSKY.)* Where on earth have you been? What brought you here? What a surprise. *(Kisses him.)* Count, you old pirate! That's not the way to behave. *(Takes him downstage by the hand.)* Why haven't you been to see us? Are you angry, or what?

SHABELSKY: And how might I come to see you, tell me? Flying on my walking stick? I don't have any horses of my own, and Nikolai won't bring me with him, he tells me to stay home with Sara, so she won't be lonely. Send me *your* horses, then I'll come…

LEBEDEV: *(Waves his hand.)* Right!…Zyuzyushka would sooner die, than lend out the horses. You are my dear dear friend, you're nearer and dearer to me than anyone! You and I are the only ones left from the good old days. *(Sings.)* "In you I love my days of suffering,/In you I mourn my long-lost youth…" All joking aside, look, I'm almost weeping…*(Kisses the COUNT.)*

SHABELSKY: Let me go, please! You've been down in the wine cellar, I can tell…

LEBEDEV: My dear man, you can't imagine how lonely it is without my friends!

I could hang myself from the loneliness… *(Softly.)* Zyuzyushka has driven away all the respectable people with her money-lending, and all that is left, as you can see, are the "zulu" people . . these Dudkins and Budkins…whatever…Now, let's have some tea…

GAVRILA brings the COUNT tea.

ZINAIDA SAVISHNA: *(Worried, to GAVRILA.)* Wait, how are you serving that? Bring in some kind of preserves…why not gooseberry?. . .

SHABELSKY: *(Laughs loudly; to IVANOV.)* Didn't I tell you? *(To LEBEDEV.)* I made a bet with him on the way over, that the moment we arrive, Zyuzyushka would start to serving us gooseberry preserves…

ZINAIDA SAVISHNA: Count, you are such a mocker…*(Sits.)*

LEBEDEV: They made twenty barrels of it, so what are we going to do with it?

SHABELSKY: *(Sits near the table.)* So, tell me, Zyuzyushka, are you still making money? What do you have by now, a million?

ZINAIDA SAVISHNA: *(With a sigh.)* I know, from the outside it appears that we're richer than other people, but where does the money come from? From talk, that's all…

SHABELSKY: Yes, of course!…we know…We know what a poor player you are…*(To LEBEDEV.)* Pasha, tell me the truth, what do you have, a million?

LEBEDEV: I don't know, really. Ask Zyuzyushka…

SHABELSKY: *(To BABAKINA.)* And our plump little pompom here will soon have a million, too! She gets prettier and plumper — not by the day, by the hour. That's what a lot of money does to you…

BABAKINA: Thank you very much, your excellency, but I don't like to be made fun of.

SHABELSKY: My sweet little treasury, really, do you think I'm mocking you? No, it's simply a cry from the heart, I'm moved to speak from an excess of feeling…I love you and Zyuzyushka infinitely…*(Gaily.)* What rapture!…What ecstasy!…I can't look at either of you without feeling overcome…

ZINAIDA SAVISHNA: You haven't changed a bit. *(To YEGORUSHKA.)* Yegorushka, blow out the candles! Why waste candles, if you're not playing?

YEGORUSHKA trembles; he extinguishes the candles and sits down.

ZINAIDA SAVISHNA: *(To IVANOV.)* Nikolai Alekseevich, how is your wife's health?

IVANOV: Poor. Today the doctor diagnosed her with consumption…

ZINAIDA SAVISHNA: Really? What a pity! *(Sighs.)* And we all love her so...

SHABELSKY: It's all nonsense, I tell you, sheer and utter nonsense! She doesn't have consumption, she has nothing of the sort, it's medical fraud, it's quackery. He wants to hang around like Aesculapius, so he dreams up the diagnosis of consumption. It's a good thing her husband isn't jealous.

(IVANOV makes an gesture of impatience.)

SHABELSKY: As far as Sara herself is concerned, I don't believe a thing she says or does. All my life I've never trusted doctors, lawyers, or women. Nonsense, nonsense, charlatanry, and trickery!

LEBEDEV: *(To SHABELSKY.)* You are an amazing character, really you are, Matvey!...You parade around here like some kind of misanthrope and you make a great big song and dance of it. Why, you're just a man like anyone else, but as soon as you talk, it's all bile and venom.

SHABELSKY: Well, what do you expect me to do, make love to these rogues and scoundrels, or what?

LEBEDEV: What rogues and scoundrels?

SHABELSKY: Present company excluded, of course, only...

LEBEDEV: "Only" what...There you go again...It's a pose, that's all.

SHABELSKY: A pose...that's easy for you to say, you have no philosophy of life.

LEBEDEV: What do you mean, "philosophy of life"? I'm just sitting around here waiting to become a corpse, that's my philosophy of life. We have not time to think of philosophies, my friend. And so it goes...*(Shouts.)* Gavrila!

SHABELSKY: Enough already with Gavrila...Look at the color of your nose!

LEBEDEV: *(Drinks.)* Never mind, my dear fellow, this is not my wedding day.

ZINAIDA SAVISHNA: Doctor Lvov hasn't been to see us in a long time. He's forgotten about us.

SASHA: God, my walking nemesis. The honorable doctor. He can't ask for a glass of water or smoke a cigarette without showing you how honorable he is. He walks and talks, while right on his forehead is inscribed: "I am an honorable man!" He's a bore.

SHABELSKY: Right you are, he's Doctor Righteous! *(Imitates.)* "Make way for the honest physician." Every step he takes, he squawks like a parrot, he thinks he's the second Dobrolyubov. And anyone who doesn't sing his song is a scoundrel. If a peasant is prosperous and lives like a human being, then that mean's he's a scoundrel and a profiteer. I walk around in a velvet smoking jacket and let my servant dress me — and that means I'm a scoundrel and a serf-owner. Honesty is as honesty does, but this man oozes honesty from every pore. He doesn't know what to do with himself. I'm actually afraid of him...no, really, it's the truth!...You get the feeling that he might punch you in the face or call you a scoundrel, all out of a sense of duty.

IVANOV: He gets on my nerves, but nevertheless I like him; he is very sincere.

SHABELSKY: I'll say, he's sincere! Yesterday evening he came up to me and said: "Count, I dislike you intensely!" Well, I most humbly thank you! And not just a pure and simple "I dislike you"— no, with such affectation: with trembling voice, and fiery eyes, I mean, he was shaking in his shoes...To hell with this false sincerity! All right, I'm repulsive to him, he loathes me, that's natural...I know all that, really, but why tell me to my face? I am a worthless, rotten good-for-nothing, but whatever they may say, I am still an old man...No, it's a cruel and callous honesty!

LEBEDEV: Come, come, come!...You were young once, you understand.

SHABELSKY: Yes, I was young and foolish once, I played "Chatsky" in my time, I unmasked villains and frauds in my day too, but never did I call a thief "a thief" to his face, never did I speak of rope in the house of a hanging man. After all, I am a man of culture. But as for your fatuous physician, he must have felt it his call of duty, his divine right, so to speak, as if fate had ordained him, in the name of principle and higher human ideals, to give me a punch in the face or a kick in the ribs in public.

LEBEDEV: Young people all have their ways. I once had an uncle, a disciple of Hegel... He used to gather people into his home, and after a couple of drinks he'd stand on a chair like this and say: "You ignoramuses! You are the forces of darkness! This is the dawn of a new life!" and on and on and on he'd go, blah blah blah. How he loved to lecture...

SASHA: And what about the guests?

LEBEDEV: Nothing...They'd listen and get drunk themselves. Although once I challenged him to a duel, yes, my very own uncle. It was all about Bacon. I remember, God help me, I was sitting, just like this, like Matvey, and Uncle was standing right there, where Nikolasha is, with poor Gerasim Nilich, may his soul rest in peace...And so, my friend, Gerasim Nilich asked a question...

Enter BORKIN, dressed in dandified clothing, a parcel in his hands; he comes in the right door, skipping and humming a tune. There is a murmur of approval.

FIRST GUEST: Mikhail Mikhailovich!...

LEBEDEV: Michel Michelich! Speaking of the devil...

BORKIN: And here I am! *(Runs up to SASHA.)* Congratulations, senorita, and may I dare to congratulate the entire universe on the birth of such a marvelous flower as yourself...As a gesture of my joy, I take the liberty of presenting to you *(gives her the parcel)* these specially made fireworks and sparklers. They will light up the night just as you illuminate the darkness of the darkest domain. *(Bows theatrically.)*

SASHA: I thank you.

LEBEDEV: *(Laughs loudly; to IVANOV.)* Why don't you fire this Judas?

BORKIN: *(To LEBEDEV.)* Pavel Kirilich! *(To IVANOV.)* Boss… *(Sings.)* Nicolas voilà, la di da! *(Makes the rounds.)* Most honorable Zinaida Savishna…Most divine Marfa Yegorovna…Most ancient Avdotya Nazarovna…Most high and mighty Count…

SHABELSKY: *(Laughs loudly.)* The life of the party…No sooner does he come in, and the atmosphere gets livelier. Can't you feel it?

BORKIN: Ugh, I'm all tired out…I've said "hello" to everyone, haven't I? So what's new, ladies and gentlemen? Anything in particular, the scent of something special, perhaps? *(Animated, to ZINAIDA SAVISHNA.)* Ach, just listen to this, Mama…On my way over here…*(To GAVRILA.)* Give me some tea, Gavryusha, only no gooseberry preserves! *(To ZINAIDA SAVISHNA.)* On my way, I saw some peasants by the river, stripping bark away from your willow bushes. Why don't you go out and lease your bushes for that purpose?

LEBEDEV: *(To IVANOV.)* Why don't you fire this Judas?

ZINAIDA SAVISHNA: *(Startled.)* You know, you're right, I never even thought of it!…

BORKIN: *(Exercises his arms.)* I can't live without physical exercise…Let's play a little game, Mamasha, shall we? Marfa Yegorovna, I'm in excellent shape…I'm quite exalted, actually! *(Sings.)* "Again before you I stand…"

ZINAIDA SAVISHNA: Yes, do something, would you, everyone's so bored.

BORKIN: Ladies and gentlemen, really, why are you looking so dejected? You're sitting there like a jury!…Come on, let's think up something. So what do you want to play? Charades, a game of tag, dancing, fireworks?

GUESTS: *(Clapping their hands.)* Fireworks, fireworks! *(They run out into the garden.)*

SASHA: *(To IVANOV.)* Why are you so depressed tonight?…

IVANOV: My head aches, Shurochka, and yes, I'm depressed…

SASHA: Come, let's go into the drawing room.

They exit out the right door; everyone has gone into the garden, except for ZINAIDA SAVISHNA and LEBEDEV.

ZINAIDA SAVISHNA: Now there's a young man for you — he's here no more than two minutes, and already he's cheering everyone up. *(Turns down the large lamp.)* While everyone's in the garden, there shouldn't be any candles burning needlessly. *(Extinguishes the candles.)*

LEBEDEV: *(Follows her around.)* Zyuzyushka, we ought to feed our guests something…

ZINAIDA SAVISHNA: Look how many candles there are…no wonder people think we're so rich. *(Extinguishes them.)*

LEBEDEV: *(Following her around.)* Zyuzyushka, we really should feed our guests something…They're young people, poor things, they're starving, no doubt…Zyuzyushka…

ZINAIDA SAVISHNA: The count didn't finish his tea. And all that sugar wasted. *(She exits through the left door.)*

LEBEDEV: Tfoo!…*(Exits into the garden.)*

Enter SASHA and IVANOV.

SASHA: *(Enters with IVANOV through the right door.)* Everyone's gone into the garden.

IVANOV: And that's the way it is, Shurochka. Before I used to work a lot, think a lot, and never get fatigued; and now I do nothing, I think nothing, and I'm weary, body and soul. Day and night my conscience torments me, I feel a terrible guilt, but exactly of what I am guilty, I do not know. And then there's my wife's illness, the lack of money, the endless squabbling, the gossip, the useless conversations, that foolish Borkin…My own home is loathsome to me, to live there is worse than torture. I tell you the truth, Shurochka, even the company of my own wife is unbearable, the wife who loves me. You are an old friend, you won't be angered by my honesty. I've come here to divert myself, but I'm depressed even here, and I long to go home. Forgive me, I'll slip away quietly.

SASHA: Nikolai Alekseevich, I understand you. You are unhappy because you are lonely. You need someone near you whom you love and who understands you. Only love can restore you.

IVANOV: Really, Shurochka! That would be the limit, for a has-been like me, to get involved in a love affair! God save me from such a misfortune! No, my clever one, a love affair is not the answer. I say before God that I can bear anything: anxiety, depression, ruination, loneliness, loss of my wife, premature old age, but what I cannot bear is my own self-loathing. I shall die with shame from the thought that I, a strong, healthy man, have become a Hamlet, a Manfred, one of those "alienated" men…or God only knows what! There are pitiful people who are flattered to be called Hamlet or "alienated" — to me it's disgraceful! It offends my pride, I'm overcome with shame, and I suffer…

SASHA: *(Playfully, through tears.)* Nikolai Alekseevich, let's run away to America.

IVANOV: Here I am, too weary to walk to the door, and you want to go to America…*(They walk toward the exit into the garden.)* Really, Shura, it's too difficult for you to live here! When I look at the people around you, I'm terrified: Who is there for you to marry here? I have only one hope—that some passing lieutenant or student might capture you and carry you off…

ZINAIDA SAVISHNA enters from the left door with a jar of preserves.

IVANOV: Forgive me, Shurochka, I'll talk to you later…

SASHA exits into the garden.

IVANOV: Zinaida Savishna, I have a favor to ask of you…

ZINAIDA SAVISHNA: What is it, Nikolai Alekseevich?

IVANOV: *(Hesitates.)* The fact of the matter is, you see, that the day after tomorrow my loan to you is due. I would be very much obliged if you might grant me an extension or else permit me to attach the interest to the capital. I have absolutely no money at this time…

ZINAIDA SAVISHNA: *(Frightened.)* Nikolai Alekseevich, really, how could I possibly? What are you suggesting? No, really, don't even think of it, for God's sake, don't torture me, I'm a poor, unfortunate woman…

IVANOV: Forgive me, forgive me…*(Exits into the garden.)*

ZINAIDA SAVISHNA: Good heavens, how he frightened me!…I'm trembling…trembling all over!…*(Exits through the right door.)*

Enter KOSYKH.

KOSYKH: *(Enters through the left door and crosses the stage.)* I was holding an ace, king, queen, jack, and seven more diamonds, an ace of spades and one, only one little heart, and she, confound her, couldn't even bid a small slam! *(Exits through the right door.)*

Enter AVDOTYA NAZAROVNA and the FIRST GUEST from the garden.

AVDOTYA NAZAROVNA: I'd like to tear her apart, the miser…that's right, tear her apart! It's a joke, I've been sitting here since five o'clock, and she hasn't even offered me a moldy piece of herring!…What a household!…What hospitality!…

FIRST GUEST: I'm so bored, I could bang my head against a wall! What people, God help them!…I'm so starving I could howl like a wolf and start devouring people.

AVDOTYA NAZAROVNA: I'd like to tear her apart.

FIRST GUEST: I'll have a drink first, old girl, and then I'm off! I don't need any of your maidens here, thank you very much. How in hell can a man even think of love if he hasn't had a thing to drink since dinner?

AVDOTYA NAZAROVNA: Shall we have a little look around, or what?…

FIRST GUEST: Shhh!…Softly! I think there's some schnapps on the buffet in the dining room. Let's go find Yegorushka…Shhh!…

They exit by the left door. Enter ANNA PETROVNA and LVOV from the right door.

ANNA PETROVNA: Really, they'll be glad to see us. There's no one here. They're probably in the garden.

LVOV: The question is, why did you bring me here, to this vulture's nest! This is no place for us! Honest people can't survive in this atmosphere!

ANNA PETROVNA: Listen, O righteous one! It is unseemly for a gentleman to escort a lady and talk to her of nothing but his own integrity! You may be honest, but you're also tiresome, to say the least. Never tell women about your virtues. Let them discover them on their own. When my Nikolai was in the company of ladies at your age, he sang songs, he told tales, and yet all the while they knew what kind of man he was.

LVOV: Oh, please don't talk to me about your Nikolai, I understand him very well!

ANNA PETROVNA: You're a good man, really you are, but you understand nothing. Let's go into the garden. Never, ever would he say: "I'm honest!" or "I'm suffocating in this atmosphere!" or "Vultures! Owls' nest! Crocodiles." No, he'd leave the menagerie alone, and when he'd get exasperated, all I ever heard him say was: "How unjust I was tonight!" or "Anyuta, I feel sorry for this man!" And that was all, while you…

They exit. AVDOTYA NAZAROVNA and the FIRST GUEST enter from the left door.

FIRST GUEST: There's nothing in the dining room, so it must be somewhere in the pantry. We've got to find Yegorushka. Let's go through the drawing room.

AVDOTYA NAZAROVNA: I'd like to tear her apart!…

They exit through the right door. Enter BABAKINA and BORKIN, running and laughing, from the garden, followed by the COUNT, tripping after them, laughing and rubbing his hands together.

BABAKINA: How boring! *(Laughs loudly.)* How positively boring! They're all sitting around like dummies! My bones are stiff with boredom. *(Jumps.)* I have to stretch my legs!…

BORKIN grabs her by the waist and kisses her cheek.

SHABELSKY: *(Laughs loudly and snaps his fingers.)* Well, I'll be damned! *(Clears his throat.)* As I was saying…

BABAKINA: Let go of me, let go of me, you shameless man, what in the world will the Count think! Leave me alone…

BORKIN: Angel of my soul, carbuncle of my heart!…*(Kisses her.)* Lend me two thousand three hundred rubles!…

BABAKINA: No, no, no…When it comes to money, then thank you very much…But no, no, and no again! Let go of my hand!…

SHABELSKY: *(Skips around.)* Little pompom…Isn't she charming…

BORKIN: *(Seriously.)* Enough. Let's get down to business. We'll discuss it in a businesslike fashion. Give me a straight answer, without beating around the bush: yes or no? Listen! *(Points to the COUNT.)* He needs money, a minimum of three thousand a year. You need a husband. Wouldn't you like to be a countess?

SHABELSKY: *(Laughs loudly.)* What an incredible cynic!

BORKIN: Do you want to be a countess? Yes or no?

BABAKINA: *(Anxiously.)* You're making this all up, Misha, really…And anyway, things like this aren't done in such an offhanded fashion…If the count wishes to, he can ask me himself, and…and anyway, I don't know, really, it's all so sudden…

BORKIN: Let's not confuse the issue! It's strictly business…Yes or no?

SHABELSKY: *(Laughing and rubbing his hands.)* Really?…Well, I'll be damned, shall I play this nasty little charade? eh? Little pompom…*(Kisses BABAKINA on the cheek.)* Coquette!…My cucumber!

BABAKINA: Stop it, stop, you're alarming me…Go away, go away!…No, wait, don't go yet!…

BORKIN: Quickly! Yes or no? We're running out of time…

BABAKINA: Do you know what, Count? Come stay with me for a few days… We'll have fun at my place, it's not like here…Come tomorrow…*(To BORKIN.)* You were only teasing, weren't you?

BORKIN: *(Angrily.)* Who would want to joke about serious matters like this?

BABAKINA: Stop it, stop it…I feel faint! I feel quite faint! A countess…I feel ill! I'm going to faint!

BORKIN and THE COUNT, laughing, take her by the arm, and kissing her on the cheek, they lead her out through the right door. IVANOV and SASHA come rushing in from the garden.

IVANOV: *(In despair, holding his head.)* It can't be! Don't, Shurochka, don't!…My God, don't do this!…

SASHA: *(Passionately.)* I love you madly…Without you, my life makes no sense, no sense at all, there's no joy, no happiness! You're everything to me…

IVANOV: Why, why! My God, I understand nothing…Shurochka, don't do this!…

SASHA: You were the only joy of my childhood; I loved you, I loved you heart and soul, more than I loved myself, and now…I still love you, Nikolai Alekseevich…I'll follow you anywhere, to the ends of the earth, wherever you want to go, to the grave, even, only for God's sake, let's go now, as soon as possible, or else I shall suffocate…

IVANOV: *(Bursts into peals of laughter.)* What is this? What are you saying, start life all over again? Really, Shurochka?…My happiness! *(He draws her close to him.)* My youth, my inspiration!…

ANNA PETROVNA enters from the garden, and upon seeing her husband and SASHA, stands, as if rooted to the ground.

IVANOV: To live again, do you mean it? Yes? To work again?

They kiss. Afterwards, they glance around and see ANNA PETROVNA.

IVANOV: *(Horrified.)* Sara!

END OF ACT TWO

ACT THREE

IVANOV's study. A writing table, with books, papers, official-looking envelopes, knickknacks, revolvers, strewn about; beside the papers is a lamp, a decanter with vodka, a plate with herring and pieces of bread and cucumber. On the walls are maps, paintings, firearms, pistols, sickles, riding whips, and so forth. — It is midday.

SHABELSKY and LEBEDEV sit on either side of the writing table. BORKIN sits on a chair upstage center. PYOTR stands by the doors.

LEBEDEV: In France, the politics are clearly defined. The French know what they want. They want to skin the sausage-makers, that's all. In Germany, on the the other hand, they sing a different tune. Germany has other things on its mind besides France…

SHABELSKY: Nonsense!…In my opinion, the Germans are cowards, and the French are cowards too…They just shake their fists at one another. Believe me, it won't go beyond that. They'll never fight.

BORKIN: And why fight, in my opinion? Why all the fuss — the arms, the congresses, the expenditures? Know what I'd do? I'd round up all the dogs in the kingdom, I'd inject them all with a good dose of Pasteur's virus, and then set them loose on enemy territory. All my enemies would go mad in a month.

LEBEDEV: *(Smiling.)* He has a small head, you know, but it's packed with as many ideas as there are fishes in the sea.

SHABELSKY: A genius!

LEBEDEV: God bless you, you make me laugh, Michel Michelich! *(Stops laughing.)* Well, gentlemen, all this talk, and not a word about vodka. "Repetatur!" *(Fills three glasses.)* To your health…*(They drink and eat.)* Herring…God love it, it's the delicacy of delicacies.

SHABELSKY: No it's not, cucumbers are better…Scientists have been contemplating this problem ever since the world began and have come up with nothing better than the salted cucumber…*(To PYOTR.)* Pyotr, go brings us some more cucumbers and tell them out in the kitchen to bake us four onion pies. And make them really hot.

PYOTR exits.

LEBEDEV: Caviar tastes good with vodka, too. Only do you know how to serve it? With intelligence, that's how…You take a quarter of a pound of pressed caviar, two bulbs of green onions, a little olive oil, you mix all these ingredients together, you know, like this…and then you top it off with a little lemon juice! It's lethal! You can go mad from the aroma.

BORKIN: Another delicious delicacy after vodka is fried gudgeon. Only you have to know how to fry it. First you clean it, then you roll it in crushed bread-crumbs, then you fry it to a crisp, so that they're crispy and crunchy and they crackle when you eat them, like this…crackle, crackle, crackle…

SHABELSKY: Last evening at Babakina's they served an excellent delicacy — white mushrooms.

LEBEDEV: I'll say…

SHABELSKY: Only they were specially prepared. You know, with onion, and bay leaf, and all sorts of spices. When you lift the lid of the saucepan, what a fragrance…pure bliss!

LEBEDEV: And so, gentlemen? "Repetatur!" *(They drink up.)* To our health… *(Looks at his watch.)* I can't wait for Nikolasha today. I must be on my way. At Babakina's they served mushrooms, you say, and I haven't seen one in my house yet. Kindly tell me, why the devil do you go to Marfutka's so often?

SHABELSKY: *(Nods at BORKIN.)* He wants me to marry her…

LEBEDEV: You, marry? How old are you?

SHABELSKY: Sixty-two years old.

LEBEDEV It's time you got married. And Marfutka's the match for you.

BORKIN: It's not a question of Marfutka, it's a question of Marfutka's money…

LEBEDEV: Marfutka's money…what do you want next, the moon?

BORKIN: And when this man gets married and stuffs his pockets, then you'll see how to get the moon. You'll be licking your lips…

SHABELSKY: He's serious. This genius is convinced that I'm going to listen to him and get married…

BORKIN: What do you mean? You're not sure?

SHABELSKY: Are you out of your mind? When was I ever sure of anything! Come on…

BORKIN: Well thank you, then…I'm much obliged! You're letting me down, is that it? First you will, then you won't…God only knows what you're doing, and meanwhile I've given my word! So that means you're not getting married?

SHABELSKY: *(Shrugs his shoulders.)* He's serious…What an astonishing man!

BORKIN: *(Indignant.)* In that case, why would you upset an honest woman? She went crazy over the idea of being a countess, she doesn't sleep, she doesn't eat…Is this something to joke about? Is this an honorable thing to do?

SHABELSKY: *(Snaps his fingers.)* It's a nasty little charade, really, but why not play it! Eh? Just for spite. I'll do it. Word of honor…Just for fun!

Enter LVOV.

LEBEDEV: Aesculapius, our most humble servant…*(Gives LVOV his hand and sings.)* "Doctor, oh doctor, save me, I'm scared to death of my dying day…"

LVOV: Nikolai Alekseevich still hasn't arrived yet?

LEBEDEV: No, and I've been waiting for him for over an hour myself.

LVOV paces the stage impatiently.

LEBEDEV:My dear man, how is Anna Petrovna?

LVOV: She's doing poorly.

LEBEDEV: *(Sighs.)* May I pay my respects?

LVOV: No, please, I'm sorry, don't go in there. I think she's asleep…

Pause.

LEBEDEV: A lovely woman, a splendid woman…*(Sighs.)* Ever since Shurochka's birthday, when she fainted at our house, I looked at her face and I understood then, that she did not have long to live, poor woman. I still don't understand: What was the matter with her then? I ran in and I saw her: pale, lying there on the floor, Nikolasha kneeling there beside her, pale, too, Shurochka in tears. After that incident, Shurochka and I were quite shaken, we walked around for a week in a trance.

SHABELSKY: *(To LVOV.)* Tell me, most honorable high priest of science, which great scientist discovered the fact that the condition of a woman with chest ailments can be improved by frequent visits from a young physician? That was a tremendous discovery! Truly tremendous! Would you consider that it falls in the category of allopathy or homeopathy?

LVOV wishes to respond, but instead gives him a contemptuous look and exits.

SHABELSKY: What an annihilating glance…

LEBEDEV: What the devil made you say that? Why did you offend him?

SHABELSKY: *(Irritated.)* Then why did he lie? With consumption, there is no hope, she'll die…He's lying, I tell you! I can't bear it!

LEBEDEV: But why do you think he's lying?

SHABELSKY: *(Stands and walks around.)* I cannot tolerate the thought that a living human being, suddenly, for no reason, ceases to be. Let us quit this conversation!

Enter KOSYKH.

KOSYKH: *(Running in, panting.)* Is Nikolai Alekseevich home? Hello! *(Hurriedly shakes everyone's hand.)* Is he home?

BORKIN: No, he is not.

KOSYKH: *(Sits, then jumps up again.)* In that case, then, good-bye! *(Pours a glass of vodka and eats hurriedly.)* I'll be moving on…Business, you know…I'm all worn out…Can hardly stand on my feet…

LEBEDEV: And where did you blow in from?

KOSYKH: From Barabanov. We played cards all night long, we just finished…I lost everything I had…That Barabanov, he plays like a cobbler. *(In a tearful voice.)* Just listen to this: I'm holding hearts…*(Turns to BORKIN, who hides from him.)* He bids diamonds, and I bid hearts again, he bids diamonds…And no trump. *(To LEBEDEV.)* We were playing in clubs. I'm holding the ace, queen, and six in my hand, the ace, ten, and three of spades…

LEBEDEV: *(Holds his hands over his ears.)* Spare me, spare me, for Christ's sake, spare me!

KOSYKH: *(To the COUNT.)* Think of it: the ace, queen, six of clubs, the ace, ten and three of spades…

SHABELSKY: *(Waves him away.)* Go away, I don't want to hear any more of this!

KOSYKH: And then suddenly, disaster strikes: The ace of spades is trumped in the first round…

SHABELSKY: *(Seizes the revolver from the table.)* Get out of here, or else I'll shoot!…

KOSYKH: *(Waves his hand.)* What in hell…Can't I talk to anyone around here? It's like living in Australia: There is no commonality, no solidarity…It's every man for himself… Never mind, I've got to go…it's time. *(Takes his cap.)* Time is precious…*(Gives LEBEDEV his hand.)* Pass!…

Laughter. KOSYKH exits and collides with AVDOTYA NAZAROVNA at the door.

AVDOTYA NAZAROVNA: *(Cries out.)* To hell with you, you almost knocked me off my feet!

ALL: Aaahhhh!…Madame Ubiquitous!…

AVDOTYA NAZAROVNA: And here they are, I've been looking for you all over the house. Hello, my fine friends, and *guten appetit…(Greets them.)*

LEBEDEV: And why are you here?

AVDOTYA NAZAROVNA: Business, my dear, business! *(To the COUNT.)* A matter concerning you, your excellency. *(She bows.)* I have been commissioned to extend to you the warmest greetings and to inquire after your health…And she, the sweet little darling, has also asked me to tell you that if you do not come to see her this evening, she will cry her little eyes out. "Take him aside and whisper it to him in his ear," the little darling said. But why such secrecy? We're all friends here. After all, we're not stealing chickens, we're conducting business, properly, according to the laws of love and civil obedience. You know, I never drink, old sinner that I am, but perhaps on such on occasion I just might!

LEBEDEV: And so shall I. *(Pours.)* You're holding up well, you old bird, you. You've been an old lady these last thirty years that I've known you…

AVDOTYA NAZAROVNA: Who's counting…I've buried two husbands, and I would have had a third, but no one gets married nowadays without a dowry. I've had eight or so children…*(Takes the glass.)* Well, we've got something going here, so God help us finish it off! They'll live happily ever after, and we'll wish them love and joy, and give them good advice…*(Drinks.)* This is wicked vodka!

SHABELSKY: *(Laughing, to LEBEDEV.)* It's fascinating, you know, really, they're taking all this seriously, they think that I…Amazing! *(Stands.)* No, really, Pasha, shall I play this nasty little charade? Out of spite, then…Here, drink up, you old dog! So, Pasha?

LEBEDEV: You're talking nonsense, Count. The task at hand is to prepare ourselves for the grave, you've long since missed your chance for Marfutka and her money…Our time is past.

SHABELSKY: No, I'll do it! Word of honor, I'll do it!

Enter IVANOV and LVOV.

LVOV: I beg of you, give me just five minutes.

LEBEDEV: Nikolasha! *(Goes to greet IVANOV and kisses him.)* Hello, my friend…I've been waiting you for an entire hour.

AVDOTYA NAZAROVNA: *(Bows.)* Greetings, sir!

IVANOV: *(Bitterly.)* Gentlemen, you've turned my office into a tavern again!… I've asked you one and all a thousand times not to do this…*(Goes to the writing table.)* Look at this, vodka spilled on my papers…crumbs…cucumbers… It's disgusting, really!

LEBEDEV: So sorry, Nikolasha, so sorry…Forgive me. I must speak to you about a matter of great urgency, my friend…

BORKIN: Me, too.

LVOV: Nikolai Alekseevich, May I have a word with you?

IVANOV: *(Pointing at LEBEDEV.)* He needs me. I'll talk to you in a minute…*(To LEBEDEV.)* What do you want?

LEBEDEV: Gentlemen, I wish to talk in private. I beg of you…

The COUNT and AVDOTYA NAZAROVNA exit, followed by BORKIN, and then LVOV.

IVANOV: Pasha, go ahead, drink, as much as you want, it's your illness, but I ask you please, do not let my uncle drink. He never used to drink before. It's bad for him.

LEBEDEV: *(Frightened.)* But my dear man, really, I had no idea…I didn't even notice…

IVANOV: God forbid that old baby should die, what would you care, but as for me…Now what do you want?…

Pause.

LEBEDEV: You see, my dear friend…I don't know how to begin, or how to say it tactfully. Really, Nikolasha, I'm ashamed, look, I'm blushing, I'm tongue-tied, but, my dear man, put yourself in my place, please, understand, I'm a subservient, a spineless subordinate…forgive me…

IVANOV: What are you talking about?

LEBEDEV: My wife has sent me…Have mercy on me, be so kind as to pay her the interest you owe! Believe me, she's been aggravating me, harassing me, nagging me, tormenting me to death! For God's sake, get her off your back!…

IVANOV: Pasha, you know very well that I have no money.

LEBEDEV: I know, I know, but what can I do? She won't wait. If she takes you to court, how can Shurochka and I look you in the face?

IVANOV: I'm so ashamed, Pasha, I wish I could vanish into the earth…but where can I possibly get it? Tell me: where? There is only one solution: to wait until autumn, when I can sell the harvest.

LEBEDEV: *(Shouts.)* She doesn't want to wait!

Pause.

IVANOV: Your situation is awkward, it's delicate, to say the least but mine is even worse. *(Walks and thinks.)* And there's nothing I can think of…Nothing I can sell…

LEBEDEV: Why not go and ask Millbach, you know he owes you 16,000.

(IVANOV waves his hand in despair.) Tell you what, Nikolasha…I know you'll be angry with me, but…out of respect for an old souse! Out of friendship… Look upon me as a friend…We're educated men, we're liberals…Common ideas and interests…We've both studied at Moscow University…Our alma mater… *(Takes out his wallet-portfolio.)* Here are my secret savings, not a soul at home knows about it. Take it as a loan…*(Takes the money out and places it on the table.)* Throw away your pride, for friendship's sake. I'd take it from you, truly I would… *(Pause.)* Here it is, on the table: one thousand one hundred rubles. Take it to her today, give it to her with your own hands. "Here you are, Zinaida Savishna," say to her, "I hope you choke on it." Only be careful not to let on, that you got it from me, for God's sake! Or else I'll be up to my neck in gooseberry preserves! *(Scrutinizes IVANOV's face.)* Oh, all right, then, never mind! *(Quickly takes the money from the table and hides it in his pocket.)* Never mind! I was only joking…Forgive me, for Christ's sake! *(Pause.)* Are you upset?

IVANOV waves his hand.

LEBEDEV: Yes, business…*(Sighs.)* This is a bad time for you, your troubles are only beginning. A man, my friend, is like a samovar. He doesn't always sit in a nice cool place on a shelf, sometimes he gets stoked up, and then: "Pshhh…Pshhh"! To hell with that comparison, it's not very good anyway, but I couldn't think of a cleverer one…*(Sighs.)* Misfortunes strengthen the soul. I don't pity you, Nikolasha, you'll overcome it, it will pass, but I'm fed up, really I am, my friend, I'm angry at what people are saying…Tell me, will you, where is all this gossip coming from! You're the scandal of the district, my friend, it even looks as if the local prosecutor might be after you…They're calling you a murderer, a parasite, an extortionist…

IVANOV: It's all nonsense, my head is aching.

LEBEDEV: It's because you think too much.

IVANOV: I'm not thinking of anything.

LEBEDEV: Listen, Nikolasha, don't you give a damn about any of this, you come and see us. Shurochka loves you, she's devoted to you, she understands and appreciates you. She's a good and kind person, Nikolasha. She's not like her mother or father at all — who *does* she resemble, some passing stranger?… There are times, my friend, when I look at her, and I can't believe that an old red-nosed souse like me could have such a treasure. Come over, have an enlightening conversation with her — it will cheer you up. She's a fine person, loyal and true…

Pause.

IVANOV: Pasha, my dear friend, leave me alone…

LEBEDEV: I understand, I understand…*(Hurriedly looks at his watch.)* I understand. *(Kisses IVANOV.)* Good-bye. I must attend the consecration of a school. *(Goes to the door and stops.)* What an intelligent girl…Yesterday we were talking about slander, Shurochka and I. *(Laughs.)* And what a wise thing she said: "Papa," she said, "Fireflies illuminate the night, only so that night birds might more easily find and eat them; so too do good people exist, only so that gossip and slander can prey upon them." Can you imagine that? A genius! A true Georges Sand!…

IVANOV: Pasha! *(Stops him.)* What's the matter with me?

LEBEDEV: I wanted to ask you that myself, but, I confess, I was ashamed, I'm too shy. I don't know, my friend! On the one hand, I think that many misfortunes have overcome you, and on the other hand, I know that you're not the kind to be defeated by your misfortunes. No, there's something else, Nikolasha, but what that is — I do not know!

IVANOV: I do not know myself. I think…no, never mind! *(Pause.)* Here is what I want to say. I once had a worker named Semyon, you may remember him. Once, during threshing time, he wanted to dazzle the young girls with his strength, so he hoisted two huge sacks of rye upon his back, and his back broke under the strain. He died soon thereafter. And so it seems that I, too, have broken under the strain. Education, university, then farming, building schools, all kinds of plans and projects…I held different beliefs from others, I married differently, I had passions, I took risks, I threw my money around right and left, as well you know, I was happy, and, yes, I suffered, like no one else in the entire district. And all these, Pasha, these are my sacks of rye. I lifted these burdens upon my back, and suddenly it snapped. In our twenties we are heroes, we undertake anything, we can do anything, but by thirty we're already weary, we're good for nothing. How do you explain this weariness, how? Ah well, perhaps that's not it…that's not it at all!…Go, Pasha, God be with you, you must be tired of me.

LEBEDEV: *(Animated.)* I know what it is! It's your surroundings that are destroying you.

IVANOV: That's stupid, Pasha, stupid and stale, too. Go on, go!

LEBEDEV: Yes it is, it is stupid. It is, I see it myself. I'm going, I'm going!… *(Exits.)*

IVANOV: *(Alone.)* A worthless soul am I, pitiful, paltry, insignificant. You'd have to be as worn-out, as dissipated, as pitiable as Pasha, to love and to admire me. How I despise myself, my God! How deeply I detest the sound of my own voice, my footsteps, my hands, the clothes I wear, my very thoughts. Ludicrous, isn't it, and enraging, too. Not even one year ago, I was vital and strong, my mood was high, I worked tirelessly, passionately, with my own two hands; I waxed eloquent till fools were moved to tears, I wept when faced with sorrow and grief, I cried out in protest against evil. I myself knew inspiration, I knew the pleasure and poetry of gentle nights, alone at my desk from dusk until dawn, alone with my dreams to excite me. I had faith, I looked to the future, as into the eyes of my own precious mother…And now, oh dear God! I'm weary, I'm lost, I believe no more, paralysis is with me day and night. My brain and hands and feet no longer obey me. The estate has gone to rack and ruin, the forests fall under the stroke of the ax. *(Weeps.)* My own beloved land gazes at me with the eyes of an orphan. I have no expectations, no regrets, my soul trembles with terror at the coming of each day…And what about Sara? I vowed love eternal, I promised her happiness, I opened her eyes to a future she'd never dared to dream of. And she believed me. For five years I've seen her bowing under the terrible burden of self-sacrifice, exhausted from the struggles of conscience, and, as God is my witness, not one look askance at me, not even one word of reproach!…And what did I do? I fell out of love with her…How? Why? For what reason? I do not know. And now she suffers, her days are diminishing, and, coward that I am, I flee from her pale face, her sunken chest, her imploring eyes…For shame, for shame! *(Pause.)* Sasha, that child, is touched by my sorrows. She speaks to me of love, me, an old man, almost, and I'm intoxicated, I forget about everything else on earth, I'm hypnotized by it, as if by music, and I cry: "A new life! happiness!" And yet the very next day I believe in this life and this happiness as much as I believe in ghosts…What is wrong with me? Into what abyss do I hurl myself? Where does this fatal flaw in me come from? What has become of my nerves? My poor ill wife has only to look at me the wrong way, or a servant displease me, or a gun misfire, and I become rude and ill-tempered, I'm no longer myself…*(Pause.)* I don't understand, I don't understand, I don't understand! I feel like putting a bullet through my brain!…

Enter LVOV.

LVOV: I must have a word with you, Nikolai Alekseevich!
IVANOV: Doctor, if we had words with each other every single day, it would be
    more than I could bear.
LVOV: Are you willing to hear me out?

IVANOV: I hear you out every day and still don't understand a single word: What precisely do you want from me?

LVOV: I'll speak clearly and distinctly, and only he who has no heart will not understand me...

IVANOV: I have a wife at death's door, that I know; I am irreparably guilty, that I also know; you are an honest, upright man, I know that, too. What more do you want from me?

LVOV: Human cruelty devastates me...A woman is dying. She has a father and mother, whom she loves and wishes to see before her death; they know full well that she is soon to die and that she loves them dearly, but still they continue to curse her. What contemptible cruelty! Do they wish to astonish us with their religious zeal? You are the man for whom she has sacrificed everything — her home, her peace of mind, and yet every day, in plain sight and in cold blood, you go off to the Lebedevs with the clearest of intentions.

IVANOV: For God's sake, I haven't been there in two weeks...

LVOV: *(Not hearing him.)* With people like you, one must speak directly and plainly, and if you don't care to listen, then don't! I am accustomed to calling things by their proper names...You need this death for your new exploits; so be it, but is there any reason why you simply can't wait? If only you'd let her die naturally, instead of torturing her to death with your insidious and deadly cynicism, do you really think you'd lose Lebedev and her dowry? And, who knows, in a year or two you might even succeed in turning the head of another sweet young thing and taking possession of *her* dowry, just as you're doing now, debonair Tartuffe that you are...What's your hurry? Why do you need your wife to die just now, instead of in a year or two?

IVANOV: This is torture...Doctor, you're a pretty poor physician if you think that a man has no limits. I'm exercising terrific self-control not to respond to your insults.

LVOV: Oh come, come, who do you think you're fooling? Enough. Throw off the mask.

IVANOV: You're an intelligent man, think about it: As far as you're concerned, there's nothing easier than to figure me out! Right? I married Anna, to get my hands on her sizeable dowry...Her dowry was not forthcoming, I lost that game, so now I'm torturing her to death so that I can get married to someone else and get a dowry that way...Right? How clear and uncomplicated...A man is such a simple and uncomplicated machine...No, Doctor, in each of us there are too many cogs and wheels, too much complex apparatus to judge one another on first impression or superficialities. I don't understand you, you don't understand me, we don't understand one another. An excellent physician you may be, and yet at the same time you know nothing of the human soul. Admit it, and don't be so sure of yourself.

LVOV: And do you really think you're so opaque and I'm so naive that I can't tell perversity from honesty?

IVANOV: Evidently, we'll never agree…For the last time, I ask you, now answer me, please, without digressing: What exactly is it that you want from me? What are you driving at? *(Irritated.)* And with whom do I have the honor of talking so candidly: with my prosecutor, or with my wife's doctor?

LVOV: I am a doctor, and as a doctor, I demand that you behave differently… You're killing Anna Petrovna!

IVANOV: But what can I do? What? If you understand me better than I understand myself, than tell me clearly: What can I do?

LVOV: At least, behave more discreetly.

IVANOV: Oh, my God! Do you know what you're saying? *(Drinks water.)* Leave me alone. I'm guilty, a thousand times over, I shall answer before God — but who has given you the right to torture me like this day after day?…

LVOV: And who has given you the right to offend me? You've exhausted me, you've poisoned my soul. Until I came to this district, I tolerated the fools, the madmen, the fanatics of the world, but never ever did I believe that there existed in this world people, cruel, calculating criminals who consciously and cold-bloodedly plotted evil…I loved and respected mankind, until I met you…

IVANOV: I've heard this already!

Enter SASHA, wearing a riding habit.

LVOV: Have you, really? *(He sees SASHA entering.)* In that case, I trust, we understand each other perfectly! *(Shrugs his shoulders and exits.)*

IVANOV: *(Frightened.)* Shura, you're here?

SASHA: Yes, I am. Hello. Weren't you expecting me? Why haven't you been to see us in such a long time?

IVANOV: Shura, for God's sake, this is indiscreet! Your presence here might have a terrible effect on my wife.

SASHA: She won't see me. I came in the back entrance. I'll go, right away. But I've been so worried: Are you all right? Why haven't you come to see me in so long?

IVANOV: My wife is wounded enough as it is, she's almost dying, and here you come to see me. Shura, Shura, this is irresponsible, it's inhuman!

SASHA: But what was I to do? You haven't been to see us in two weeks, you haven't answered my letters. I'm exhausted from the anxiety. I thought you were suffering unbearably, that you were ill, that you had died. I haven't slept one single night in peace…I'll go…At least tell me, though: Are you all right?

IVANOV: No, I torment myself, and others torment me, too, endlessly…I can bear it no longer! And now you're here! How unnatural, how bizarre it all is! The guilt is mine, Shura, the guilt is mine!…

SASHA: How you love to say terrible and pitiful things! You are guilty? Really? Guilty? Of what? Tell me!

IVANOV: I don't know, I don't know…

SASHA: That is not an answer. Every sinner must know how he has sinned. Have you forged bank notes, is that it?

IVANOV: That's not a clever answer!

SASHA: Guilty, then, for falling out of love with your wife? Perhaps, a man is not master of his soul, after all, you didn't *want* to stop loving her. Guilty, then, that she witnessed my declaration of love for you? But no, you didn't *want* her to witness it…

IVANOV: *(Interrupting.)* Etcetera, etcetera, etcetera…I fell in love, I fell out of love, I am not the master of my soul — what platitudes, what trite phrases, none of which help the situation…

SASHA: It's tiring to talk to you. *(Looks at the painting.)* How well that little dog has been painted! Is it from real life?

IVANOV: Yes, from real life. And our little romance is a platitude, it's hackneyed and trite: "He lost his way, he lost heart. And she appears, a spirit bright and strong, and holds out a helping hand." How very pretty, indeed, but these things only happen in novels, not in real life…

SASHA: They do, it's all the same.

IVANOV: I see, how astutely you understand life! My *ennui* inspires in you a reverential awe, I'm your fantasy, you imagine you've found the second Hamlet, but no, not really: I believe this glorious psychosis of mine, with all its symptoms, has made me into a laughing stock, and nothing more! They ought to be laughing to death at my affectations, and meanwhile, you — you cry "help!" You want to save me, to play the heroine! I'm enraged with myself today! My tension is at its peak…I'm ready to break something, or else…

SASHA: That's right, do it, you must. Break something, do, smash something, shout…You are angry with me, I've done a foolish thing, coming here today. So rant at me, rave at me, stamp your feet. Well? Go on, get angry…*(Pause.)* Well?

IVANOV: You're ridiculous!

SASHA: Wonderful! We're smiling, it seems! Do be so kind as to deign to smile again!

IVANOV: *(Laughs.)* I couldn't help noticing: When you're trying to save me and you start spouting wisdom, your face glows with innocence, and your eyes grow larger, as if they've seen a shooting star. Wait, there's just a bit of dust on your shoulder. *(Brushes the dust from her shoulder.)* A man who is naive is a fool. But when a woman affects naiveté, it seems so sweet, so warm, so wholesome — not foolish at all. But why are you this way? When a man is healthy, and happy, and strong, you pay him not the slightest attention, but no sooner does he start to disintegrate and to bemoan his fate, you hang around his neck. To be the wife of a strong and courageous man, is it really worse than to be nurse to some sort of lachrymose failure?

SASHA: It is worse!

IVANOV: But why? *(Laughs.)* Lucky for you that Darwin can't hear you, he'd set you straight! You are corrupting mankind. Your kindness and mercy is nurturing a breed of neurotics and psychopaths.

SASHA: There is so much that men don't understand. Every young woman is attracted to a failure more than to a happy man, because what she wants is a vital love…You understand? A vital love. A man has his work, and love is incidental. To talk with his wife, to stroll with her in the garden, to pass the time pleasantly, to weep at her grave — that's all. But for us, our love is our life. I love you, that means that I dream of how I'd cure you of your despair, how I'd follow you to the ends of the earth…If you climb a mountain, I climb a mountain; if you plunge into an abyss, I plunge, too. What joy it would bring me just to copy your papers, for example, or stand watch over you all night, so that no might awaken you, or walk with you for miles and miles and miles. I remember once, three years ago, at threshing time, you came to us all dusty and burnt by the sun, exhausted, and you asked for a drink of water. I brought you a glass, and there you were, stretched out on the sofa, sound asleep. You slept for the rest of the day, and I stood watch over you the whole time by the door, so that no one might come in. How wonderful it was! The greater the effort, the greater the love, provided you feel it deeply.

IVANOV: Vital love…Hm…It's a spell that's cast, a maiden's fantasy, or perhaps, it is as it should be…*(Shrugs his shoulder.)* God only knows! *(Joyfully.)* Shura, I give you my word, I am a decent man!…You be the judge: I have always loved to philosophize, but never in my life have I said: "Our women are depraved," or: "They're going down the primrose path!" I've always been grateful, and nothing more! Nothing more! My child, my lovely child, how funny you are! And what a fool am I! I trouble the righteous, I bemoan my fate. *(Laughs.)* And I weep and I weep! *(Suddenly he steps aside.)* Go away, Sasha! We're forgetting ourselves…

SASHA: Yes, it's time to go. Farewell! I'm afraid your righteous doctor, out of a feeling of duty, might inform Anna Petrovna that I'm here. Listen to me: Go to your wife, and stay by her side, and stay, and stay…If necessary, stay for a year. And if it is ten years, then stay for ten years. Fulfill your duty. Grieve, and beg her forgiveness, and weep — do what should be done. But the main thing is, do not forsake your work.

IVANOV: Again, I feel ill. Again!

SASHA: And God bless you! Don't think about me! In a week or so, send me a line or two — I'll be grateful. And I'll write, too…

BORKIN looks through the door.

BORKIN: Nikolai Alekseevich, may I? *(Sees SASHA.)* Forgive me, I didn't notice… *(Enters.)* Bonjour! *(Bows.)*

SASHA: *(Embarrassed.)* Hello…

BORKIN: You're getting plumper and prettier every day.

SASHA: *(To IVANOV.)* So, I'm going, Nikolai Alekseevich…I'm going. *(Exits.)*

BORKIN: A vision of loveliness! I come for prose, and what do I find, but poetry…*(Sings.)* "You fly to me, like a bird flies into the light…"

IVANOV paces the stage, upset.

BORKIN: *(Sits.)* Do you know, *Nicolas, mon cher,* she's got something others haven't got. Isn't that right? Something special…phantasmagorical…*(Sighs.)* In essence, she's the richest bride in the district, but her mama's such a radish that no one wants anything to do with her. After her death, everything goes to Shurockha, but until her death her mother'll only give her a lousy 10,000, and maybe a curling iron here and a flatiron there, and she'll have to get on her knees for that. *(Digs into his pockets.)* Want to smoke a delosmajoros? Do you? *(Offers his cigar case.)* Quite a good smoke.

IVANOV: *(Approaches BORKIN, choking with anger.)* Get out of my house this minute! Don't you dare set foot in here again! This minute!

BORKIN raises himself slightly and drops his cigar.

IVANOV: Out! This minute!

BORKIN: *Mon cher Nicholas,* what does this mean? Why are you so angry?

IVANOV: Why? Where did you get those cigars? And do you really think that I don't know where you take that old man every day, and what for?

BORKIN: *(Shrugs his shoulders.)* Why do you even care?

IVANOV: You scoundrel! You dishonor my name in my own district with your vile, nasty little schemes! I'll have nothing more to do with you, and I ask that you leave my house this instant! *(Paces in agitation.)*

BORKIN: You're speaking this way because you're annoyed, I know, I know, that's why I'm not angry with you. Go on, insult me as much as you like…*(Picks up his cigar.)* But it's time to snap out of this depression. You're not a student…

IVANOV: What did I just say? *(Trembling.)* Are you playing games with me?

Enter ANNA PETROVNA.

BORKIN: Look, Anna Petrovna's here…I'm leaving. *(Exits.)*

IVANOV stops by the table, and stands, hanging his head.

ANNA PETROVNA: *(After a pause.)* Why did she come here? *(Pause.)* I'm asking you: Why did she come here?

IVANOV: Don't ask, Anyuta… *(Pause.)* I'm completely to blame. Devise whatever punishment you like, I can endure anything, but…don't ask…I haven't the strength.

ANNA PETROVNA: *(Angrily.)* Why was she here? *(Pause.)* So, that's the kind of man you are! Now I understand you. Low, dishonest…Do you remember, how you came to me and lied and said you loved me…I believed you, I left my own father and mother, I gave up my faith and followed you… Everything you said about truth, about goodness, about your noble plans, I believed every word, and you lied to me…

IVANOV: Anyuta, I have never lied to you…

ANNA PETROVNA: I have lived with you for five years, I've been ill and in anguish, but I've loved you and have never left your side for one minute…I idolized you…And why? All this time you've been deceiving me brazenly…

IVANOV: Anyuta, don't say it, it isn't the truth. I have made many mistakes, yes, it's true, but I've never lied to you, not once in my life…You cannot reproach me for that…

ANNA PETROVNA: Now I understand everything…You married me and you thought that my father and mother would forgive me and give me money… That's what you thought…

IVANOV: Oh my God! Anyuta, why are you doing this to me... *(Weeps.)*

ANNA PETROVNA: Be quiet! When you saw that there was to be no money, you started to play a new game...Now I remember everything, I understand everything. *(Weeps.)* You've never loved me and you haven't been faithful to me...ever!...

IVANOV: Sara, that's a lie!...Say whatever you like, but don't insult me with lies...

ANNA PETROVNA: You low, dishonest man...You owe money to Lebedev, and now, to avoid your debt, you want to turn his daughter's head, to deceive her, just as you've deceived me. Isn't that the truth?

IVANOV: *(Gasping.)* Be quiet, for God's sake! I cannot vouch for what I might say...I'm choking with rage and I...I might offend you...

ANNA PETROVNA: You've been deceiving me brazenly, always, and not me alone...You've blamed all your dishonest deeds on Borkin, and now I know whose they are...

IVANOV: Sara, be quiet, go away, or I'll lose control and say something I wish I hadn't! Something terrible and offensive... *(Shouts.)* Be quiet, Jew!...

ANNA PETROVNA: I will not be quiet...You've deceived me for too long, for me to be silent now...

IVANOV: So you won't be quiet? *(Struggles with himself.)* For God's sake...

ANNA PETROVNA: Go on, go on and deceive Lebedev now...

IVANOV: Then you should know, that soon...you will die...The doctor told me, soon you will die...

ANNA PETROVNA: *(Sits, her voice fails her.)* When did he tell you?

Pause.

IVANOV: *(Grabs his head in his hands.)* I am to blame. Dear God, I am to blame! *(Sobs.)*

END OF ACT THREE

ACT FOUR

Approximately one year has passed. One of the drawing rooms in LEBEDEV's house. Center stage, there is an archway separating the hall from the drawing room, to the right and left are doors. There are antique bronzes and family portraits. There are decorations for a celebration. There is a piano with a violin lying on it, and a cello standing alongside. Throughout the entire act guests pass through the hall, dressed in evening attire.

LVOV: *(Entering, looking at his watch.)* Five o'clock. I suppose the blessing will begin shortly…The blessing, and then the wedding ceremony. Here you have it, a celebration of virtue and justice! He didn't succeed in robbing Sara, he tortured her, he sent her to the grave, and now he's found another. And he'll deceive her, and rob her, and send her to the grave as well, she'll lie right alongside of poor Sara. It's the same old story of greed and corruption…*(Pause.)* He's in seventh heaven, beyond bliss, he'll live to a ripe old age, and die with a clear conscience…But you won't get away with this, oh no, you won't, I'm going to expose you! When I tear away the cursed mask, for all to see what sort of predator you are, you'll be hurled from your heaven into such an abyss that even the devil can't rescue you! I am an honest man, my mission is to intervene and open the eyes of the blind. I shall fulfill my duty and tomorrow I shall quit this accursed district! *(Thoughtfully.)* But what shall I do? Talk to Lebedev — a waste of time. Challenge him to a duel? Start a brawl? My God, I'm as nervous as a child, I've lost my powers of imagination. What shall I do? A duel?

Enter KOSYKH.

KOSYKH: *(Ecstatic, to LVOV.)* Yesterday I bid a small slam in clubs, and then I made a grand slam. Only that fellow Barabanov ruined the whole thing again. We're playing, see? And I bid: no trump. And he passed. And I bid two clubs. And he passed. Then I bid two diamonds…three clubs…and then, would you believe it, I mean, would you *believe* it, I bid a slam, and he doesn't show his ace. If that idiot had only shown his ace, I could have bid a grand slam in no trump…

LVOV: Forgive me, I don't play cards, and therefore I cannot share in your joy. Are they having the blessing soon?

KOSYKH: I suppose so. They're trying to bring Zyuzyushka around. She's crying her eyes out over that wretched dowry.

LVOV: And not about her daughter.

KOSYKH: No, about the dowry. She's in a rage. If they get married, that means he won't pay off his debt. I mean, you can hardly drag your own son-in-law to court over an unpaid debt.

Enter BABAKINA, all dressed up. She crosses the stage past LVOV and KOSYKH; the latter stifles a laugh; she glances around.

BABAKINA: Fool!

KOSYKH grabs her around the waist and laughs loudly.

BABAKINA: Peasant! *(She exits.)*

KOSYKH: *(Laughs loudly.)* That woman's gone off her rocker. Before she aspired to be a countess, she was just another woman, but now you can't even get near her. *(Teases.)* Peasant!

LVOV: *(Agitated.)* Listen, tell me the truth: What's your opinion of Ivanov?

KOSYKH: Not much. He plays cards like a cobbler. Let me give you an example: last year, during Lent, we sat down to play: the Count, Borkin, he and I. I bid —

LVOV: *(Interrupting.)* Is he a good man?

KOSYKH: Who, Ivanov? He's a real operator! He knows his way around. He and the Count — they're two of a kind. They have a real sixth sense for a good opportunity. He came up empty-handed with the little Jewess, he didn't succeed there, so now he's sniffing around Zyuzyushka's treasure chests. Damn me if I'm wrong, but I'll bet you anything that in a year's time he'll bring Zyuzyushka to rack and ruin. He'll do it to Zyuzyushka, and the Count will do it to Babakina. They'll take the money and run, and live happily ever after. Doctor, why do you look so pale today? You look awful.

LVOV: It's nothing, really. I drank too much last night.

Enter LEBEDEV with SASHA.

LEBEDEV: Let's talk here for a moment. *(To LVOV and KOSYKH.)* Be off with you, fellows, go find the ladies in the ballroom. We need to talk in private.

KOSYKH: *(Passing by SASHA, he snaps his fingers enthusiastically.)* Pretty as a picture! A queen of trumps!

LEBEDEV: Go on, you caveman, get out of here!

LVOV and KOSYKH exit.

LEBEDEV: Sit here, Shurochka, that's right…*(Sits and glances around.)* Now listen carefully, and with all due respect, of course. The fact is, that your mother has ordered me to tell you the following…Do you understand? This is not coming from me, but from your mother.

SASHA: Papa, please, come to the point!

LEBEDEV: Your dowry is set at 15,000 rubles in silver…And there it is…So there won't be any future discussion about it! Wait, don't say a word! That's only the flower, there's still the fruit. Your dowry has been set for 15,000, but, bearing in mind that Nikolai Alekseevich owes your mother 9,000, a deduction will be made from your dowry…And then, in addition…

SASHA: Why are you telling me this?

LEBEDEV: Your mother ordered me to.

SASHA: Leave me alone! If you had any respect either for yourself or for me, you wouldn't permit yourself to talk to me like this. I don't need your dowry! I never asked for it, and I'm not asking for it now!

LEBEDEV: What are you attacking me for? The two rats in Gogol's play, even *they* sniff around before going away, but you, you don't even sniff first, you attack. The emancipated woman.

SASHA: Leave me alone, don't offend me with your petty calculations.

LEBEDEV: *(Flying into a rage.)* Hah! You and your mother, you'll have me either stabbing myself or someone else! The one wails and howls and nags and counts kopeks, day after day after day; the other, Mademoiselle Emancipation, with her intelligence and compassion, doesn't even understand her own father! I insult *you!* Can't you see that before I came here to insult you, how *I* was insulted *(indicates the door)*, how I was hanged and quartered. She can't possibly understand me! I'm so confused, my head is spinning…To hell with you! *(Goes to the door and stops.)* I don't like it, I don't like it at all!

SASHA: What don't you like?

LEBEDEV: Any of it! I don't like any of it!

SASHA: What are you talking about?

LEBEDEV: Do you want me to sit down right here before you and tell you? I like nothing about it, and I don't want to be witness to this marriage! *(Goes to SASHA, affectionately.)* Forgive me, Shurochka, perhaps your marriage is sensible, pure, lofty, sublime, even, I don't know, but there's something wrong, there's something wrong! It isn't like other marriages. You're young, fresh, pure, sparkling, crystalline, while he — he is a widower, worn out, fraying at the edges. And I don't understand him, bless his soul. *(Kisses his daughter.)*

Shurochka, forgive me, but there is something impure about it all. Many people have been saying so. As soon as his Sara died, suddenly for some reason he wanted to marry you…*(Quickly.)* Never mind, I'm just an old crow, that's what I am. I'm turning into an old maid. Don't listen to me. Don't listen to any one, only to yourself.

SASHA: Papa, really, I've felt it myself, that there was something wrong…Wrong, wrong, all wrong. If only you knew how miserable I've been! It's unbearable! I feel awkward and I'm terrified to talk about it. Papa, dear, help me, please… tell me, what to do.

LEBEDEV: What did you say? What?

SASHA: I'm more terrified than I've ever been! *(Glances about.)* I feel that I don't understand him, and never shall. The whole time that I have been engaged to him, he has never once smiled at me, never once looked me straight in the eye. He's forever complaining, or repenting for something, he hints at some great guilt, he trembles…I'm exhausted from it all. There are moments when I feel…that I don't love him as much as I ought to. And when he comes to see us or talks to me, I start to feel depressed. What does it mean, Papa? It's terrible!

LEBEDEV: My darling, my only child, listen to your old father. Refuse him!

SASHA: *(Frightened.)* What are you saying? What are you saying?!

LEBEDEV: That's right, Shurochka. There will be a great scandal, gossip spreading all over the district, but better to endure a scandal than to ruin your life.

SASHA: Don't talk like that, Papa, please don't! I don't want to listen. I must struggle with these dark thoughts. He is a good man, an unhappy and complicated man: I shall love him, and understand him, and put him on his feet again. I shall fulfill my mission. It's done!

LEBEDEV: It's not a mission, it's madness.

SASHA: That's enough. I've confessed to you, what I didn't even want to confess to myself. Tell no one. We shall forget.

LEBEDEV: I understand nothing. Either I'm growing numb with old age, or you all have gotten awfully clever, but damned if I understand any of it.

Enter SHABELSKY.

SHABELSKY: Damn me and everyone else together! It's disgraceful!

LEBEDEV: What's the matter with you?

SHABELSKY: No, really, I must do something so base, so low, that everyone will be disgusted, myself included. And so I shall. Word of honor! I told Borkin to announce my engagement today. *(Laughs.)* If everyone else is going to be vile, then so shall I be.

LEBEDEV: I'm tired of you! Listen, Matvey, keep talking and they'll take you away to the madhouse, forgive me for saying so.

SHABELSKY: The madhouse — is that so very much worse than this house or any other house, for that matter? Be so kind as to take me there, immediately. Please. We're all so low, and small, and base, and worthless, and I am too, I hate myself, I don't believe a single word I say…

LEBEDEV: Do you know what, my friend? Put a wick in your mouth, light it, and go breathe fire on everyone. Or here's one better: Take your hat and go home. We're having a wedding here, everyone's celebrating, and you're cawing away like a crow. Yes, I mean it…

SHABELSKY leans against the piano and sobs.

LEBEDEV: My God!…Matvey!…Count!…What is wrong with you? Matyusha, my friend, my angel…Have I offended you? Forgive an old fool…Forgive a worthless drunk…Have a drink of water…

SHABELSKY: No, I don't want any. *(Lifts his head.)*

LEBEDEV: Why are you crying?

SHABELSKY: It's nothing, really…

LEBEDEV: No, Matyusha, don't lie to me: Why? Tell me the reason.

SHABELSKY: Just now, I was looking at this cello…and it reminded me of the little Jewess!…

LEBEDEV: For God's sake, what a time to remember! She is in heaven, may her soul rest in peace, but now isn't the time to remember…

SHABELSKY: We used to play duets together…A marvelous, wonderful woman!

SASHA sobs.

LEBEDEV: Now you? Enough! My God, they're both sobbing, and I…I…Look, why don't you go someplace where the guests won't see you!

SHABELSKY: Pasha, when the sun shines, you can even feel cheerful in a graveyard. When there is hope, you can feel happy, even in old age. But I have no hope, none, none!

LEBEDEV: Yes, things have turned out rather badly for you…You've no children, no money, no profession…But, what can you do? *(To SASHA.)* And what are you crying for?

SHABELSKY: Pasha, give me some money. I'll settle with you in the next world.

I'll go to Paris, and visit my wife's grave. I've given away plenty in my life-time, half of my fortune, I have the right to ask. And anyway, I'm asking it of a friend…

LEBEDEV: *(Dismayed.)* But my dear, I haven't even a kopek! Oh, all right, all right, never mind! Mind you, I'm not promising anything, you under-stand…very well, then, very well! *(Aside.)* They've worn me out!

Enter BABAKINA.

BABAKINA: Where is my suitor? How dare you leave me alone, Count? You're disgraceful! *(She strikes the COUNT on the hand with her fan.)*

SHABELSKY: *(Squeamishly.)* Leave me alone! I despise you!

BABAKINA: *(Dumbstruck.)* What?…Eh?

SHABELSKY: Get out of here!

BABAKINA: *(Falls into an armchair.)* Ach! *(Weeps.)*

ZINAIDA SAVISHNA *(Entering, in tears.)* Some one's coming…I think it's the best man. It's time for the ceremony…*(Sobs.)*

SASHA: *(Imploring.)* Mama!

LEBEDEV: Now everyone's weeping! A veritable quartet! They're starting a flood! Matvey!…Marfa Yegorovna!…If you keep this up, I'll cry myself…*(Weeps.)* Lord!

ZINAIDA SAVISHNA: If you no longer need your mother, if you won't obey her…oh, do what you like, I give you my blessing…

Enter IVANOV; he is wearing a dress coat and gloves.

LEBEDEV: This is the last straw! What is it?

SASHA: Why are you here?

IVANOV: Forgive me, ladies and gentlemen, permit me to speak with Sasha in private.

LEBEDEV: It is improper to see the bride before the wedding! You should be on your way to church!

IVANOV: Pasha, please…

LEBEDEV shrugs his shoulders; he, ZINAIDA SAVISHNA, the COUNT, and BABAKINA exit.

SASHA: *(Sternly.)* What do you want?

IVANOV: I'm seething with rage, but I'll try keep control. Listen to me. As I was dressing just now for the wedding, I looked at myself in the mirror, and what did I see...temples of gray. Shura, we must not do this! Let's put a stop to this senseless comedy before it is too late...You're young and pure, you have your whole life before you, while I...

SASHA: This is nothing new, I've heard it a thousand times, and I'm tired of it! Go to the the church, the people mustn't be kept waiting.

IVANOV: I'm going home now, announce to your family and friends that there is to be no wedding. Explain to them, somehow. It is time to come to our senses. I've been acting Hamlet, you're the pure and noble ingenue — and the play is over.

SASHA: *(Blushing.)* What are you saying? I refuse to listen.

IVANOV: And I'm speaking, and shall go on speaking.

SASHA: Why did you come here? Your whining is becoming an mockery and an insult.

IVANOV: No, I'm not whining any more! A mockery? Yes, I mock. Would that I could mock myself one thousand times over, and have the whole world mock me as well, then I'd do it! I looked at myself in the mirror, and something inside me shattered! I laughed and laughed at myself, it's a wonder I didn't go mad from the shame of it! *(Laughs.)* Depression! O, noble anguish! Inexplicable grief! The next thing is, I'll be writing poetry about it! Complaining, bemoaning my fate, making everyone else miserable in the process, knowing that my vitality is lost, evaporated, forever, that I'm stale and worn out, that I've outlived my time on earth, that I've succumbed to cowardice, that I'm drowning in this foul melancholy — knowing this, when all the while the sun shines brightly, when even the lowest creature on earth is bearing his burden with contentment — no, thank you very much! Seeing, how one man calls you a charlatan, while a second one pities you, and a third one lends you a helping hand, but the fourth — and this is the worst of all — listens to your sighs with reverence, looks upon you as the next Mahomed, and waits for you to announce the second coming at any moment...No, thank God, I still have some pride, some conscience left! On my way over here, I was laughing at myself, and it seemed to me that all the birds were laughing too, and the trees were laughing...

SASHA: This is not anger, this is madness!

IVANOV: You think so, really? No, I'm not mad, not all all. Now I see things in their true light, and my thoughts are as clear and as pure as your conscience. We love one another, but our wedding is not to be! I myself may rant and rave whenever I like, but I've no right to ruin the lives of others! I poisoned my own wife during the last precious year of her life with my complaining. Since our engagement, you've forgotten how to laugh, and you've aged five years. Your father, for whom life was once so clear, thanks to me has stopped understanding people. Wherever I go — to visit, to hunt, to attend a gathering, no matter, I carry my cloud of doom, dissatisfaction, and despondency. Stop, don't interrupt me! I'm speaking harshly, brutally, I am, but, forgive me, the anger is choking me to death, and I cannot speak otherwise. I've never meant to lie or to rant and rail at life, but since I've become a grumbler, against my will, without even knowing it, I curse at life, I curse my fate, I pity myself, and all who listen to me are infected with this loathing for life and they begin to curse it, too. And what an attitude! Can't you tell? I'm doing nature a favor to live in this world. Curse me!

SASHA: Wait a moment…What you've just said, it means that you're tired of complaining, that it's time to start a new life!…How wonderful!…

IVANOV: I see nothing wonderful in it at all. What new life? I'm ruined, irrevocably! It's time we both saw that. A new life!

SASHA: Nikolai, get hold of yourself! Where is there proof that you're ruined? What sort of cynicism is this? No, I will not speak of it, I will not listen…Go to the church!

IVANOV: I'm ruined!

SASHA: Don't shout like that, the guests will hear you!

IVANOV: If an intelligent, educated, and healthy man for no apparent reason starts to bemoan his fate and starts going downhill, he will continue to go downhill and there is no saving him! Where is my salvation, tell me? In what? I don't drink — wine makes my head ache; I can't even write bad poetry; I can't dignify this spiritual torpor and call it something noble. Inertia is inertia, and weakness is weakness, — there are no other names for them. I'm ruined, ruined — there can be no argument! *(Glances about.)* Someone might disturb us. Listen to me. If you love me, than help me. Now, this minute, give me up! Right now…

SASHA: Oh, Nikolai, if only you knew how weary you make me! How you torment my soul! You're a good, intelligent man, judge for yourself, how you can ask such a thing? Not a day goes by when there is not a crisis, one after another…I wanted a vital love, but this is martyrdom!

IVANOV: And when you become my wife, the problems will be compounded. Give me up! Please understand: This is not love inside you, it's determination, it's your pure and steadfast nature. You've made up your mind to rescue me, to redeem me, you get satisfaction from performing such a feat…Now you're ready to withdraw, but there is some false feeling inside you which prevents you. Please understand!

SASHA: What a strange and crazy logic! How can I give you up? Tell me, how?

You have nobody — no mother, no sister, no friends…You're ruined, they're pilfering your estate, they're vilifying you…

IVANOV: What a fool I was to have come here. I should have done what I wanted to do…

Enter LEBEDEV.

SASHA: *(Runs to meet her father.)* Papa, for God's sake, he comes bursting in here like a madman, and he's tormenting me! He's asking me to give him up, he doesn't want to ruin me. Tell him I don't want his magnanimity! I know what I am doing.

LEBEDEV: I don't understand…What magnanimity?

IVANOV: There will be no wedding!

SASHA: Oh, yes, there will! Papa, tell him there will be a wedding!

LEBEDEV: Wait, wait!…Why don't you want this wedding to take place?

IVANOV: I've explained to her why, but she doesn't want to understand.

LEBEDEV: Never mind her, explain it to me, so that I might understand! Ach, Nikolai Alekseevich! May God be your judge! You've brought darkness to our lives, I feel as if I'm living in a nightmare: I look and I understand nothing…What punishment!…So what am I supposed to do about this, old man that I am? Challenge you to a duel, or what?

IVANOV: There is no need for a duel here. You only need a head on your shoulders and an understanding of the Russian language.

SASHA: *(Paces the stage in agitation.)* This is terrible, terrible! He's acting like a child!

LEBEDEV: One can only throw up one's hands in despair, that's all. Listen to me, Nikolai! You may think this is all terribly intellectual and sophisticated and psychologically correct, but I think it will bring nothing but disgrace and heartbreak. Listen to an old man, once and for all! Here's what I want to say to you: Give that mind of yours a rest! Look at life more simply, like the rest of us! In this world, everything is simple. Walls are white, boots are black, sugar is sweet. You love Sasha, she loves you. If you love her — stay, if you don't — then go, we'll bear you no grievance. It's all that simple, really! You're both healthy, intelligent, decent people, you don't go hungry, thank God, you've clothes on your backs…What else do you need? No money? What does it matter! Money doesn't bring happiness…Of course, I understand…Your estate is mortgaged, you haven't the money to pay the interest, but I am her father, I understand…Her mother does as she likes, God bless her; if she won't give you money, so what! Shura says she doesn't need a dowry. Principles,

Schopenhauer…It's all nonsense…I have 10,000 stashed away in the bank. *(Looks around.)* Not a soul knows about it…It was your grandmother's…It's for both of you…Take it, only promise me this: Give Matvey a thousand or two…

The guests are gathering in the hall.

IVANOV: Pasha, there's no point in discussing it. I shall do what my conscience tells me to do.

SASHA: And I shall do what *my* conscience tells me. Say whatever you like, I won't let you go. I'll go call Mama. *(Exits.)*

LEBEDEV: I don't understand…

IVANOV: Listen to me, my poor old fellow…I won't even try to explain who I am to you — honest or base, sane or insane. I couldn't make you understand. Once I was young, passionate, honorable, brilliant; I loved, I hated, I believed differently than the rest, I worked and struggled with energy enough for ten men, I jousted at windmills, I beat my head against stone walls; not knowing my own strength, not listening to reason, not understanding life, I lifted a burden upon my back, and suddenly my muscles tore, my spine snapped; I raced through my youth, I drank too much, I worked too hard, I got excited, I chased my dreams; I knew no moderation. And tell me: Should it have been otherwise? There are so few of us, and so much work to be done, so much! My God, how much! And now how cruelly that life, the life that I defied, avenges itself upon me! I've cracked under the strain! And now, in my thirties, I'm old, and hungover, I've donned the dressing gown of old age. With a heavy head and heart, fatigued, strained, broken-down, with no faith and no love and no hope, like a shadow I flit among my fellow men, not knowing who I am, why I'm alive, or what I want! And already I feel that love is nothing but nonsense, sweet sugary caresses, that work is fruitless, that song and passionate oratory are banal and outdated. And everywhere I go, I bring this misery, this chilling boredom, this discontent, this loathing for life…I'm ruined, hopelessly ruined! Before you stands a man of thirty-five years, who is already dissatisfied, disillusioned, disenchanted, discouraged by his worthless and pathetic deeds, burning with shame, and mocking his own absurd weakness…Oh, how my pride rebels in me, how I suffocate with rage! *(Sways.)* I exhaust myself, I'm swaying on my feet…I'm weak. Where is Matvey? Let him take me home.

VOICES: *(In the ballroom offstage.)* The best man has arrived!

Enter SHABELSKY.

SHABELSKY: Here I am, in someone else's shabby tails…with no gloves on…oh, how they snickered and sneered at me, and made stupid remarks… Abominable pygmies!

BORKIN: *(Rushes in with a bouquet; he is wearing tails, with a best man's boutonier.)* Ach! Where is he? *(To IVANOV.)* We've been waiting forever for you in church, and you're here conducting a philosophical discourse. What a clown you are! My God, what a clown! You know very well that you're not supposed to go to the church with the bride, you're supposed to go with me, separately, and then I come back and get the bride and take her myself. You really don't understand how it works? What a complete clown!

LVOV: *(Enters, to IVANOV.)* What, you're here? *(Aloud.)* Nikolai Alekseevich Ivanov, I announce publically, for all the world to hear, that you are a scoundrel!

IVANOV: *(Coldly.)* I humbly thank you.

General embarrassment and confusion.

BORKIN: *(To LVOV.)* Sir, that is low! I challenge you to a duel!

LVOV: Mister Borkin, I consider you more than too lowly to fight with, you're too lowly even to speak with! And as for Mister Ivanov, he can have satisfaction from me, whenever he wants.

SHABELSKY: Sir, *I* challenge you to a duel!

SASHA: *(To LVOV.)* Why? Why did you insult him? Gentlemen, please, let him tell me: why did he do it?

LVOV: Aleksandra Pavlovna, I did not insulted him without cause. I came here, as an honorable man, to open your eyes, and ask you to hear me out.

SASHA: But what can you possibly say to me? That you are an honorable man? The whole world knows that. Better you should tell me with a clear conscience whether you understand yourself or not! You've come here now, as an honorable man, and insulted him horribly, which has nearly killed me; before, when you haunted him like a shadow and interfered in his life, again you were convinced you were fulfilling your duty, as a honorable man. You interfered in his private affairs, you slandered him, condemned him, and wherever possible, you deluged me and your acquaintances with anonymous letters, all the while thinking that you were an honorable man. In the name of honor, doctor, you also did not spare his ailing wife, you gave her no rest from your suspicions. And no matter what violence, what vile deeds you inflict upon others, you do so in the name of honor, as an honest and righteous man of progress!

IVANOV: *(Laughing.)* This is not a wedding, it's a parliament! Bravo, bravo!…

SASHA: *(To LVOV.)* And now, just think about it: Do you understand yourself better or don't you? You're a blind and heartless man! *(Takes IVANOV by the hand.)* Let's go away from here, Nikolai! Father, come!

IVANOV: Where, where is there to go to? Wait a moment, I'll put an end to all of this, once and for all! The youth in me is awakened anew, the young Ivanov speaks once more! *(Pulls out a revolver.)*

SASHA: *(Leaps up.)* I know what he wants to do! Nikolai, for God's sake!

IVANOV: I've been going downhill for too long now, it's time to stop! Enough, I've overstayed my welcome! Stand back! Thank you, Sasha!

SASHA: *(Cries out.)* Nikolai, for the love of God! Someone stop him!

IVANOV: Leave me alone! *(Runs to the side and shoots himself.)*

END OF PLAY

1887–1889

THE WOOD DEMON

A Comedy in Four Acts

CAST OF CHARACTERS

ALEKSANDR VLADIMIROVICH SEREBRYAKOV, a retired professor

YELENA ANDREEVNA, his wife, aged twenty-seven

SOFYA ALEKSANDROVNA (SONYA), his daughter from a first marriage, aged twenty

MARYA VASILYEVNA VOYNITSKAYA, widow of a privy councillor, mother of the professor's first wife

YEGOR PETROVICH VOYNITSKY, her son

LEONID STEPANOVICH ZHELTUKHIN, a former student of technology, now a very rich man

YULYA STEPANOVNA, his sister, aged eighteen

IVAN IVANOVICH ORLOVSKY, a landowner

FYODOR IVANOVICH, his son

MIKHAIL LVOVICH KHRUSHCHOV, a landowner with a medical degree

ILYA ILYICH DYADIN

VASILY, Zheltukhin's servant

SEMYON, a worker at the mill

The Wood Demon

ACT ONE

The garden of ZHELTUKHIN's estate. A large house with a terrace, before which are two tables: a large one, set for lunch, and a smaller one with hors d'oeuvres. It is three o'clock in the afternoon.

YULYA: You ought to have worn your grey outfit. This one doesn't suit you, you know.

ZHELTUKHIN: Who cares. It's all nonsense.

YULYA: Why so sullen, Lyonechka? And on your birthday, too. Shame on you!… *(Lays her head on his chest.)*

ZHELTUKHIN: A little less affection, please. Do you mind?

YULYA: *(In tears.)* Lyonechka!

ZHELTUKHIN: You smother me with kisses and give me gadgets I don't need, like a foolish little watch stand, for example. And then you don't even do what I ask you to do. Why haven't you written to the Serebryakovs?

YULYA: But I have written, Lyonechka!

ZHELTUKHIN: To whom?

YULYA: To Sonyechka. I asked her to come today without fail…at one, I said. Without fail. I *did* write. Honestly.

ZHELTUKHIN: But it's after two, and they're not here yet…Whatever! I don't care! Forget about it, what's the point, nothing will come of it…Only pain, humiliation, that's all…She pays no attention to me, none whatsoever. I'm unattractive, uninteresting, unromantic. She'd marry me for one reason only… money!

YULYA: What makes you think you're unattractive?…

ZHELTUKHIN: What am I, blind? Look how my beard grows out of my neck, it's not normal…And what about my moustache…and my nose…!

YULYA: Why are you holding your cheek?

ZHELTUKHIN: It hurts again, under my eye.

YULYA: You're right, it's swollen. Let me kiss it and make it better.

ZHELTUKHIN: Don't be ridiculous!

Enter ORLOVSKY and VOYNITSKY.

ORLOVSKY: When are we eating, my dear? It's after two o'clock!

YULYA: But the Serebryakovs haven't come yet, godfather!

ORLOVSKY: How much longer do we have to wait? I'm hungry, my sweet. And Yegor Petrovich is hungry, too...aren't you?

ZHELTUKHIN: *(To VOYNITSKY.)* Is your family really coming?

VOYNITSKY: When I left home, Yelena Andreevna was still getting dressed.

ZHELTUKHIN: So what does that mean?

VOYNITSKY: You never know. Our Professor might suddenly have an attack of gout, or one of his whims...in which case they'll stay home.

ZHELTUKHIN: In which case, let's eat! Why wait? *(He shouts.)* Ilya Ilyich! Sergey Nikodimich!

Enter DYADIN.

ZHELTUKHIN: Please, everyone, come. Help yourselves. *(Next to the buffet.)* The Serebryakovs haven't arrived, Fyodor Ivanich hasn't arrived, the Wood Demon hasn't arrived, even...They've all forgotten us!

YULYA: A little vodka, godfather?

ORLOVSKY: Just a little. That's it...Enough. Fine.

DYADIN: *(Tying a napkin around his neck.)* What a wonderful establishment you have here, Yulya Stepanovna! When I drive through your fields, when I walk through your shady gardens, when I behold his table, everywhere I see the power of your enchanting little hand. To your excellent health!

YULYA: It's all such a nuisance, really, Ivan Ilyich! Last night, for example, Nazarka forgot to shoo all the turkeys into the shed, they were out all night in the garden, and this morning five of the turkeys died.

DYADIN: That should never have happened. A turkey is a very sensitive bird.

VOYNITSKY: *(To DYADIN.)* Waffles, cut me a piece of ham!

DYADIN: With the utmost of pleasure. This ham is superb! Right out of the *Arabian Nights! (Slices some.)* I shall slice you some, Georgenka sweet, as artfully as I can. Beethoven himself couldn't slice it as finely. Nor could Shakespeare. Only the knife's a bit blunt. *(He sharpens the knives together.)*

VOYNITSKY: *(Shudders.)* Brrrrr!...Stop it, Waffles. I can't bear that sound!

ORLOVSKY: Come on, Yegor Petrovich. Tell us what's going on at your place?

VOYNITSKY: Absolutely nothing's going on.

ORLOVSKY: What's new?

VOYNITSKY: Nothing's new. It's all old. Whatever was, is. No different this year from last. As usual, I talk a lot and do absolutely nothing. My dear *maman*, the old crow, still babbles on and on all the time about women's emancipation;

she's got one foot in the grave, and the other in her beloved library searching for the dawn of a new life.

ORLOVSKY: And Sasha?

VOYNITSKY: The professor? The moths haven't eaten him yet, unfortunately. As always, from dawn till deepest night, he sits in his study and writes. And writes.

> "A writer toils through endless days,
> Yet hears he not a word of praise.
> Though brow be knit, though mind be strained,
> Nobody cares, so what is gained?"

The poor, poor paper! And Sonya, as always, spends her time reading very clever books and keeps a very clever diary.

ORLOVSKY: Darling Sonyechka.

VOYNITSKY: With my keen powers of observation, I ought to write a novel. What subject matter — it's simply begging to be put down on paper. A retired old professor, listen to this, a dried up old stick, a scholarly old trout…Gout, rheumatism, migraines, jaundice, and all kinds of other nonsense…Jealous as Othello, too…Lives here on the estate of his first wife, this old trout does, lives here against his will, mind you, because living in town is far more than he can possibly afford. Forever complains about his misfortunes, although, truth be told, he is a very very fortunate man, oh yes, abnormally so.

ORLOVSKY: Come, come!

VOYNITSKY: Of course he's fortunate. You can't even imagine how fortunate! Let's not even mention the fact that he, the son of a simple sexton, a seminarian, goes and gets himself a doctoral degree, a faculty chair, a title of your excellency, a senator for a father-in-law, and so on and so on and so on, blah blah blah. But never mind, forget about that. Now, here comes the good part. This is a man who for twenty-five years precisely has been reading and writing about art, while understanding absolutely nothing about art. For twenty-five years he regurgitates someone else's theories on realism, naturalism, and all other kinds of ridiculous nonsense; for twenty-five years precisely he reads and writes about things that intelligent people have already known for a long, long time, and stupid people find boring anyway; in other words, for twenty-five years he's been pouring from one empty vessel into another. And all the while behold, what success! What notoriety! And what for? Why? What right has he to have earned it?

ORLOVSKY: *(Bursts out laughing.)* You're jealous! That's what you are! Jealous!

VOYNITSKY: Of course I'm jealous. And what success with women! Don Juan himself never knew such success! His first wife, my sister, a lovely, gentle creature, pure as that blue sky up above, noble, warm-hearted, with far more admirers than he ever had students, loved him as only the purest of angels above can love others as pure and perfect as themselves. My mother, his mother-in-law, worships him till this day, till this very day he inspires in her a kind of religious awe. His second wife, a beauty, a fine woman — you just saw her, — married him when he was already an old man, gave up her youth for him, her beauty, her freedom, her radiance. What for? Why? And meanwhile, what talent, what artistry she has! How gloriously she plays the piano!

ORLOVSKY: It's a gifted family. An unusual family.

ZHELTUKHIN: Yes. Sofya Aleksandrovna, for example, has a magnificent voice. An amazing soprano! I've never heard anything like it, not even in Petersburg. Only sometimes, you know, she forces the high notes. Pity! Give me those high notes! If only she could hit those high notes, I'll stake my life on it, she'd simply soar…You receive my meaning…Forgive me, my friends, just a word or two with Yulya. *(Takes Yulya aside.)* Send a messenger over. Tell them if they can't come now, then they must come for supper. *(Softer.)* And write that note properly, don't make a fool out of me…There are two *p*'s in supper, for example. *(Loudly and sweetly.)* Please, my dear.

YULYA: Fine. *(Exits.)*

DYADIN: They say that the professor's wife, Yelena Andreevna, whom I do not have the honor of knowing, is distinguished not only by spiritual beauty, but by physical beauty as well.

ORLOVSKY: Yes, she's a wonderful woman.

ZHELTUKHIN: Is she faithful to the professor?

VOYNITSKY: Unfortunately, yes.

ZHELTUKHIN: Why unfortunately?

VOYNITSKY: Because this fidelity is false from start to finish. It has rhyme, but no reason. To betray an old husband whom you can't stand any more — that's immoral; to suffocate the youth and the vitality living and breathing inside you — that's *not* immoral? Tell me, please, where is the logic in that?

DYADIN: *(In a plaintive voice.)* Georgenka, I don't like it when you talk that way. Really…Look, I'm trembling, even…Forgive me, gentlemen, I don't have the gift of flowery speech, but allow me to tell you honestly without ornate expression…Gentlemen, he who betrays his wife, or husband, he is an unfaithful soul, one who is capable of betraying his own country.

VOYNITSKY: Oh dry up, Waffles!

DYADIN: Allow me to continue, Georgenka…Ivan Ivanich, Lyonechka, my dear dear friends, take note, if you will, of the vicissitudes of my fate. It's no secret, and no, it's not shrouded in any cloak of mystery, that my own wife ran away from me the day after our wedding with her lover, because of my unattractive appearance…

VOYNITSKY: No wonder.

DYADIN: Gentlemen, please! Still, even after this incident, I have never broken my vow to her. I have loved her to this very day and have remained faithful to her. I've helped her however I can, I've even bequeathed my own property to the children she brought into this world with her lover. My happiness I have lost, but I've kept my pride. And she? Her youth has since gone, her beauty has faded according to nature's laws, her lover has died, bless his soul…What more does she have left? *(Sits.)* I'm talking seriously, and meanwhile you're laughing at me.

ORLOVSKY: You're a good man, really you are, warmhearted too, but God! you're long-winded, and you talk with your hands…

FYODOR IVANOVICH comes out of the house. He wears a coat of fine cloth and high boots. On his chest there are decorations, medals, and a massive gold chain with charms hanging from it; on his fingers are expensive rings.

FYODOR IVANOVICH: Greetings, everyone!

ORLOVSKY: *(Overjoyed.)* Fedyusha, my dear dear son!

FYODOR IVANOVICH: *(To ZHELTUKHIN.)* Happy birthday…and many happy returns of the day…*(Greets everyone.)* Esteemed parent! Greetings, Waffles! And good appetite to all.

ZHELTUKHIN: Where have you been? You're late!

FYODOR IVANOVICH: It's hot! I could use a drop of vodka.

ORLOVSKY: *(Gazing at him in admiration.)* My dear, dear fellow, your beard is magnificent…Isn't it, ladies and gentlemen? Look at him! Isn't it magnificent?

FYODOR IVANOVICH: Many happy returns of the day! *(Drinks.)* The Serebryakovs aren't here yet?

ZHELTUKHIN: Not yet.

FYODOR IVANOVICH: Hm…and where's Yulya?

ZHELTUKHIN: I haven't the faintest idea. It's time to serve the meat pie. I'll go and call her. *(Exits.)*

ORLOVSKY: And Lyonechka, our birthday boy, seems to be out of sorts today. He's moody.

VOYNITSKY: He's a beast.

ORLOVSKY: His nerves are shot, and there's nothing to be done about it…

VOYNITSKY: He's self-centered, that's all. Praise the herring, tell him it's tasty, and he's insulted you're not praising *him*. He's a good-for-nothing. And here he comes.

Enter YULYA and ZHELTUKHIN.

YULYA: Greetings, Fedyenka! *(Kisses FYODOR IVANOVICH.)* Come have something to eat, help yourself, dear fellow. *(To IVAN IVANOVICH.)* Look at the present I gave Lyonechka, godfather! *(Shows him the watch case.)*

ORLOVSKY: My dear, sweet child, a watch case! Well, I'll be damned…

YULYA: The gold thread alone cost eight rubles fifty kopeks. Just look at the edge: pearls, pearls, and more pearls…And there's his name: Leonid Zheltukhin. And the embroidered insignia: "To whom I love, to him I give…"

DYADIN: Let me see, let me see! How lovely!

FYODOR IVANOVICH: Come on, that's enough! Yulya, bring out the champagne!

YULYA: But Fedyenka, that's for the evening!

FYODOR IVANOVICH: "That's for the evening!" — Listen to her! Bring it now, or else I'm leaving. Word of honor. Where do you hide it? I'll get it myself.

YULYA: You're always turning my household upside down, Fedya. *(To VASILY.)* Vasily, go get the key! The champagne's in the pantry, in a basket in the corner near the sack of raisins. Only mind that it doesn't break.

FYODOR IVANOVICH: Three bottles, Vasily! Hurry!

YULYA: You'll never learn to run a household properly, Fedyenka…*(Serves everyone pie.)* Help yourselves to your hearts' content, everyone…There won't be any dinner till almost six…You'll never amount to anything, Fedya. You're hopeless.

FYODOR IVAVNOVICH: That's telling me off, isn't it!

FOYNITSKY: Someone's coming, I think…Do you hear?

ZHELTUKHIN: Yes…It's the Serebryakovs, at last!

VASILY: The Serebryakovs!

YULYA: *(Shrieks.)* Sonyechka! *(Runs offstage.)*

VOYNITSKY: *(Sings.)* Let's go meet them, let's go meet them…*(Exits.)*

FYODOR IVANOVICH: Overjoyed, aren't they?!

ZHELTUKHIN: Some people have no tact! He's in love with the professor's wife, and doesn't even bother to hide it.

FYODOR IVANOVICH: Who is?

ZHELTUKHIN: George is. The way he was carrying on about her before you got here — why, it was downright indecent.

FYODOR IVANOVICH: How do you know he's in love with her?

ZHELTUKHIN: What am I, blind?…The whole district's talking about it…

FYODOR IVANOVICH: Nonsense. No one's in love with her, at least not yet, but *I* soon shall be…Do you hear me? *I* shall!

Enter SEREBRYAKOV, MARYA VASILYEVNA, VOYNITSKY with YELENA ANDREEVNA on his arm, SONYA, and YULYA.

YULYA: *(Kisses SONYA.)* Darling! Darling!

ORLOVSKY: *(Goes to greet them.)* Sasha, greetings, my dear, greetings, my sweet! *(Kisses the professor.)* Are you well? Thank God!

SEREBRYAKOV: And what about you, old man? You look splendid, simply splendid! So good to see you. Have you been here long?

ORLOVSKY: Since Friday. *(To MARYA VASILYEVNA.)* Marya Vasilyevna! And may I inquire "How are you," dear lady? *(Kisses her hand.)*

MARYA VASILYEVNA: My dearest…*(Kisses the top of his head.)*

SONYA: Godfather!

ORLOVSKY: Sonyechka, my darling! *(Kisses her.)* My sweet little canary…

SONYA: You look the same as ever, so kind, and dear, and sweet…

ORLOVSKY: And you're all grown up, and prettier than ever, my pet…

SONYA: Tell me, how are you? Are you well?

ORLOVSKY: Terribly well, terribly!

SONYA: Good for you, godfather! *(To FYODOR IVANOVICH.)* And I didn't notice your excellency. *(Kisses him.)* All shaggy and sunburned…like a spider!

YULYA: Darling!

ORLOVSKY: *(To SEREBRYAKOV.)* How are things, my good man?

SEREBRYAKOV: Not bad, not bad…And you?

ORLOVSKY: What can I say? I'm living it up! I gave the estate to my son, I gave my four daughters away, and now I haven't care in the world. I'm free!

DYADIN: *(To SEREBRYAKOV.)* Your excellency is somewhat on the late side. The temperature of the meat pie has been reduced significantly. Allow me to present myself: Ilya Ilyich Dyadin or, as some have so cleverly named me, owing to my pockmarked face, Waffles.

SEREBRYAKOV: Pleased to meet you.

DYADIN: *Madame! Mademoiselle! (Bows to YELENA ANDREEVNA and SONYA.)* We're all among friends here, your excellency. Once I, too, was well situated, but then owing to domestic circumstances, or as they say in literary circles, under conditions where the editor takes no responsibility, I have had to relinquish my holdings to my own brother, who owing to an unfortunate occurrence found himself deprived of seventy thousand rubles of state money. My profession is that of exploiting the stormy elements. I compel the turbulent waves to turn the wheel of the windmill, which I lease from my friend the Wood Demon.

VOYNITSKY: Oh dry up, Waffles!

DYADIN: I always bow down with reverence *(bows)* before learned luminaries who adorn our country's horizon. Forgive the audacity of my hopes to visit your excellency and delight in the pleasures of conversation of the latest scholarly discoveries.

SEREBRYAKOV: With pleasure. I'd be delighted.

SONYA: So tell us, godfather…Where did you hide yourself this winter? You disappeared!

ORLOVSKY: My dear, I've been in Gmunden, in Paris, in Nice, in London…

SONYA: Wonderful! How fortunate!

ORLVSKY: Come with me this autumn! Why don't you?

SONYA: *(Sings.)* "And lead me not into temptation…"

FYODOR IVANOVICH: Don't sing at the table, or you'll make a fool of your husband.

DYADIN: A bird's-eye view of this table — how fascinating! Such an entrancing floral arrangement! A combination of grace, beauty, profound erudition…

FYODOR IVANOVICH: Such entrancing language! I don't understand what the hell you're saying! You speak as if someone were running a carpenter's plane down your spine…

Laughter.

ORLOVSKY: *(To SONYA.)* So, my dear, you're still not married yet…

VOYNITSKY: Have mercy on her, please, who would she marry? Humboldt's dead already, Edison's in America, Lassalle's dead, too…The other day, I found her diary on the table: a tome as big as this! I opened it and read: "No, I'll never fall in love. Love is an egotistical attraction of the self to a member of the opposite sex…" What hasn't she thought of? "Transcendental, cumulative point of the integrating principle"…ugh! Where did you dig that up?

SONYA: Spare the irony, Uncle George, it doesn't suit you.

VOYNITSKY: What are you so angry about?

SONYA: One more word, and one of us will have to go home. You or me…

ORLOVSKY: *(Bursts out laughing.)* Temper, temper!

VOYNITSKY: Yes, I'll say, temper…*(To SONYA.)* Come on, give me your hand! *(Kisses her hand.)* Peace and harmony…I'll be good. I promise.

Enter KHRUSHCHOV.

KHRUSHCHOV: *(Coming out of the house.)* Why aren't I an artist! What a magnificent gathering!

ORLOVSKY: *(Joyfully.)* Misha! My dear god son!

KHRUSHCHOV: Congratulations! Hello, Yulyechka, how lovely you're looking today! Godfather! *(He embraces ORLOVSKY.)* Sofya Aleksandrovna… *(Greets everyone.)*

ZHELTUKHIN: Why are you so late? Where have you been?

KHRUSHCHOV: With a patient.

YULYA: The meat pie's cold by now.

KHRUSHCHOV: Never mind, Yulyechka, I'll eat it cold. Where do you want me to sit?

SONYA: Here…*(Points to the seat next to hers.)*

KHRUSHCHOV: The weather's superb today, I've built up a wicked appetite… Wait, let me have some of that vodka…*(Drinks.)* Congratulations! I'll have a little of that pie…Yulyechka, kiss the pie, it'll taste better.

She kisses it.

KHRUSHCHOV: *Merci.* How are you, godfather? Haven't seen you in a long time.

ORLOVSKY: No, you haven't. I've been abroad, you know.

KHRUSHCHOV: So I've heard…How I envy you. And how are you, Fyodor?

FYODOR IVANOVICH: Fine, thanks to you, we're holding up…

KHRUSHCHOV: And how's business?

FYODOR IVANOVICH: Can't complain. We're getting on. Only there's so much traveling. I'm all worn out. From here to the Caucasus from the Caucasus here, and again to the Caucasus — and on and on, it never ends, I gallop back and forth like a madman. I have two estates there, you know!

KHRUSHCHOV: I know.

FYODOR IVANOVICH: I run the estate, and catch tarantulas and scorpions. Things are going fine, but when it comes to "be still, my passion's fire" — it's pretty much as always.

KHRUSHCHOV: So you're in love, is that it?

FYODOR IVANOVICH: Let's drink to that, O Wood Demon. *(Drinks.)* Gentlemen, never fall in love with married women! Word of honor, better to have a bullet clean through the shoulder and the foot, just like your humble servant here, than to love a married woman…It's simply awful…

SONYA: Is it hopeless, then?

FYODOR IVANOVICH: Listen to her! Hopeless, indeed…There's nothing hopeless in this world. Hopelessness, unhappiness in love, sighing and swooning, it's all a lot of self-indulgence. One only has to set one's mind to it…I don't want my gun to misfire, and it doesn't…I do want a certain lady to love me, and she does. And so it goes, Sonya, my dear. And once I set my eyes on someone, then she's as much a chance of leaping over the moon as she does in fleeing from me.

SONYA: You're a terrible man, really you are…

FYODOR IVANOVICH: She'll never get away from me, never! I've only to say three words to her, and she's already in my power…Yes…I've only to say to her: "Mademoiselle, whenever you gaze out a window, anywhere, remember me. That's the way I want." And she'll be thinking of me a thousand times a day. Besides, I bombard her with letters hourly.

YELENA ANDREEVNA: Letters — now there's a hopeless method. She may receive them, but perhaps she doesn't even read them.

FYODOR IVANOVICH: Really? Hm…I've lived on this earth for thirty years, and yet I've never met a woman so remarkable that she had the power to resist opening a letter.

ORLOVSKY: *(With admiration.)* You see? That's my son! Isn't he handsome? I was just like him once, you know. A mirror image! Only I never fought in the war, but I did drink vodka and squander my money to an extreme.

FYODOR IVANOVICH: No really, dead seriously, Misha, I love her terribly…Let her say the word and I'd give her everything I have…I'd take her away to my estate in the Caucasus, in the mountains, and we'd live in clover…You know, Yelena Andreevna, I'd guard her like a bloodhound, and I'd sing her the song that one of our locals sings: "Your rule shall be divine, O loyal mistress mine!" She doesn't know how lucky she is, really!

KHRUSHCHOV: And who's the lucky lady?

FYODOR IVANOVICH: "What you don't know won't hurt you," as they say…But, never mind. Let's sing another song, shall we? I remember, ten years ago — Lyonya was still in school then — and we were celebrating his birthday, just as we are today. I was riding home with Sonya on my right and Yulya on my left, both of them holding onto my beard. Come, everyone, let's drink to the loves of my youth, Sonya and Yulya!

DYADIN: *(Bursts out laughing.)* Delightful! Delightful!

FYODOR IVANOVICH: Once, after the war, I got drunk with a Turkish pasha in Trapezond… And he asked me…

DYADIN: *(Interrupting.)* Gentlemen, a toast to good relations! Long live friendship! To life!

FYODOR IVANOVICH: Stop, stop stop! Sonya, your attention please! I'll make a bet with you, damn it! Three hundred rubles I'll stake you! Let's go play croquet after lunch, and I'll bet you that with one shot I make it through all the hoops and back again.

SONYA: I accept, only I don't have three hundred rubles.

FYODOR IVANOVICH: If you lose, you must sing to me forty times.

SONYA: Fine.

DYADIN: Delightful! Delightful!

YELENA ANDREEVNA: *(Looks at the sky.)* What kind of bird is that?

ZHELTUKHIN: A hawk.

FYODOR IVANOVICH: Gentlemen, let's drink to the hawk! Good health!

SONYA bursts out laughing.

ORLOVSKY: What got *her* started?

KHRUSHCHOV bursts out laughing.

ORLOVSKY: Now you, too?

MARYA VASILYEVNA: Sofya, it's unseemly!

KHRUSHCHOV: Oh, dear, sorry, everyone…I'll stop, really I will, right away…

ORLOVSKY: As they say in the scriptures, that's the laughter of fools.

VOYNITSKY: You only have to lift your little finger, and they're laughing their heads off. Sonya! *(Shows her his finger.)* You see?!…

KHRUSHCHOV: Enough! *(Looks at his watch. Addresses himself.)* So, Father Mikhail, we sang, we drank, and now it's time to go.

SONYA: Where to?

KHRUSHCHOV: To see a patient. I'm sick of medicine, it's like an dreary wife, or a long, long winter…

SEREBRYAKOV: But still, medicine is your profession, your calling, so to speak…

VOYNITSKY: *(Ironically.)* He has another profession. He digs peat on his land.

SEREBRYAKOV: What?

VOYNITSKY: Peat. One engineer calculated that the peat on his land is worth seven hundred twenty thousand rubles, without any doubt. Seriously.

KHRUSHCHOV: I don't dig peat for money.

VOYNITSKY: Then what do you do it for?

KHRUSHCHOV: So that you won't cut down the forests.

VOYNITSKY: Why not cut them down? To hear you speak, you'd think the forests exist only for young lovers.

KHRUSHCHOV: I never said that.

VOYNITSKY: Everything I've had the honor of hearing you say in defense of the forests is, to my mind, old hat — it's superficial and opinionated. Forgive me, please. I don't say this frivolously, either, I know all your speeches almost by heart…Listen to this one, for example…*(Speaks in a theatrical tone, as if to imitate KHRUSHCHOV.)* "O people, you are destroying the forests, the forests which grace the earth, which teach man to appreciate beauty and inspire in him a kind of majesty. The forests temper the more severe climate. Where the climate is milder, less energy is expended on the struggle with nature, and there you find a gentler, warmer temperament. In countries where the climate is mild, the people are beautiful, free-spirited, lighthearted, their speech is refined, their movements are graceful. Learning and art flourish, their philosophy of life isn't so pessimistic, their attitudes toward women are endowed with refinement and gentility." And so on and so on and so on…All this is very lovely indeed, but not very convincing, so allow me to continue to stock my stove with kindling and build my barn with wood.

KHRUSHCHOV: You can cut down trees from necessity, but it's time to stop destroying the forests. The Russian forests are falling under the stroke of the axe, billions of trees are being destroyed, wildlife and birds are deserting their dwellings, rivers are drying up, our wonderful countryside is disappearing forever, and all because one lazy man doesn't have sense enough to bend down and pick up fuel from the earth. You have to be a senseless barbarian to burn this beauty in your stove *(points to the trees)*, to destroy that which we can't create. Man is endowed with reason, creativity, and strength to increase that which has been given to him, but up until now, he hasn't created, he's only destroyed. The forests are fewer and fewer, rivers are drying up, wildlife is becoming extinct, the climate is spoiled, and each and every day the earth is growing poorer and uglier. You look at me with irony, and yes, perhaps what I'm saying seems obvious and trivial, but when I walk through the countryside past the forests which I've rescued from devastation, when I hear the sounds of the young forests planted by my very own hands, I realize that the forces of nature are somehow within my power, too, and that if in a thousand years people will find happiness, then in some small way I shall be responsible for it. When I plant a birch tree, and then watch it grow and turn green and sway in the wind, my soul fills with pride from the knowledge that I've helped God create a living organism.

FYODOR IVANOVICH: *(Interrupting.)* To your good health, Wood Demon!

VOYNITSKY: All this is very good, very good indeed, but if you look at it less from a critical point of view, and rather from a scientific point of view, then…

SONYA: Uncle George, this is unpleasant. Be quiet, please!

KHRUSHCHOV: Really, Yegor Petrovich, let's not talk about it any more. I beg of you.

VOYNITSKY: Whatever you say.

MARYA VASILYEVNA: Ach!

SONYA: What is it, grandmother?

MARYA VASILYEVNA: *(To SEREBRAYKOV.)* I forgot to tell you, Aleksandr…it slipped my mind…today I received a letter from Kharkov, from Pavel Alekseevich…He sends his regards…

SEREBRYAKOV: I'm delighted, thank you.

MARYA: He sent his newest pamphlet and asks me to show it to you.

SEREBRYAKOV: Is it interesting?

MARYA VASILYEVNA: Interesting, but also somewhat strange. Imagine, he refutes what he advocated only seven years ago. How typical that is of our times. Never before could one's convictions be so easily changed as today. It's terrible!

VOYNITSKY: Nothing is terrible. Try the fish, *maman,* why don't you?

MARYA VASILYEVNA: But I want to talk!

VOYNITSKY: But we've already been talking for fifty years, talking of trends and tendencies and movements, and now it's time to stop.

MARYA VASILYEVNA: For some reason you find it unpleasant to listen, when I speak. Forgive me, George, but in the past year you've changed so much I hardly know you at all. You used to be a man of clear convictions, an enlightened individual…

VOYNITSKY: Oh yes! I was an enlightened individual, an individual who enlightened no one. Allow me to stand. I was an enlightened individual…What a cruel joke! I am now forty-seven years old. Up until last year I tried so desperately, as you did, I deluded myself with all kinds of abstraction and pedantry, my eyes were blinded so that I could not see life as it truly is — and I thought I was doing "good." And now, if you only knew how foolish I feel that I've wasted my time so stupidly, that I might have had everything my old age now denies me!

SEREBRYAKOV: Wait a minute. You're blaming everything on your former convictions…They're not to blame, you are. You've forgotten that convictions themselves are nothing without deeds. You should have done something.

VOYNITSKY: *Done* something? Not everyone is clever enough to be *perpetuum mobile*…a perpetual writing machine, that is to say…

SEREBRYAKOV: And what's that supposed to mean?

VOYNITSKY: Nothing. Let's cut this conversation short. We're not at home.

MARYA VASILYEVNA: It simply slipped my mind…I forgot to remind you to take your medicine before lunch, Aleksandr. I brought it, but I completely forgot about it…

VOYNITSKY: Never mind. I don't need it.

MARYA VASILYEVNA: But Aleksandr, you're ill, you know! You're *very* ill!

SEREBRYAKOV: Well, you don't have to make an announcement about it, do you? Old, ill, old, ill…that's all I ever hear! *(To ZHELTUKHIN.)* Leonid Stepanich, I'd like to get up and go inside, if I may. It's gotten awfully hot, and the mosquitoes are biting.

ZHELTUKHIN: Go right ahead. We've finished with lunch, anyway.

SEREBRYAKOV: I thank you. *(Exits into the house; MARYA VASILYEVNA follows.)*

YULYA: *(To her brother.)* Go with the professor! This is most awkward!

ZHELTUKHIN: *(To YULYA.)* Blast him! *(Exits.)*

DYADIN: Yulya Stepanovna, allow me to thank you from the bottom of my heart. *(Kisses her hand.)*

YULYA: Don't mention it, Ilya Ilyich! You hardly ate anything…

Everyone thanks her.

YULYA: You're welcome everyone. But really, you hardly ate anything!

FYODOR IVANOVICH: And what shall we do now, ladies and gentlemen? Play a game of croquet…and then what?

YULYA: Then we'll have dinner.

FYODOR IVANOVICH: And then what?

KHRUSHCHOV: Then we'll go to my place. We can fish on the lake in the evening.

FYODOR IVANOVICH: Splendid!

DYADIN: Delightful!

SONYA: All right, everyone…Let's go play a game of croquet now…Then we'll have an early dinner here at Yulya's and at seven we'll go to the Wood De — I mean, to Mikhail Lvovich's. Lovely. Come, Yulyechka, let's go find the croquet balls. *(Exits with YULYA into the house.)*

FYODOR IVANOVICH: Vasily, bring the wine to the croquet lawn! We'll drink to the health of the winner. So, O revered father, shall we partake of this noble game?

ORLOVSKY: Wait a minute, my boy, I have to spend five minutes with the professor, or else it wouldn't look right. One must stick to etiquette. Meanwhile, you play my ball, I'll be right there…*(Exits into the house.)*

DYADIN: Come, let's sit at the feet of the learned Aleksandr Vladimirovich. I anticipate the extreme pleasure which —

VOYNITSKY: You tire me out, Waffles. Go.

DYADIN: I'm going, sir. *(Exits into the house.)*

FYODOR IVANOVICH: *(Goes into the garden, singing.)* "Your rule shall be divine, O loyal mistress mine!…" *(Exits.)*

KHRUSHCHOV: I'll go now, quietly. *(To VOYNITSKY.)* Yegor Petrovich, I beg of you in earnest, please let's not talk of the forests, nor of medicine. I don't know why, but whenever you turn the conversation in that direction, I have a very bad taste in my mouth for the rest of the day. I wish you good day. *(Exits.)*

VOYNITSKY: What a narrow-minded man. I don't care when people talk nonsense, but I *do* care if they do it with feeling.

YELENA ANDREEVNA: You've behaved abominably again, George. Was it really necessary to quarrel with Marya Vasilyevna and with Aleksandr, and talk of *perpetuum mobile?!* How petty it is!

VOYNITSKY: But what if I hate him?

YELENA ANDREEVNA: Why hate Aleksandr, he's like everyone else…

SONYA and YULYA pass through the garden with croquet balls and mallets.

VOYNITSKY: If only you could see your expression, your movements…What an idle creature you! Too idle to live!

YELENA ANDREEVNA: Yes, idle and bored! *(Pause.)* Everyone finds fault with my husband right in front of me, they don't even care if I'm there. Everyone looks at me with pity: Poor woman, what an old husband she has! Even the most sympathetic ones wish that I'd leave Aleksandr… The compassion, the knowing glances, the pitying sighs, they all mean just what your Wood Demon says. You're all recklessly destroying the forests, and soon there will be nothing left on this earth. In just the same way you're recklessly destroying each other, and soon there will be no purity, no fidelity, and no devotion left, either. Why can't you look at a woman who doesn't belong to you without wanting her? Because, — and he's right, this Wood Demon, you're all possessed by the demon of destruction. You don't care about forests, about wildlife, about women, not even about each other.

VOYNITSKY: I don't like this philosophizing!

YELENA ANDREEVNA: And tell this Fyodor Ivanich that I'm tired of his impertinence. Really, it's offensive. To look at me straight in the eye and loudly proclaim his love for some married woman — what kind of behavior is that!

(Voices from the garden: "Bravo! Bravo!") How charming that Wood Demon is, isn't he?! He comes here so often, but I'm shy, I haven't talked to him properly, haven't treated him kindly. He must think I'm too proud, or else simply awful! That's why we're such good friends, you and I, George, because we're both such awful, boring people! Yes, boring! Don't look at me like that, I don't like it.

VOYNITSKY: How else can I look at you, if I love you? You're my happiness, my life, my youth!…I know that my chances you'll return my love are nil, nonexistent; but I need nothing, if only you'll let me look at you, listen to your voice…

SEREBRYAKOV: *(At the window.)* Lyenochka, where are you?

YELENA ANDREEVNA: Here.

SEREBRYAKOV: Come sit with us, darling…*(Disappears again.)*

YELENA ANDREEVNA goes to the house.

VOYNITSKY: *(Follows after him.)* Let me speak of my love, don't drive me away, it alone can bring me the greatest happiness.

END OF ACT ONE

ACT TWO

The dining room in Serebryakov's house. There is a buffet, and in the center of the room, a dining room table. It is after one o'clock in the morning. The watchman can be heard tapping in the garden.

SEREBRYAKOV sits dozing in an armchair before an open window, and YELENA ANDREEVNA sits next to him, also dozing.

SEREBRYAKOV: Who's there? Is that you, Sonya?

YELENA ANDREEVNA: It's me...

SEREBRYAKOV: You, Lyenochka...the pain is unbearable!

YELENA ANDREEVNA: Your blanket fell on the floor...*(Covers his feet.)* I'll close the window, Aleksandr.

SEREBRYAKOV: No, it's stifling in here...I just dozed off, and dreamed that my left leg belonged to someone else...I awoke in excruciating pain. No, this is not gout, this is more like rheumatism. What time is it?

YELENA ANDREEVNA: Twenty after one.

Pause.

SEREBRAKOV: Go find me a copy of Batyushkov in the morning. I think we've got one in the library.

YELENA ANDREEVNA: What?

SEREBRYAKOV: Go find me a copy of Batyushkov in the morning. I remember we had one somewhere. Why is it so difficult to sleep?

YELENA ANDREEVNA: You're tired. It's the second night you haven't slept.

SEREBRYAKOV: They say that Turgenev developed *angina pectoris* from his gout. The same thing will happen to me, I fear. Abominable, detestable old age. Curse it. Ever since I've grown old, I find myself repulsive. Yes. And all of you must find me repulsive, too.

YELENA ANDREEVNA: You speak of old age as if it's all our fault.

SEREBRAYKOV: And you most of all find me repulsive.

YELENA ANDREEVNA: How depressing this is! *(Walks away and sits in the corner.)*

SEREBRYAKOV: Of course, you're right. I'm not a fool, I understand. You're young, healthy, beautiful, you want to live, and I'm an old man, a corpse, almost. You see? I understand, don't I? And how stupid it is, of course, that I'm still alive. But just wait, soon I'll liberate you all. This won't drag on much longer.

YELENA ANDREEVNA: Sasha, I can't bear it any longer. If I deserve any reward for these sleepless nights, then please at least be quiet! For God's sake, please! That's all I want from you.

SEREBRYAKOV: And now it seems, thanks to me, everyone's exhausted, everyone's miserable, everyone's youth has been wasted, only I am content and take pleasure in living. Of course!

YELENA ANDREEVNA: Be quiet! You're torturing me!

SEREBRYAKOV: I torture everyone. Of course!

YELENA ANDREEVNA: *(Weeping.)* It's unbearable! Tell me, what do you want from me?

SEREBRYAKOV: Nothing.

YELENA ANDREEVNA: Then be quiet, I beg of you.

SEREBRYAKOV: Strange, isn't it, that George can talk his head off, or that old idiot Marya Vasilyevna, and never mind, everyone listens, but no sooner do I utter one word and everyone gets depressed. Even my voice is repulsive. All right, fine, I'm repulsive, I'm egotistical, I'm a tyrant, but really, don't I have a right to be selfish in my old age? Really, haven't I earned it? My life has been difficult. Ivan Ivanich and I once were students together. Ask him. He would drink and hang around with gypsy girls…He was my benefactor, and meanwhile I lived in cheap, dirty lodgings, working day and night, like an ox, starving and suffering, living at others' expense. Then I went to Heidelberg and saw nothing of Heidelberg; I went to Paris, too, and saw nothing of Paris, either: The whole time I sat inside and slaved away. Then I attained my university chair. I've spent my life serving scholarship faithfully and truly, and do so to this very day. Now really, I ask you, haven't I the right to a tranquil old age, to the tender loving care of others?

YELENA ANDREEVNA: No one is disputing your right. *(The window rattles from the wind.)* The wind is picking up, I'll close it. *(Closes it.)* Soon it will rain. No one is disputing your rights.

Pause. The watchman in the garden knocks and sings a song.

SEREBRYAKOV: All my life I've served scholarship, I've had my study, my lecture hall, the company of distinguished colleagues — and now, suddenly, I find myself in this crypt, every day I see these stupid people, hear their worthless babble. I want to live, I love success, I love fame, society, and here it's like living in exile. Every minute mourning for the past, slavishly following the successes of others, dreading death…I can't bear it! I haven't the strength! And now they won't even forgive me for being old!

YELENA ANDREEVNA: Just wait, have patience: in five or six years I'll be old, too.

Enter SASHA.

SONYA: I don't know what's keeping the doctor so long. I told Stepan to go and get the Wood Demon if he couldn't find the local doctor.

SEREBRYAKOV: What do I need your Wood Demon for? He knows as much about medicine as I do about astronomy.

SONYA: You can't summon an entire medical faculty here for your gout.

SEREBRYAKOV: I'm not going to waste time talking to that fanatic.

SONYA: Do whatever you want. *(Sits.)* I don't care.

SEREBRYAKOV: What time is it now?

YELENA ANDREEVNA: Two o'clock.

SEREBRYAKOV: It's stifling in here…Sonya, bring me those drops from the table!

SONYA: In a minute. *(Hands him the drops.)*

SEREBRYAKOV: *(Irritated.)* Ach, not these! You can't ask for anything around here!

SONYA: Please, don't play games with me! Others may like it, but I don't, spare me, please. I don't enjoy it.

SEREBRYAKOV: She's impossible, this girl is. Why are you so angry with me?

SONYA: And why do you speak in such a wretched tone of voice? You act as if you're miserable, when in reality, you're one of the luckiest people on earth.

SEREBRYAKOV: Oh, of course! I'm so lucky!

SONYA: Of course you are…And if you have an attack of gout, you know very well that it will gone by morning. So what's all the groaning about? Really!

Enter VOYNITSKY in a dressing gown, carrying a candle.

VOYNITSKY: There's a storm rising. *(Lightning.)* So-o-o, I see! Helene and Sonya, go to bed, I have come to relieve you of your posts.

SEREBRYAKOV: *(Frightened.)* No, no, don't leave me with him! No! He'll talk me to death!

VOYNITSKY: But you must give them their rest. They haven't slept for two nights.

SEREBRYAKOV: All right, let them go to bed, but you must go, too. I beg of you. I beseech you. For the sake of our former friendship, don't argue. We'll talk about it later.

VOYNITSKY: Our former friendship…Well, that's new to me.

YELENA ANDREEVNA: Be quiet, George…

SEREBRYAKOV: Don't leave me alone with him! He'll talk me to death.

VOYNITSKY: This is getting ridiculous.

KHRUSHCHOV: *(Offstage.)* Are they in the dining room? In here? Please, have someone look after my horse.

VOYNITSKY: The doctor is here.

Enter KHRUSHCHOV.

KHRUSHCHOV: What a storm!! The rain was following fast behind me, I barely escaped it. Hello. *(He shakes hands.)*

SEREBRYAKOV: Forgive me for having disturbed you. It wasn't my idea at all.

KHRUSHCHOV: Never mind, it doesn't matter! What's up, Aleksandr Vladimirovich? You're feeling ill? Shame on you? That's not right! What's the matter?

SEREBRYAKOV: Why do doctors always patronize their patients?

KHRUSHCHOV: *(Laughs.)* My, aren't you observant! *(Tenderly.)* Come, let's get in bed. It's not comfortable here. It's warm and peaceful in bed. Come, let's go...I'll listen to your chest...and everything will be just fine.

YELENA ANDREEVNA: Go on, Sasha, do what he tells you.

KHRUSHCHOV: If it hurts too much to walk, we'll carry you in your chair.

SEREBRYAKOV: No, that's fine, I can manage...I'll walk...*(Gets up.)* They shouldn't have disturbed you, really.

KHRUSHCHOV and SONYA take him by the arm.

SEREBRYAKOV: Besides, I don't have that much faith in medication. Why are you helping me? I can walk by myself. *(Exits with KHRUSHCHOV and SONYA.)*

YELENA ANDREEVNA: He's worn me out. I can hardly stand.

VOYNITSKY: He's worn you out, I've worn myself out. It's the third night I haven't slept.

YELENA ANDREEVNA: Something is wrong in this house. Your mother hates everything except her brochures and the professor; the professor is in a wretched mood, he doesn't trust me, he's afraid of you; Sonya is angry with her father, she isn't speaking to me; you hate my husband and openly despise your own mother; I'm tense and irritable, I've burst into tears twenty times today. In a word, there's a declaration of war in this house. But what's the point, what sense does it make?

VOYNITSKY: Let's stop philosophizing!

YELENA ANDREEVNA: Something is wrong in this house. You, George, are an educated and intelligent man, you alone should know that the world will be destroyed not by crime and not by fire, but by all this seething hatred, this hostility between good people, these petty squabbles. People don't see this, they think of our house as a citadel of culture. Help me to make peace! I can't do it alone.

VOYNITSKY: First help me make peace with myself! My darling…*(Attempts to kiss her hand.)*

YELENA ANDREEVNA: Let me go! *(Takes her hand away.)* Go away!

VOYNITSKY: Soon the rain will pass, and everything in nature is refreshed and revived, everything breathes anew. I alone am not refreshed by the storm. Day and night, one thought haunts me, haunts me like an apparition — the thought that my life is lost beyond hope. There is no past, it has been wasted on foolishness, and the present is terrifying in its absurdity. And there you have it — my life and my love: What can I do with them, what will become of them? My love is lost, like a ray of sunlight disappearing into a dungeon, and I am lost…

YELENA ANDREEVNA: When you speak to me of love, I simply grow numb, I don't know what to say. Forgive me, I have nothing to say to you. *(Wants to go.)* Good night!

VOYNITSKY: *(Blocks her way.)* And if only you know how I suffer from the thought that, right here in the same house, another life is lost along with mine — yours! What are you waiting for? What cursed philosophy forbids you? Face it — you're stifling your youth and suppressing your passions…Is that a moral way of life?

YELENA ANDREEVNA: *(Gazes intently at him.)* George, you are drunk.

VOYNITSKY: It's possible, it's possible…

YELENA ANDREEVNA: Is Fyodor Ivanovich here?

VOYNITSKY: He's spending the night. It's possible, it's possible. Everything is possible!

YELENA ANDREEVNA: And tonight you've gotten drunk? What for?

VOYNITSKY: At least I feel alive…Don't try to stop me, Hélène!

YELENA ANDREEVNA: You never used to drink and you never you used to talk so much. Go to bed! You bore me. And tell your friend Fyodor Ivanich that if he doesn't stop bothering me, I intend to do something about it. Now go!

VOYNITSKY: *(Bends down to kiss her hand.)* My darling…my marvelous one!

Enter KHRUSHCHOV.

KHRUSHCHOV: Yelena Andreevna, Aleksandr Vladimirovich has been asking for you.

YELENA ANDREEVNA: *(Takes her hand away from VOYNITSKY.)* Coming! *(Exits.)*

KHRUSHCHOV: *(To VOYNITSKY.)* Is there nothing that is sacred to you? You and that lovely lady who just left, you might remember that her husband was once married to your own dear sister and that now you have a young girl living under the same roof! The whole province has been talking about your little affair. It's disgraceful! *(He exits to see his patient.)*

VOYNITSKY: *(Alone.)* She's gone. *(Pause.)* Ten years ago it was, when I met her, at my poor late sister's. She was seventeen, I was thirty-seven. Why couldn't I have fallen in love with her then, why couldn't I have proposed to her? It would have been possible, oh yes! And now, she would be my wife...Yes... Now we would both be awakened by the storm; she would be frightened by the thunder, and I would hold her in my arms and whisper: "Don't be afraid, I am here." Oh, wonderful thoughts, how lovely, look, I'm laughing...But my God, how these thoughts get muddled up in my head...Why am I old? Why doesn't she understand me? Her talk, her idle moralizing, her absurd, idle views on the destruction of the world — I despise it all, deeply... *(Pause.)* Why am I so terrible? How I envy that crazy Fyodor or that foolish Wood Demon! They're simple, sincere, and straightforward...Not poisoned by this accursed irony...

FYODOR IVANOVICH appears at the door, wrapped in a blanket.

FYODOR IVANOVICH: *(At the door.)* Are you alone here? No ladies present? *(Enters.)* The storm woke me up. Quite a downpour. What time is it?

VOYNITSKY: Who the hell knows!

FYODOR IVANOVICH: I thought I heard Yelena Andreevna's voice.

VOYNITSKY: She was just here.

FYODOR IVANOVICH: A gorgeous woman! *(Looks at the phial bottle on the table.)* What are these, peppermints? *(Eats some.)* Yes, a gorgeous woman...Is the professor really ill?

VOYNITSKY: Yes.

FYODOR IVANOVICH: Yes. I don't understand this kind of existence. They say that the ancient Greeks would toss their weak and sickly young over a precipice on Mont Blanc. That's what we should do with his kind!

VOYNITSKY: *(Irritated.)* No, it's not Mont Blanc, it's the Tarpeian Rock. What gross ignorance!

FYODOR IVANOVICH: All right, so it was a rock...so what, who cares? Why are we so depressed today? Feeling sorry for the professor, are we?

VOYNITSKY: Leave me alone.

Pause.

FYODOR IVANOVICH: Or perhaps we're in love with the professor's wife? Are we? Well, why not…pine away, then…only listen: If I find out that there's even an ounce of truth in all the gossip that's going around this district, then don't ask for mercy. I'll hurl *you* off the Tarpeian Rock…

VOYNITSKY: She's my friend.

FYODOR IVANOVICH: Already?

VOYNITSKY: What do you mean "already"?

FYODOR IVANOVICH: A woman is a man's friend only in the following order: first an acquaintance, then a lover, then a friend.

VOYNITSKY: A vulgar philosophy.

FYODOR IVANOVICH: In that case, let's drink to that. Let's see, I think there's a spot of Chartreuse left. We'll have a little nip of it. And come dawn, we'll go to my place. "Right-o?" I've got this steward named Luka, who never says "all right" but instead he says "right-o"… A real rogue…So, "right-o"? *(Sees SONYA entering.)* Saints alive, forgive me, I don't have a tie on! *(Runs offstage.)*

SONYA: Uncle George, you've been drinking champagne with Fedya again and riding around in the troika. Two fine-feathered friends. All right, he's incorrigible, he was born that way, but what about you? At your age it doesn't suit you.

VOYNITSKY: What does age have to do with it? When you have no real life, you live an illusion. It's better than nothing.

SONYA: Our hay's not in yet; Gerasim said today that it's going to rot in all the rain, and you speak of illusions. *(Frightened.)* Uncle, you've got tears in your eyes!

VOYNITSKY: What tears? It's nothing…nonsense…You looked at me just now, the way your poor dear mother used to. My darling…*(Eagerly kisses her hands and face.)* My sister…my darling sister…Where is she now? If only she knew! Oh, if only she knew!

SONYA: What? Uncle, knew what?

VOYNITSKY: How painful, how futile…Never mind…

Enter KHRUSHCHOV.

VOYNITSKY: Later…Never mind…I'm leaving…*(Exits.)*

KHRUSHCHOV: Your father won't listen to me at all. I tell him — gout, he says — rheumatism; I tell him to lie down, he sits up. *(Picks up his cap.)* It's nerves.

SONYA: He's spoiled. Put down your cap. Wait for the rain to stop. Would you like a little something to eat?

KHRUSHCHOV: All right.

SONYA: I love to nibble at night. There's something to eat in the buffet, I think…*(Rummages around in the buffet.)* What does he need a doctor for? What he really needs is a dozen young women sitting beside him, gazing into his eyes and sighing: "Professor!" Here, have some cheese…

KHRUSHCHOV: You shouldn't talk about your own father like that. It's true, he's a difficult man, but compared to all the others, to Uncle George and Ivan Ivanich, they aren't worth his little finger.

SONYA: Here's a bottle of something. I wasn't speaking of him as a father, but rather as a great man. I love my father, but great men and all the homage one must pay them — it's tiresome. *(Sits.)* What a storm! *(Lightning.)* Listen!

KHRUSHCHOV: The storm's passing, we'll just catch the edge of it.

SONYA: *(Pours.)* Drink.

KHRUSHCHOV: May you live to be a hundred. *(Drinks.)*

SONYA: Are you angry that we have disturbed your evening?

KHRUSHCHOV; On the contrary. If you hadn't sent for me, I'd be asleep for now, and it's much nicer seeing you awake than in my dreams.

SONYA: Then why do you look so angry?

KHRUSHCHOV: Because I am angry. There's no one here, we can talk openly. With such pleasure I'd take you away from this place in a minute, Sofya Aleksandrovna. I couldn't breathe in this atmosphere, and it seems that's it's poisoning you, too. There's your father with his books and his gout and his complete self-absorption, your Uncle George, and finally, your stepmother…

SONYA: What about my stepmother?

KHRUSHCHOV: There are things one simply can't talk about. No! My darling, there's so much I don't understand about people. I always think people should be beautiful in every way: in their faces, in the way they dress, in their thoughts and their innermost souls. Oh, I've seen beautiful faces and dresses, my head has been turned many times, but as for their minds and their souls — my God! Under all that loveliness there sometimes lurks a soul so black that no cosmetic can conceal it…Forgive me, I'm getting all excited…You're really very dear to me, you know…

SONYA: *(Drops a knife.)* I dropped it…

KHRUSHCHOV: *(Picks it up.)* Never mind… *(Pause.)* You know, when you walk through the forest in the darkness of the night and there's a small light shining in the distance, your soul feels so full of hope that somehow you don't feel the fatigue, or the darkness, or the sharp branches beating against your face. I work from morning until late at night, winter and summer, I know no rest, I rail against those who don't understand me, at times I suffer unbearably…but still I see my light shining in the distance. I'm not going to declare that I love you more than anything in the world. Love isn't everything for me in life…it's my reward. And my dearest darling, there's no greater reward for he who works, and struggles, and suffers…

SONYA: *(Agitated.)* Forgive me… May I ask you something, Mikhail Lvovich?

KHRUSHCHOV: What is it? Tell me quickly…

SONYA: Look…you come here very often, and sometimes I come to visit you. Admit it: You just can't forgive yourself for it…

KHRUSHCHOV: Meaning what?

SONYA: Meaning this…that your principles are compromised by your acquaintanceship with us. I had an exclusive education, Yelena Andreevna is an aristocrat, we dress fashionably, whereas you hold these democratic beliefs…

KHRUSHCHOV: Now wait…let us not speak of this. It's not the time!

SONYA: The point is, you're digging peat, you're planting forests…and it's all rather strange. You're somewhat of a populist…

KHRUSHCHOV: Democrat, populist…Sofya Aleksandrovna, are you really being serious? Your voice is quivering.

SONYA: Of course I'm serious, I'm absolutely serious…

KHRUSHCHOV: No, you're not…

SONYA: I'll bet you anything that if I had a sister, say, and you fell in love with her and proposed to her, that you'd never forgive yourself, that you couldn't look your fellow doctors (men and women alike) in the eye, that you'd be ashamed to love a preparatory-school girl, a proper young lady with a fancy education and a fashionable wardrobe. I know that very well…I can see it in your eyes that it's the truth! In a word, to put it plainly, your forests, your peat, your Russian clothes — all that's a pretense, an affectation and nothing more.

KHRUSHCHOV: Why are you saying this? My child, why do you offend me? Never mind, I'm a fool. It serves me right for not knowing my place! Farewell! *(Goes to the door.)*

SONYA: Good-bye…Those were harsh words. Forgive me, please.

KHRUSHCHOV: *(Returning.)* If only you knew how oppressive and stuffy the atmosphere is here! You're surrounded by people who sneak up on you, size you up, saying you're either a populist, or a psychopath, or a sycophant — anything other than human! "Oh, he's a psychopath!" they say, and they're delighted. Or: "He's a sycophant!" — and they're as pleased as if they'd discovered

America! And when they can't figure out what label to paste on my forehead, they don't blame themselves for it, they blame me and say: "This man is strange, strange!" You're only twenty, but already you're as old and as stuffy as your father and Uncle George, and I wouldn't be in the least bit surprised if you summoned me to cure your gout, too. You mustn't live like that! Whoever I might be, you should look me straight in the eye, clearly, without any preconceived notion, without an agenda, and above all see the human being in me, otherwise you'll never truly relate to people. Good-bye! And remember this: With such shrewd, suspicious eyes as yours, you'll never fall in love!

SONYA: That's not true!

KHRUSHCHOV: It *is* true!

SONYA: No, it *isn't* true! And just to show you…I am in love, so there! I'm in love, and suffering terribly, terribly! Leave me alone! Go away, I beg of you… Don't come here any more, don't…

KHRUSHCHOV: I wish you a very good evening! *(Exits.)*

SONYA: *(Alone.)* He's angry. I pray to God I never have a temper like his! *(Pause.)* How beautifully he speaks, but who can assure me it's not a lot of rhetoric? All he thinks about and talks about are his woods, and planting his trees…That's fine, but perhaps it's an obsession…*(Covers her face with her hands.)* I don't understand anything! *(Weeps.)* He studied medicine, but he practices so much more than medicine…How strange it all is…God, please help me to make sense of it all!

Enter YELENA ANDREEVNA.

YELENA ANDREEVNA: *(Opens the window.)* The storm has passed! What lovely, fresh air! *(Pause.)* Where's the Wood Demon?

SONYA: Gone.

Pause.

YELENA ANDREEVNA: Sofi!

SONYA: What?

YELENA ANDREEVNA: How much longer will you go on being angry with me? We haven't done each other harm. Why must we be enemies? Enough…

SONYA: Oh yes, I've wanted to, myself…*(Embraces her.)* Darling!

YELENA ANDREEVNA: Good. That's good…

They are both moved.

SONYA: Has Papa gone to bed?

YELENA ANDREEVNA: No, he's still sitting in the drawing room. We don't speak for weeks at a time, God only knows why…It's enough now. *(Looks at the table.)* What's this?

SONYA: The Wood Demon was having some supper.

YELENA ANDREEVNA: And there's wine…Let's drink to our friendship — "brüdershaft."

SONYA: Yes, let's.

YELENA ANDREEVNA: From one glass…*(Pours.)* It's better like this. So now: "Friends"?

SONYA: "Friends."

They drink and kiss each other.

SONYA: I've wanted to make peace for so long, but, I don't know, somehow I was ashamed…*(Weeps.)*

YELENA ANDREEVNA: Why are you crying?

SONYA: It's nothing, I can't help it.

YELENA ANDREEVNA: Don't cry, don't…*(Weeps.)* Silly girl, now you've made me cry, too! *(Pause.)* You're angry with me, because you think I married your father for money. If you want me to, I'll swear to you, I married him for love. I was attracted to his fame and his intellect. My love wasn't genuine, it wasn't real, but believe me, I thought it was at the time. I'm not to blame. And yet ever since our wedding day you've been punishing me with those shrewd, suspicious eyes.

SONYA: Peace, peace! Let's forget. That's the second time tonight I've heard about my shrewd, suspicious eyes.

YELENA ANDREEVNA: You don't have to be so suspicious. It doesn't suit you. You must trust in others, or else life is not worth living.

SONYA: Once bitten, twice shy. I've been disappointed so often.

YELENA ANDREEVNA: By whom? Your father is a good and honest man, he works hard. Today you reproached him for being happy. If indeed he is happy, he doesn't know it, he works so hard. I've never tried to harm either you or your father. Your Uncle George is a good and honest man, but he's unhappy and dissatisfied…Whom can you trust, then?

SONYA: Tell me the truth, as a friend…Are you happy?

YELENA ANDREEVNA: No.

SONYA: I knew it. One more question. Be honest with me, wouldn't you rather have a young husband?

YELENA ANDREEVNA: What a child you are, still…Of course I would! *(Laughs.)* Go on, ask me anything…

SONYA: Do you like the Wood Demon?

YELENA ANDREEVNA: Yes, very much.

SONYA: *(Laughs.)* I look foolish now…don't I? He's gone, and I can still hear his voice, his footsteps, I look through the dark window, — and I see his face before me. Let me tell you…No, I can't, I can't say it aloud, I'm ashamed. Come to my room, we'll talk there. You think I'm foolish, don't you? Tell me…Is he a good man?

YELENA ANDREEVNA: He's a very good man…

SONYA: His forests and his peat…it all seems so strange to me…I don't understand.

YELENA ANDREEVNA: But it's not only a question of forests! Darling, don't you understand, it's about genius! And do you know what genius is? Courage, freedom of mind, breadth of vision…He plants a tree or digs peat from the earth, and already he sees it a thousand years from now, already he dreams of a future happiness for mankind. Such people are rare, they must be loved…God bless you both. You're both decent and pure, courageous and honest…He's an eccentric, you're practical and sensible. You'll complement one another beautifully…*(Stands.)* But I'm only a minor character, aren't I, and a useless one, too…In music, in my husband's house, in all my love affairs — everywhere, really, all I've ever played is a minor role. As a matter of fact, Sonya, come to think of it, I'm actually very, very unhappy! *(Paces, agitated.)* There's no happiness for me on this earth! None! Why are you laughing?

SONYA: *(Laughs, covering her face.)* I'm so happy…so happy!

YELENA ANDREEVNA: *(Wrings her hands.)* How unhappy I am, really!

SONYHA: I'm so happy…so happy.

YELENA ANDREEVNA: I feel like playing now…I want to play something…

SONYA: Play. *(Embraces her.)* I can't sleep…Play.

YELENA ANDREEVNA: I shall. But wait, your father's not asleep. When he's ill, music annoys him. Go ask. If he doesn't mind, I'll play. Hurry.

SONYA: I shall. *(Exits.)*

Outside in the garden, the watchman knocks.

YELENA ANDREEVNA: It's been such a long time since I've played the piano. I'll play and cry, cry like a fool. *(At the window.)* Is that you knocking, Yefim?

WATCHMAN: *(Offstage.)* Yoo-hoo!

YELENA ANDREEVNA: Don't knock, the master is unwell.

WATCHMAN: *(Offstage.)* Right-o, we're leaving! *(Whistles.)* Zhuchka! Trezor! Zhuchka! *(Pause.)*

SONYA: *(Returning.)* No!

 END OF ACT TWO

ACT THREE

The living room in SEREBRYAKOV's house. There are three doors: to the right, left, and center. Daytime. Offstage, YELENA ANDREEVNA is playing Lensky's aria before the duel from Eugene Onegin *on the piano.*

ORLOVSKY, VOYNITSKY, and FYODOR IVANOVICH, the latter in Circassian costume, a fur cap in his hand.

VOYNITSKY: *(Listening to the music.)* Listen…Yelena Andreevna's playing my favorite aria… *(The music stops offstage.)* Yes…A lovely aria . . It's never been so boring here before, not that I can remember…

FYODOR IVANOVICH: You don't know what boredom really is, my dear. When I was with the volunteers in Serbia, now that's what you call boredom! The heat, the dust, the dirt, the splitting headaches from all the hangovers…I remember once, I was sitting in some filthy little shed, along with a Captain Kashkinazi…We'd talked ourselves out long ago, nothing more left to say, didn't feel like drinking — in short, it was awful, enough to make you want to hang yourself! So there we sit, like two snakes, staring at each other…He stares at me, and I stare at him…I stare at him, and he stares at me…We stare at each and we don't know why…And an hour or so passes, you know, and we're still staring at each other. Suddenly for no reason whatsoever up he jumps, whips out his sabre and goes for me… "Well, hello there," I say…Of course, I draw mine right away — don't want to get killed, do I! — and we start in — click-clack, click-clack, click-clack…They had quite a time separating us…I was fine, but Captain Kashkinazi to this day wears a scar on his cheek. People can go to extremes, sometimes…

ORLOVSKY: They surely can.

Enter SONYA.

SONYA: *(Aside.)* I don't know what to do with myself…*(She walks about the stage, laughing.)*

ORLOVSKY: Where are you going, kitten? Sit with us for a moment.

SONYA: Fedya, come here…*(Takes FYODOR IVANOVICH aside.)* Come here…

FYODOR IVANOVICH: So? What are you beaming about?

SONYA: Fedya, promise you'll do what I ask of you!

FYODOR IVANOVICH: Well, what is it?

SONYA: Go to the Wood Demon's.

FYODOR IVANOVICH: What for?

SONYA: Never mind…just go…Ask him why he hasn't been to see us in so long…It's already been two weeks.

FYODOR IVANOVICH: You're blushing! You should be ashamed of yourself! Ladies and gentlemen, Sonya is blushing!

ALL: For shame! For shame!

(*SONYA covers her face with her hands and runs offstage.*)

FYODOR IVANOVICH: She drifts around from room to room like a shadow, she doesn't know what to do with herself. She's in love with the Wood Demon.

ORLOVSKY: A lovely girl…I'm very fond of her. I always dreamed that you would marry her, Fedyushka — you couldn't find a better wife, but it wasn't God's will…But it would have brought me such joy and pleasure! I'd have come to visit you, and there you would be with your wife, in the bosom of your family, and the samovar would be boiling…

FYODOR IVANOVICH: That's not my territory. And if ever I had the sudden urge to marry, I'd marry Yulya, anyway. At least she's little, and one always must pick the lesser of two evils. Oh, yes, and she's a good housekeeper, too…(*Claps his forehead.*) I've got an idea!

ORLOVSKY: What is it?

FYODOR IVANOVICH: Come, let's have some champagne!

VOYNITSKY: It's still early, and it's hot…Let's wait a while…

ORLOVSKY: (*With admiration.*) My dear sweet son…He wants champagne, the dear boy does…

Enter YELENA ANDREEVNA. She crosses the stage.

VOYNITSKY: Just look at her, roaming about, reeling with idleness. How very, very adorable!

YELENA ANDREEVNA: Stop it, George. It's bad enough without your carrying-on.

VOYNITSKY: (*Blocking her way.*) Here comes our gifted artist! But you don't look much like an artist, do you? Languid, apathetic, and as lazy as Oblomov… And so virtuous that I can't bear looking at you.

YELENA ANDREEVNA: Then don't… Leave me alone…

VOYNITSKY: Why languish away? (*Animated.*) Come, my darling, my treasure, be smart! You've got mermaid's blood coursing through those veins. Go, swim like a mermaid!

YELENA ANDREEVNA: Leave me alone!

VOYNITSKY: Let yourself go for once in your life, fall head-over-heels in love with another water-sprite…

FYODOR IVANOVICH: And dive headlong into the deep, while Herr Professor and the rest of us stand waving helplessly on the shore!

VOYNITSKY: A mermaid, eh? Let us love while we can!

YELENA ANDREEVNA: Why are you telling me what to do? I don't need you to tell me how to live! Oh, if only I had my own way, I'd fly away free as a bird, as far as I could from all of you, from your sleepy faces, your dull, endless talk, I'd forget you ever existed, and no one would dare tell me how to live, then. But I have no will of my own. I'm a coward, I'm shy, and I'm so afraid that if I were to be unfaithful, then all wives would follow my example and leave their husbands, and that God would punish me and my conscience would torture me…Oh, if only I could, I would show you how to live a free life! *(Exits.)*

ORLOVSKY: My darling, my beautiful…

VOYNITSKY: Soon I will start to despise that woman! She's as shy as a maiden, and she moralizes more than a prissy old parish priest! It's sicklier than sour cream!

ORLOVSKY: Enough, enough…Where's the professor?

VOYNITSKY: He's in his study. Writing.

ORLOVSKY: He wrote me and summoned me for some important business matter. Do you know what it's about?

VOYNITSKY: He has no business whatsoever. He writes rubbish, he grumbles, he envies people, that's about it.

Enter ZHELTUKHIN and YULYA from the right door.

ZHELTUKHIN: Greetings, ladies and gentlemen. *(Greets everyone.)*

YULYA: Hello, godfather! *(Kisses him.)* Hello, Fedyenka! *(Kisses him.)* Hello, Yegor Petrovich! *(Kisses him.)*

ZHELTUKHIN: Is Aleksandr Vladimirovich at home?

ORLOVSKY: He is. He's sitting in his study.

ZHELTUKHIN: I must go and see him. He wrote me that he wanted to talk about some business or other…*(Exits.)*

YULYA: Yegor Petrovich, did you receive the barley you ordered yesterday?

VOYNITSKY: Yes I did, thank you. How much do I owe you? We ordered some from you in the spring, I don't remember what…We must settle up. I can't bear having my accounts in disarray or confusion.

YULYA: You ordered sixty-four bushels of rye, Yegor Petrovich, two calves, one steer…and they ordered butter from your farm, too.

VOYNITSKY: Then how much do I owe you?

YULYA: How should I know? I don't have my abacus, Yegor Petrovich.

VOYNITSKY: Then I'll bring you one, if you need it…*(Exits, and returns at once with an abacus.)*

ORLOVSKY: Is your brother well, my dear?

YULYA: Yes, thank God. Wherever did you buy that tie, godfather?

ORLOVSKY: In town, at Kirpichev's.

YULYA: It's lovely. I must buy one for Lyonechka.

VOYNITSKY: Here's the abacus.

(YULYA sits and clicks on the abacus.)

ORLOVSKY: What a housekeeper! Lucky Lyonya! She's no bigger than a minute, and yet look how hard she works! Amazing!

FYODOR IVANOVICH: Yes, while he walks around clutching his cheek, and nothing more. The lazy-bones…

ORLOVSKY: A little beggar, that's what she is…She goes around wearing an old, worn-out cloak, you know. On Fridays when I go to market, there she is, weaving in and out among the carts in this old, old cloak…

YULYA: Now you've offended me.

VOYNITSKY: Let's go somewhere else, ladies and gentlemen. Into the ballroom, wherever. I'm tired of this place…*(Yawns.)*

ORLOVSKY: Fine, whatever you want…I don't care. *(Exits through the left door.)*

YULYA: *(Alone, after a pause.)* Fedyenka's in Chechnian dress…His parents simply didn't bring him up properly…He's the handsomest man in the district, he's clever, he's rich, but he simply has no sense…What a fool…*(Clicks on the abacus.)*

Enter SONYA.

SONYA: Oh…Yulya! I didn't know you were here…

YULYA: *(Kisses her.)* Darling!

SONYA: What are you doing here? Accounts? How capable you are, you make me feel quite jealous…Why don't you get married, Yulyechka?

YULYA: I don't know, really…I've had offers, but I've turned them down. No proper suitor would ever woo me.

SONYA: Why in the world not?

YULYA: Because I'm uneducated. I left school after the second year!

SONYA: Why, Yulya?

YULYA: I wasn't good enough.

SONYA laughs.

YULYA: Why are you laughing, Sonyechka?
SONYA: I have the strangest feeling...I'm so happy today, Yulyechka, so happy that I'm almost bored by it...I don't know what to do with myself...Oh, let's talk about something else, why don't we...Have you ever been in love?

YULYA nods her head affirmatively.

SONYA: Really? Is he attractive?

YULYA whispers in her ear.

SONYA: With whom have you been in love? With Fyodor Ivanich?
YULYA: *(Nods her head affirmatively.)* What about you?
SONYA: I've been in love, too...Only not with Fyodor Ivanich. *(Laughs.)* Go on, tell me more.
YULYA: I've wanted to talk with you for such a long time, Sonyechka.
SONYA: Go on, please.
YULYA: Let me explain. You see...I've always felt close to you...I have many friends, but you're the best of them all...And if you were to tell me: "Yulyechka, give me ten horses," or, let's say, "two hundred sheep" — why, I'd be delighted!...There's nothing I wouldn't do for you...
SONYA: But then why are you so embarrassed, Yulyechka?
YULYA: I'm ashamed...I like you so much...You're the nicest of all my friends... you're not in the least bit proud, or anything like that...What a lovely dress!
SONYA: Let's talk about it later...Go on...
YULYA: *(Agitated.)* I don't know how to put this properly...Allow me to ask you... I mean, it would make me happy if you...that is to say...if you...would marry Lyonechka. *(Covers her face.)*
SONYA: *(Standing.)* Let's not talk about this, Yulyechka...We mustn't, really...

Enter YELENA ANDREVNA.

YELENA ANDREEVNA: There's simply no place to go to in this house. Both the Orlovskys and George are wandering through all the rooms, and no matter where you go, there they are. It's really very depressing. What do they want here? They ought to go elsewhere.

YULYA: *(In tears.)* Hello, Yelena Andreevna! *(Goes to kiss her.)*

YELENA ANDREEVNA: Forgive me, I don't like all this kissing. Sonya, what is your father doing? *(Pause.)* Sonya, why don't you answer me? I'm asking you: What is your father doing? *(Pause.)* Sonya, why don't you answer me?

SONYA: Do you really want to know? Come here…*(Takes her aside.)* All right, I'll tell you, then…I must tell the truth today, and I can't talk to you today and continue to hide it. Here! *(Hands her a letter.)* I found it in the garden. Let's go, Yulyechka! *(Exits by the left door with Yulya.)*

YELENA ANDREEVNA: *(Alone.)* What's this? A letter from George to me? What have I done? How rude, how shameful!…She must tell the truth today, and therefore she can't talk to me…God, what an insult! My head is spinning, I feel faint…

FYODOR IVANOVICH: *(Enters from the left door and crosses the stage.)* Why do you flinch when you see me? *(Pause.)* Hm…*(Takes the letter from her hand and tears it to pieces.)* You can throw all this away. Think only of me.

Pause.

YELENA ANDREEVNA: What does this mean?

FYODOR IVANOVICH: It means that once I have my eye on someone, that she can't escape my clutches so easily.

YELENA ANDREEVNA: No, it doesn't, it means that you're stupid and impertinent.

FYODOR IVANOVICH: Tonight at seven thirty you must go to the other side of the garden and wait for me by the bridge…All right? I won't say any more…And so, my angel, until seven thirty. *(Goes to take her hand.)*

YELENA ANDREEVNA gives him a slap on the face.

FYODOR IVANOVICH: I receive your meaning…

YELENA ANDREEVNA: Get out of here.

FYODOR IVANOVICH: I hear you, yes, right away…*(Starts to go, then returns.)* I'm touched, really, I am…Let's discuss this calmly. You see…I've been around, I've done it all, I've even eaten gold fish soup once or twice… However, I've never flown in a hot air balloon, nor have I run away with the wife of a learned professor…

YELENA ANDREEVNA: Get out of here…

FYODOR IVANOVICH: I shall…Right away…Yes, I've done it all…And I'm so full of myself I don't know what to do. Anyway, what I'm saying is, if ever you need a friend or a faithful watchdog, turn to me…I'm touched, truly touched…

YELENA ANDREEVNA: I don't need a watchdog…Go away.

FYODOR IVANOVICH: I hear you…*(Moved.)* Nevertheless, I'm truly touched… really and truly…Yes…*(Exits indecisively.)*

YELENA ANDREEVNA: *(Alone.)* My head aches…Every night I have bad dreams and dreadful premonitions…How offensive this all is! These young people were born here, and raised together, they're close, they embrace; you'd think they'd live in peace and harmony, but it seems they're ready to devour one another alive…The Wood Demon saves forests, but what about people? No one can save them. *(Goes to the left door, but, seeing ZHELTUKHIN and YULYA approaching, she exits through the middle door.)*

YULYA: How unlucky we are, Lyonyechka, oh, how unlucky!

ZHELTUKHIN: But who asked you to speak to her? What are you, a match-maker? Now you've ruined everything! She'll think I can't speak for myself…how vulgar! I told you a thousand times to leave it alone. It can only lead to humiliation, and all these insinuations. It's base and vile…The old man has probably guessed I'm in love with her, and already he's taking advantage of my feelings! He wants me to buy the estate from him.

YULYA: How much is he asking for it?

ZHELTUKHIN: Sh!…They're coming…

Enter SEREBRYAKOV, ORLOVSKY, and MARYA VASILYEVNA through the left door; the latter reads a brochure as she walks.

ORLOVSKY: I haven't been all that well myself either, my dear. My head's been hurting for two days, and I ache all over…

SEREBRYAKOV: Where is everybody? I don't like this house. It's like a maze. Twenty-six enormous rooms, everybody's scattered all over the place, you can't find anyone. *(Rings.)* Ask Yegor Petrovich and Yelena Andreevna to come in!

ZHELTUKHIN: Yulya, you're not doing anything, go find Yegor Petrovich and Yelena Andreevna.

YULYA exits.

SEREBRYAKOV: One can accustom oneself to ill health, come what may, but

I simply cannot bear my present circumstances. It's as if I've fallen off the earth onto some other planet.

ORLOVSKY: I suppose you could look at it that way…

MARYA VASILYEVNA: Give me a pencil…Here's another contradiction! I must make a note of it.

ORLOVSKY: Allow me, dear lady! *(Gives her a pencil and kisses her hand.)*

Enter VOYNITSKY.

VOYNITSKY: Am I needed?

SEREBRYAKOV: Yes, George.

VOYNITSKY: And what do you want of me?

SEREBRYAKOV: What…But why are you so angry? *(Pause.)* If I have offended you in any way, then please, forgive me…

VOYNITSKY: Spare me that tone of voice…Let's get down to business…What do you want?

SEREBRYAKOV: And here is Lyenochka…Ladies and gentlemen, please be seated. *(Pause.)* I have invited you here, ladies and gentlemen, to announce that the inspector general is coming. However, all joking aside. This is a serious matter. Ladies and gentlemen, I have gathered you here to request your aid and advice, and knowing your infinite kindness, I hope I shall have them both. I am a scholarly man, a man of letters, and have always been a stranger to the practical affairs of life. Without the guidance of knowledgeable people, I cannot manage, and I look to you, Ivan Ivanich, and to you, Leonid Stepanich, and you, George…The fact is that *manet omnes una nox,* that is to say we are all in the hands of God. I am old and ill, and for that reason I find it an opportune time to settle the affairs pertaining to my property, insofar as they concern my family. My life is already over, I am not concerned with myself, but I have a young wife, and an unmarried daughter…To continue living in the country will no longer be possible for them.

YELENA ANDREEVNA: I don't care, really.

SEREBRYAKOV: We were not meant for country life. To live in town, however, on the allowance we receive from this estate, is also not possible. The other day I sold some of the forest for four thousand rubles, but that was an extraordinary measure, one we could not take every year. Such measures must be found, therefore, which would guarantee us a steady, more or less fixed yearly income. I have thought of one such measure and I have the honor of presenting it to you for your consideration. Details aside, I shall present it to you in general outline form. Our estate yields a profit, on the average, of no more than two percent. I propose to sell it. If the money we earn is converted into interest-bearing securities, then we shall receive from four to five percent, and I believe there will even be a surplus of several thousand, which will allow us to buy a small dacha in Finland…

VOYNITSKY: Wait a minute, I believe my hearing has failed me. Repeat what you just said.

SEREBRYAKOV: The money will be converted into interest-bearing securities which will allow us to buy a dacha in Finland…

VOYNITSKY: Not Finland…What you said before that.

SEREBRYAKOV: I propose to sell the estate.

VOYNITSKY: That's it…You sell the estate…Wonderful, a fabulous idea…And what do you propose to do with me and my old mother?

SEREBRYAKOV: That we can discuss in due time…There's no hurry…

VOYNITSKY: Wait a minute…Evidently, up until now, I haven't had a drop of common sense. Up until now I had the stupidity to assume that this estate belongs to Sonya. My late father bought the estate as a dowry for my sister. Up until now I have been so naive — imagine! — it was my understanding we were *not* living under Turkish law, and I thought the estate had passed down from my sister to Sonya.

SEREBRYAKOV: Yes, the estate belongs to Sonya. Who is disputing that? Without Sonya's consent I could not, in effect, sell it. It's for her very sake that I'm proposing to do so.

VOYNITSKY: This is unbelievable! Unbelievable! Either I'm going out of my mind, or…or else…

MARYA VASILYEVNA: George, don't contradict the Professor! Trust me, he knows better than we do what's right and wrong.

VOYNITSKY: No, give me some water…*(Drinks water.)* Say whatever you like, whatever you like!

SEREBRYAKOV: I don't understand why you're getting so excited, George! I didn't say my plan was ideal. If everyone finds it unsuitable, I won't insist on it.

Enter DYADIN; he is wearing tails, with white gloves and a wide-brimmed top hat.

DYADIN: How do you do, everyone. Kindly forgive me for daring to enter unannounced. I confess I am guilty, but I beg your leniency in this case, since there was nary a *domestique* in the front hall.

SEREBRYAKOV: *(Embarrassed.)* Delighted…Please…

DYADIN: *(Bowing.)* Your excellency! *Mesdames!* My intrusion into your domicile has a double purpose. Firstly, I have come here to visit and to pay my most reverential respects; secondly, in celebration of this wonderful weather, to invite all of you to conduct an expedition in my part of the world. I reside in a water mill, which has been leased to me by our mutual friend, the Wood Demon. It's a sheltered and poetic corner of the world, where at nighttime you hear the wood nymphs splashing, while in daylight…

VOYNITSKY: Wait a minute, Waffles, we're discussing business…Save it for later…*(To SEREBRYAKOV.)* Go ahead, ask him…This estate was bought from his uncle.

SEREBRYAKOV: Ach, why should I ask him? For what purpose?

VOYNITSKY: This estate was bought for ninety-five thousand at the time! My father paid only seventy thousand, so that left a mortgage of twenty-five thousand. Now you listen to me…This estate could not have been bought, had I not forfeited my inheritance on behalf of my sister, whom I dearly loved. Moreover, I worked for ten years, like an ox, and payed off the entire mortgage…

ORLOVSKY: So what's your point, my dear fellow?

VOYNITSKY: This estate is free of debt and disorder thanks only to my own personal efforts. And now that I'm old, they want to throw me out by the neck!

SEREBRYAKOV: I don't understand what you're getting at?

VOYNTISKY: For twenty-five years I've managed this estate; I've worked, I've sent you money, like the most conscientious caretaker, and in all this time not once did you ever thank me! All this time, when I was young and even now, I have received from you a salary of five hundred rubles a year — a pathetic pittance! — and it didn't even dawn on you to increase it, not once, not even by a single ruble!

SEREBRYAKOV: George, how was I to know! I'm not a practical man, I know nothing of these matters. You could have raised it yourself as much as you liked.

VOYNITSKY: Why didn't I just steal it, then? Why don't you all despise me for the fact that I didn't just steal it! It would have been just, and I wouldn't be a pauper today!

MARYA VASILYEVNA: *(Severely.)* George!

DYADIN: *(Agitated.)* Georgenka, please don't, please…I'm trembling…Why ruin good relations? *(Kisses him.)* Please don't.

VOYNITSKY: For twenty-five years I've sat here with my mother, buried like a mole within these four walls…All our thoughts and feelings were for you, and you alone. All day long we'd talk about you, about your works, we were so proud of your fame, we spoke your name with reverence; we wasted our nights reading journals and books which now I deeply despise!

DYADIN: Please don't, Georgenka, please don't…I can't bear it…

SEREBRYAKOV: I don't understand. What do you want?

VOYNITSKY: You were a being of a supreme order, we recited your articles by heart…But now my eyes are open! I see everything! You write about art, but you understand nothing about art! All your works, which I adored, aren't worth a lousy half a kopek!

SEREBRYAKOV: Ladies and gentlemen! Calm him down once and for all! I am leaving!

YELENA ANDREEVNA: George, I command you to be quiet! Do you hear me?

VOYNITSKY: I will not be quiet! *(Blocks SEREBRYAKOV's way.)* Wait a minute, I'm not finished yet! You have ruined my life! I haven't lived! I have not lived! Thanks to you, I have destroyed, wasted the best years of my life! You are my worst enemy!

DYADIN: I can't bear it…I can't…I'm going into the other room…*(Exits though the right door in great distress.)*

SEREBRYAKOV: What do you want from me! And how dare you speak to me in that tone of voice! You nonentity! If the estate is yours, go ahead, take it, I have no need for it!

ZHELTUKHIN: *(Aside.)* Things are heating up!…I'm out of here! *(Exits.)*

YELENA ANDREEVNA: If you won't be quiet, I'm leaving this hell at once! This very minute! *(Shouts.)* I can't stand it any more!

VOYNITSKY: I've wasted my life! I'm talented, intelligent, courageous…If I had lived a life, I might have been Schopenhauer, or a Dostoevsky…What am I saying? I'm raving…Matushka, I'm in despair! Matushka!

MARYA VASILYEVNA: Listen to the Professor!

VOYNITSKY: Matushka! What can I do? Never mind, don't tell me! I know myself what I must do! *(To SEREBRYAKOV.)* You will remember me! *(Exits by the center door.)*

MARYA VASILYEVNA follows after him.

SEREBRYAKOV: Ladies and gentlemen, will someone tell me what is happening here? Take this madman away from me!

ORLOVSKY: Never mind, Sasha, never mind, just let him calm down. And don't you get so excited.

SEREBRYAKOV: I cannot live with him under the same roof! He lives there, *(indicates the middle door)* right next to me, almost…Let him move to the village, to a separate wing, or else I'll move out myself, but I cannot live with him…

YELENA ANDREEVNA: *(To her husband.)* If something like this happens again, I'm leaving!

SEREBRYAKOV: Please, you're frightening me!

YELENA ANDREEVNA: I'm not trying to frighten you. But it's as if you've all conspired to make my life pure hell…I'm leaving…

SEREBRYAKOV: You know very well that you're young and I'm old, and that you're doing me a favor to live here at all…

YELENA ANDREEVNA: Go on, finish what you were saying…

ORLOVSKY: Come, come…dear friends…

KHRUSHCHOV rushes in. Meanwhile, SONYA appears at the door on the left, and listens throughout the following scene.

KHRUSHCHOV: *(Agitated.)* I'm delighted to find you at home, Aleksandr Vladimirovich…Forgive me, perhaps I've come at an inopportune time, I'm disturbing you…In any event, how are you…

SEREBRYAKOV: What do you want?

KHRUSHCHOV: Forgive me, I'm rather agitated — I've galloped here so fast… Aleksandr Vladimirovich, I've heard that you sold your forests to Kuznetsov the other day in return for timber. If that's the truth, and not just a rumor, then I beg of you not to do it.

YELENA ANDREEVNA: Mikhail Lvovich, my husband is not inclined to talk about such matters now. Let's go into the garden.

KHRUSHCHOV: But I must discuss it now!

YELENA ANDREEVNA: Whatever…I can't bear this…*(Exits.)*

KHRUSHCHOV: Allow me to go see Kuznetsov and tell him you've reconsidered…Will you? Please? You're going to fell a thousand trees, to destroy them for the sake of two or three thousand rubles, so you can indulge your wife in finery, and live in luxury!…You'll destroy them so that posterity will curse our barbarity! If you, a learned, famous man, can be so cruel, how do you expect men less privileged to behave? It's terrible!

ORLOVSKY: Later, Misha!

SEREBRYAKOV: Let's go, Ivan Ivanovich, this will never end.

KHRUSHCHOV: *(Blocks SEREBRYAKOV's way.)* In that case, Professor…Wait three months, and I'll get the money to buy it myself.

ORLOVSKY: I'm sorry, Misha, but this is most strange…You're a principled man, that we know…and we thank you humbly and we admire you deeply for it. *(Bows.)* But why raise such a ruckus?

KHRUSHCHOV: *(Flaring up.)* The elder statesman speaks! There are so many well-meaning people in this world, and that always strikes me as suspicious! And they're all so well-meaning because they just don't care!

ORLOVSKY: You've come here to quarrel, my dear man...That's not right! Principles are all well and good, my friend, but you still need this... *(Points to his heart.)* Without this contraption, my dear man, all your peat and your forests aren't worth a copper kopek...Don't be offended, but you're still so naive!

SEREBRYAKOV: *(Sharply.)* And next time, please be kind enough to come only when you're announced, and spare me your psychopathic outbursts! You've all wanted to exasperate me, and you've succeeded...So kindly leave me alone! As far as your peat and your forests are concerned, I consider it all sheer lunacy — and that's my opinion! Come, Ivan Ivanovich! *(Exits.)*

ORLOVSKY: *(Following after him.)* You didn't have to go so far, Sasha...Really, why be so hard on him? *(Exits.)*

KHRUSHCHOV: *(Alone, after a pause.)* Sheer lunacy, psychopathy...According to this learned professor, I must be mad...I bow to your excellency's authority, I shall now go home and shave my head. No, it's the planet earth that is mad for putting up with all of us!

KHRUSHCHOV goes to the right door quickly; SONYA enters from the left, where she has been listening since KHRUSHCHOV's entrance.

SONYA: *(Runs after him.)* Wait...I heard everything...Say something...Say something, quickly, or else, heaven help me, *I* will!

KHRUSHCHOV: Sofya Aleksandrovna, I've already spoken my mind. I begged your father to spare the forest, I was right, I know it, but he insulted me, and called me a madman...Fine, I'm mad!

SONYA: Enough, enough...

KHRUSHCHOV: Yes, they are not mad, they who in the guise of scholarship hide their cruelty, their cold-bloodedness, their callousness — and all in the name of great wisdom! And they are not mad, they who marry old men only to deceive them before everyone's eyes, to buy plumage and finery at the expense of the destruction of the forests!

SONYA: Listen to me, listen... *(Takes his hand.)* Let me tell you...

KHRUSHCHOV: Stop, Enough. We're different, very different, I know what you think of me already and I don't belong here. Farewell. Your friendship has been precious to me, and it's a pity that I'm left only with memories of your father's gout and your speech about my democratic sensibilities...But I'm not to blame for that...Not I...

SONYA weeps, covers her face and runs out the left door.

KHRUSHCHOV: That will teach me a lesson…I was a fool to fall in love here! I've got to get out of his crypt!

He goes to the right door; YELENA ANDREEVNA enters from the left door.

YELENA ANDREEVNA: You're still here? Wait…Ivan Ivanovich just told me that my husband was rude to you… Please forgive him, he was in a bad mood today, and he misunderstood what you said… As for me, my sentiments lie with you, Mikhail Lvovich! In all sincerity, let me say how much I respect you, and sympathize with you, and feel for you, and allow me to offer you my friendship from the bottom of my heart! *(Extends both hands.)*

KHRUSHCHOV: *(With disgust.)* Go away from me…I despise your friendship! *(Exits.)*

YELENA ANDREEVNA: *(Alone, moans.)* Why? Why?

Offstage, a shot is heard. Enter SONYA, SEREBRYAKOV, ORLOVSKY, and ZHELTUKHIN. MARYA VASILYEVNA staggers in from the center door, cries out, and falls down in a faint. SONYA rushes out through the center door.

SEREBRYAKOV, ORLOVSKY, ZHELTUKHIN: What was that?

SONYA shrieks offstage, and reenters.

SONYA: Uncle George has shot himself!

SONYA, ORLOVSKY, SEREBRYAKOV, and ZHELTUKHIN rush out through the center door.

YELENA ANDREEVNA: *(Moans.)* Why? Why?

DYADIN appears in the right door.

DYADIN: *(At the door.)* What happened?

YELENA ANDREEVNA: Take me away from here! Throw me off a precipice, kill me, but I can't stay here any more. As soon as possible, I beg of you! *(Exits with DYADIN.)*

END OF ACT THREE

ACT FOUR

The forest and the house by the watermill, which DYADIN has leased from KHRUSHCHOV.

YELENA ANDREEVNA and DYADIN sit on the bench beneath a window.

YELENA ANDREEVNA: You'll go to the post office tomorrow again, won't you, dearest Ilya Ilyich?

DYADIN: Without fail.

YELENA ANDREEVNA: I'll wait three more days. If my brother doesn't answer my letter by then, then I'll borrow some money from you and go to Moscow myself. I can't spend the rest of my life at your mill.

DYADIN: Of course not...*(Pause.)* I don't presume to advise you, dear lady, but your letters and telegrams which I'm delivering to the post office every day — well, forgive me for saying so, but they're all in vain, dear lady. No matter what response you'll receive from your brother, you'll go back to your husband anyway in the end.

YELENA ANDREEVNA: No, I won't...Let's be honest, Ilya Ilyich. I don't love my husband. The young people on the estate — I liked them very much, but they've been untrue to me all along. Why should I return there? You speak of duty...I know that full well, but, I repeat, we must be honest about it...

Pause.

DYADIN: I see...The great Russian poet Lomonosov ran away from Archangelsk province and found his fortune in Moscow. That, of course, was noble of him...But why have *you* run away? To be honest about it, you'll never find happiness...A canary should sit in its cage and look out at others who are happy. It should sit there forever, in fact.

YELENA ANDREEVNA: Perhaps I'm not a canary...Perhaps I'm a sparrow, free to fly...

DYADIN: Nonsense! You can spot a bird in flight, dear lady...These past two weeks any other lady would have been spotted in ten towns and thrown dust in everyone's eyes, while you got as far as this mill, and are quite exhausted at that....Where can you go, indeed! Live here a while, rest to your heart's content, and then go back to your husband. *(Listens.)* Someone's coming in the carriage. *(Stands.)*

YELENA ANDREEVNA: I'm going.

DYADIN: I'll trouble you no longer with my presence...I'm going to the mill to have a little rest...I arose this morning before Aurora, even.

YELENA ANDREEVNA: When you wake up, come back, and we'll have some tea. *(Exits into the house.)*

DYADIN: *(Alone.)* If I lived among the *literati*, what a fine caricature I'd make for a journal. Imagine the caption: Good heavens! Elderly gent of unattractive appearance runs off with the young wife of a famous professor! Delightful! *(Exits.)*

Enter SEMYON, carrying buckets. Enter YULYA.

YULYA: Hello, Senka, how are you! Is Ilya Ilyich at home?

SEMYON: He is. He went to the mill.

YULYA: Go call him.

SEMYON: Right away. *(Exits.)*

YULYA: He's sleeping, most likely...*(Sits on the bench beneath the window and sighs deeply.)* Some sleep, others walk, while I'm on my feet all day long...No rest for the weary. *(Sighs even more deeply.)* Dear Lord, are there any creatures on this earth more stupid than that Waffles! I was just passing by his barn, and a little black pig came out of the door. If the pigs get into his barn and start tearing his corn sacks, that will teach him a lesson...

Enter DYADIN.

DYADIN: *(Putting on his frock coat.)* Is that you, Yulya Stepanovna? Forgive me, I'm in a state of *deshabilé*...I was just going to rest a while in the arms of Morpheus.

YULYA: Hello.

DYADIN: Forgive me for not inviting you inside...The place is a mess, etcetera etcetera...If you like, we'll go over to the mill...

YULYA: I'll just stay here for a bit. Here's why I've come to see you, Ilya Ilyich. Lyonechka and the professor wanted to plan an outing, and they'd like to have a picnic at the mill today, have a little tea...

DYADIN: I'd be absolutely delighted.

YULYA: I've come to tell you in advance...The others will be here soon. Please have a table brought out here, oh, and of course, a samovar, too...And ask Senka to take the picnic basket out of my carriage.

DYADIN: Without fail. *(Pause.)* So? How are things at home?

YULYA: Bad, Ilya Ilyich…I'm worried sick about it, believe me. You know that the professor and Sonyechka are staying with us now, don't you?

DYADIN: I do.

YULYA: After Yegor Petrovich took his own life, they couldn't live in his house any more…They were afraid. It wasn't so bad during the day, but in the evenings, they'd all gather in one room and sit there till dawn. They were terrified that Yegor Petrovich's ghost might appear…

DYADIN: They're superstitious…Do they ever speak of Yelena Andreevna?

YULYA: Of course they do. *(Pause.)* She's vanished.

DYADIN: Yes, a subject worthy of the brush of Ayvazovsky… She's up and vanished.

YULYA: Yes, and no one knows where… Perhaps she's gone away, or perhaps she took desperate measures and…

DYADIN: God is kind, Yulya Stepanovna! Everything will be all right.

Enter KHRUSHCHOV with a portfolio and a drawing case.

KHRUSHCHOV: Hey! Is anyone home? Semyon?

DYADIN: Over here!

KHRUSHCHOV: Ah!…Hello, Yulyechka!

YULYA: Hello, Mikhail Lvovich.

KHRUSHCHOV: I've come to do some work, Ilya Ilyich. I can't just sit at home. Please ask them to put my table under this tree, just as it was yesterday, and tell them to have two lamps ready, too…It's already getting dark…

DYADIN: Yes, your honor.

KHRUSHCHOV: How are things, Yulyechka?

YULYA: Oh, all right…

Pause.

KHRUSHCHOV: Are the Serebryakovs staying with you?

YULYA: They are.

KHRUSHCHOV: Hm…And what is Lyonechka doing?

YULYA: He stays at home…and spends his time with Sonyechka…

KHRUSHCHOV: I'll bet he does! *(Pause.)* He ought to marry her.

YULYA: Yes…*(Sighs.)* If only he would, please God! He's an educated man, he's respectable, and she comes from a good family, too…I have always wished this for her…

KHRUSHCHOV: She's a fool…

YULYA: You mustn't say that.

KHRUSHCHOV: And your Lyonechka's such an intellect…You've got quite an assortment over there, haven't you! A meeting of great minds!

YULYA: You haven't had lunch today, have you…

KHRUSHCHOV: Why?

YULYA: You're in a very bad mood…

Enter DYADIN and SEMYON, carrying a small table.

DYADIN: You do know how to pick your places, Misha. It's a lovely spot that you've found here for your work. An oasis! A veritable oasis! Imagine that it's surrounded by palm trees — Yulyechka's a gentle doe, you're a lion, and I'm a tiger.

KHRUSHCHOV: You're a good fellow, a fine fellow, Ilya Ilyich, but where are your manners? You sputter sweet words, shuffle your feet, shrug your shoulders…Anyone who didn't know you would think you're not human…God only knows what you are…It's a shame…

DYADIN: And so I was meant to be…It was preordained.

KHRUSHCHOV: There you go again, "preordained." Forget about it. *(Pins a drawing on the table.)* I'll be staying the night with you.

DYADIN: I'm exceedingly delighted. You may be in a bad mood, Misha, but I feel inexpressibly happy! As if a little bird was nestled in my bosom and singing a little song.

KHRUSHCHOV: Well, enjoy it while it lasts. *(Pause.)* You have a bird tucked in your bosom, while I've got a toad. It's one crisis after another! Shimansky's sold his forest for timber…That's one! Yelena Andreevna left her husband, and no one knows where she is. That's two! And every day I feel more stupid, and petty, and dull…That's three! Yesterday, I wanted to tell you something, but I hadn't the courage to do so. You may congratulate me. Yegor Petrovich left a diary behind. First it fell into the hands of Ivan Ivanich, and I went over and read it through ten times…

YULYA: We read it, too.

KHRUSHCHOV: George's little affair with Yelena Andreevna was the talk of the district, but it turned out to be nothing but nasty, sordid gossip…I believed it, too, and joined them in their onslaught of slandering, mudslinging, insulting…

DYADIN: Of course, and that wasn't right.

KHRUSHCHOV: I heard it all first from your brother, Yulyechka! A fine friend I am! I don't really respect your brother, but I believed him, whereas I didn't believe the woman who in fact was acting nobly before my very eyes. I readily believe in evil instead of good, and I don't see farther than my own nose. And that means I'm as mediocre as all the rest.

DYADIN: *(To YULYA.)* Let's go to the mill, my child. Leave our grumbler to his work, we'll take a walk. Come…To work, Mishenka. *(Exits with YULYA.)*

KHRUSHCHOV: *(Alone; mixes some paints in a saucer.)* One night, I saw him take her hand and press it to his face. He writes of that night in detail in his diary, of how I came in, and what I said to him. He repeats what I said, and calls me a narrow-minded fool. *(Pause.)* Too thick…I ought to make it lighter…And then he scolds Sonya for loving me…She never loved…Now I've made a blot…*(Scrapes the paper with his knife.)* And even if there were some truth in it, there's no point thinking about it now…It began foolishly, it ended foolishly…

SEMYON and the workers enter, carrying a large table.

KHRUSHCHOV: What are you doing? What's that for?

SEMYON: Ilya Ilyich's orders. The company from Zheltukyin's estate are arriving for tea.

KHRUSHCHOV: I humbly thank you, then. That means I'll have to set aside my work…I'll pack up everything and go home.

Enter ZHELTUKHIN with SONYA on his arm.

ZHELTUKHIN: *(Sings.)* "Against my will, to these sad shores, a mysterious force allures me…"

KHRUSHCHOV: Who's there? Ah! *(Hurries to pack his drawing materials in the case.)*

ZHELTUKHIN: One question, dear Sofi…Do you remember your birthday lunch at our place? When you laughed at me? You thought I looked so funny.

SONYA: Enough, Leonid Stepanich. Must you? I was laughing for no reason, that's all.

ZHELTUKHIN: *(Sees KHRUSHCHOV.)* Ah, look who's here! You, too! Hello.

KHRUSHCHOV: Hello.

ZHELTUKHIN: Are you working? Excellent, excellent…Where's Waffles?

KHRUSHCHOV: Over there…

ZHELTUKHIN: Where?

KHRUSHCHOV: I thought I made it clear…Over there, at the mill.

ZHELTUKHIN: Let's go and call him. *(Walks off, singing.)* "Against my will to these sad shores…"

SONYA: Hello…

KHRUSHCHOV: Hello.

Pause.

SONYA: What are you drawing?

KHRUSHCHOV: Oh…nothing interesting.

SONYA: Is that a chart?

KHRUSHCHOV: No, it's a map of the forests in our district. I made it myself. *(Pause.)* The green colors represent the places where there were forests in our forefather's time; the light green represents where forests have been cut down in the last twenty-five years, — oh, and the blue shows where they still remain…Yes… *(Pause.)* And how are you? Are you happy?

SONYA: Now is not a time to think of happiness, Mikhail Lvovich.

KHRUSHCHOV: What should we think about, then?

SONYA: Our sorrow comes from thinking too much of happiness…

KHRUSHCHOV: I see.

Pause.

SONYA: Good and evil go hand in hand. Sorrow has taught me something. One must forget one's own happiness, Mikhail Lvovich, and think only of the happiness of others. All of life must be a sacrifice.

KHRUSHCHOV: Yes, I suppose… *(Pause.)* Marya Vasilyevna's son has shot himself, and still she searches for contradictions in those damned brochures of hers. A tragedy has befallen us, and you delude yourself by trying to spoil your own life in the name of sacrifice…You have no heart…None of you do…And neither do I…We don't do the right thing, and everything's reduced to ashes…I'll go away, I won't interfere with you and Zheltukhin…Why are you crying? I didn't mean to make you cry.

SONYA: Never mind, never mind…*(Wipes her eyes.)*

Enter YULYA, DYADIN, and ZHELTUKHIN. SEREBRYAKOV's voice is heard offstage: "A-oo! Where is everyone?"

SONYA: *(Shouting.)* Over here, papa!

DYADIN: They're bringing the samovar! Delightful! *(DYADIN and YULYA busy themselves at the table.)*

Enter SEREBRYAKOV and ORLOVSKY.

SONYA: Here we are, papa!

SEREBRYAKOV: I see you, I see you...

ZHELTUKHIN: *(Loudly.)* Ladies and gentlemen, the meeting has come to order! Waffles, uncork the liqueur!

KHRUSHCHOV: *(To SEREBRYAKOV.)* Professor, let's forget what has happened between us! *(Extends his hand.)* I offer you my apology...

SEREBRYAKOV: I thank you. Delighted, I'm sure. You must forgive me, as well. After the incident, I tried to think over what had happened the very next day. When I remembered our conversation, I felt very badly, indeed...Let's be friends. *(Takes him by the arm and walks to the table.)*

ORLOVSKY: It's about time, my dear man. A bad peace is better than a good war.

DYADIN: Your excellency, I'm delighted that you've visited me in my oasis. I'm delighted beyond words!

SEREBRYAKOV: I thank you, dear sir. It is a lovely place, indeed. Truly, an oasis.

ORLOVSKY: Do you love nature, Sasha?

SEREBRYAKOV: Enormously. *(Pause.)* Let us keep the conversation going, ladies and gentlemen. In our situation, it's the best thing to do. We must look misfortune straight in the eye with courage, I more than the rest of you, because I'm the most unfortunate of all. I must be positive!

YULYA: I'm not serving sugar, ladies and gentlemen; so drink your tea with jam.

DYADIN: *(Bustling among the guests.)* Delighted, simply delighted.

SEREBRYAKOV: I have lived through so much lately, Mikhail Lvovich, and I've given the matter considerable thought, so much so that I believe I could write an entire treatise for the benefit of posterity on how we must live our lives. We're never too old to learn, and misfortune is the greatest teacher of all.

DYADIN: Let bygones be bygones. God is kind, it will all turn out well.

SONYA shudders.

ZHELTUKHIN: What are you shuddering for?

SONYA: I heard someone shouting.

DYADIN: The peasants are catching crayfish on the river.

Pause.

ZHELTUKHIN: Ladies and gentlemen, we all agreed to spend the evening as if nothing had happened…And yet, there is tension in the air…

DYADIN: Your excellency, I have not only the utmost reverence for learning, but I have a kindred feeling for it as well. My brother Grigory Ilyich's wife's brother, perhaps you might know him, Konstantin Trofimovich Lakedemonov, has a master's degree in foreign literature.

SEREBRYAKOV: I've never met him, but I've heard of him.

Pause.

YULYA: Tomorrow it will be fifteen days exactly, since Yegor Petrovich died.

KHRUSHCHOV: Yulyechka, we're not going to talk about it.

SEREBRYAKOV: Positive, be positive!

Pause.

ZHELTUKHIN: All the same, there's a feeling of tension in the air, somehow…

SEREBRYAKOV: Nature abhors a vacuum. She has robbed me of two precious friends and, to compensate for this loss, she will soon send me new ones. I drink to your health, Leonid Stepanovich!

ZHELTUKHIN: I thank you, dear Aleksandr Vladimirovich! And for my part, allow me to drink to the success of your scholarly endeavors.
> "Sow the seeds of good and reason,
> Sow them now for every season,
> Russia thanks you from her heart!"

SEREBRYAKOV: Your gesture is deeply appreciated. And I wish with all my heart that the time may come soon that our friendship will grow even closer.

Enter FYODOR IVANOVICH.

FYODOR IVANOVICH: What have we here! A picnic!

ORLOVSKY: My dear sweet son — you handsome boy, you!

FYODOR IVANOVICH: Hello. *(Kisses SONYA and YULYA.)*

ORLOVSKY: I haven't seen you in weeks. Where have you been? What's happening?

FYODOR IVANOVICH: I've just been to Lyonya's, and they told me you were here, so here I am.

ORLOVSKY: But what have you been doing?

FYODOR IVANOVICH: I haven't slept in three nights…Last night, Father, I lost five thousand in cards. I kept drinking and losing, and I've been to town five times…I thought I was losing my mind.

ORLOVSKY: Well done! I suppose you're a bit drunk now?

FYODOR IVANOVICH: Not at all, not at all. Yulka, tea! Only straight, with a little lemon…How about George, eh? All of a sudden, for no reason at all, bang! Right in the forehead! And with a Lefoche revolver! Why didn't he use a Smith and Wesson?

KHRUSHCHOV: Be quiet, you swine!

FYODOR IVANOVICH: Swine I may be, but at least I'm a pedigree. *(Smooths his beard.)* My beard alone is worth a fortune…I may be a swine, and a fool, and a rascal, too, but I can have any bride I want. Sonya, will you marry me?! *(To KHRUSHCHOV.)* Oh, sorry…*Pardon…*

KHRUSHCHOV: Stop all this foolishness.

YULYA: You're a good-for-nothing, Fedyenka! You're the worst drunk and spendthrift in the province. You're pathetic even to look at…a menace. You're perversity itself!

FYODOR IVANOVICH: Oh, stop complaining! Come, sit next to me…right here. I'm coming to stay with you for a week or two…Must get some rest. *(Kisses her.)*

YULYA: Shame on you! You ought to be comforting your father in his old age. Instead you disgrace him. You lead a crazy life, that's all I can say about it.

FYODOR IVANOVICH: I renounce drinking! Basta! *(Pours himself a drink.)* Is this plum brandy or cherry?

YULYA: Don't drink, don't.

FYODOR IVANOVICH: Just one little glass. *(Drinks.)* I'll give you a pair of horses and a rifle, Wood Demon. I'm going to stay at Yulya's for two weeks…

YULYA: Come on, drink some tea!

DYADIN: And have some biscuits with it, Fedyenka.

ORLOVSKY: *(To SEREBRYAKOV.)* Sasha, my friend, I lived a life, just like Fyodor's, for forty years. Once, dear fellow, I even started to calculate how many hearts I'd broken in my time. I got as far as seventy, and I stopped. Then, suddenly, as soon as I reached forty, something happened. I felt depressed, and out of place, in a word, I was completely lost, and that's all there is to it. I tried reading, and working, and traveling — but nothing helped! So, my dear, I went to visit my good friend, the late Prince Dmitry Pavlovich. And we dined together, we ate this and that…And after dinner, instead of taking a nap, we went outside for some target practice. An immense crowd of people were gathered there. Waffles was among them, too.

DYADIN: I was there, I was there…I remember.

ORLOVSKY: Imagine, I was so depressed — good God! I couldn't stand it any longer. Suddenly, I burst into tears, I staggered across the yard and yelled at the top of my voice: "My friends, dear friends, forgive me, for Christ's sake!" And at that moment I felt so tender, and pure, and warm inside, and since that time, my dear fellow, there has never been a happier man in the district. You should try it yourself sometime.

SEREBRYAKOV: What?

A glow appears in the sky.

ORLOVSKY: Do just as I did. Capitulate. Surrender.

SEREBRYAKOV: A fine example of armchair philosophy. You're advising me to ask forgiveness. For what? Let others apologize to me!

SONYA: But Papa, it is *we* who are guilty!

SEREBRYAKOV: Really? Ladies and gentlemen, at this moment you're all thinking of my attitude toward my wife, evidently. Am I really to blame, in your opinion? Why, that's ridiculous, ladies and gentlemen. She has broken her vows, she has left me at the most difficult moment in my life…

KHRUSHCHOV: Aleksandr Vladimirovich, listen to me…You've been a professor for twenty-five years, you've served scholarship, while I've planted trees and practiced medicine, but to what avail, if we are not kind to those for whom we toil? We say that we serve humanity, and yet at the same time we're destroying one another. For example, what did we do, you and I, to save George? Where is your wife, whom we've all insulted? Where is your peace of mind, and your daughter's, too? It's all disappeared, destroyed, and all for naught. Ladies and gentlemen, you call me the Wood Demon, but I'm not the only one, you know. There's a demon inside all of you, you're all wandering alone in the dark forest, finding your way. And you're all just about good and bright and clever enough to ruin your own lives and everyone else's.

YELENA ANDREEVNA enters from the house unnoticed, and sits on the bench under the window.

KHRUSHCHOV: I thought I was a man of principle, a humanist, when really I was intolerant and malicious like everyone else. When, for instance, your wife truly offered me her friendship, I replied: "Go away from me! I despise your friendship!" What condescension and self-righteousness! And that is what I am. A demon lives inside me, he is petty, mediocre, and blind — and you're no paragon, either! Yet all the women in the district think I'm a hero and a visionary, while you're known throughout all of Russia. And if men like me are heroes, and if men like you are famous, that means that in the land of the blind, the one-eyed man is king, and that there are no true heroes, no geniuses, no one to lead us out of the dark forest, to purify what we have spoiled, and that no — there are no true paragons who merit honor and glory...

SEREBRYAKOV: Forgive me...I haven't come to argue with you, nor to defend my claim to fame.

ZHELTUKHIN: We might think of changing the subject, Misha.

KHRUSHCHOV: In a minute...then I'll go. Yes, I'm mediocre, but you're no paragon either, professor! And poor George who couldn't find anything better to do than to put a bullet through his brain, he's mediocre too. We're all mediocre. And as for the women...

YELENA ANDREEVNA: *(Interrupting.)* As for the women, they're no better. Yelena Andreevna left her husband, and do you think she made any use of her freedom? Don't worry...She'll return...*(Sits at the table.)* And so I have...

General confusion.

DYADIN: *(Bursts out laughing.)* Delightful! Ladies and gentlemen, I beg of you, a word before the execution, please! Your excellency, it was I who stole off with your wife, as Paris once abducted fair Helen! I! All right, so Paris wasn't pockmarked, but then again, "There are more things in heaven and earth, Horatio, than are dreamt of in your philosophy!"

KHRUSHCHOV: I don't understand it...Can this really be you, Yelena?

YELENA ANDREEVNA: I've spent the past two weeks at Ilya Ilyich's...Why do you all look at me like that? Hello, everyone...I was sitting by the window, I heard everything. *(Embraces SONYA.)* Come, let's make peace. Hello, my dear girl . ... Peace and harmony!

DYADIN: *(Rubbing his hands.)* Delightful!

YELENA ANDREEVNA: *(To KHRUSHCHOV.)* Mikhail Lvovich. *(Gives him her hand.)* Let bygones be bygones. Hello, Fyodor Ivanich...Yulyechka...

ORLOVSKY: Darling wife of our dear professor, lovely lady...She's come home to us...

YELENA ANDREEVNA: I've missed you so. Hello, Aleksandr! *(Extends her hand to her husband, who turns away.)* Aleksandr!

SEREBRYAKOV: You've broken your vows.

YELENA ANDREEVNA: Aleksandr!

SEREBRYAKOV: I can't hide the fact that I'm pleased to see you and am prepared to talk to you, but at home, not here…*(Moves away from the table.)*
ORLOVSKY: Sasha!

Pause.

YELENA ANDREEVNA: I see…And so, Aleksandr, the solution to our problem is that there isn't one. Very well, then, so be it! I'm only a minor character, and my happiness is the kind a canary in a cage has, the kind any
woman has who sits all day at home, who eats, drinks, sleeps, who listens
to talk about gout, about rights, about just deserts. Why do you hang your
head, are you embarrassed? Come, let's have a glass of wine? What about it?
DYADIN: Everything will be just fine. It will all turn out in the end.
FYODOR IVANOVICH: *(Approaches SEREBRYAKOV, anxiously.)* Aleksandr
Vladimirovich, I'm truly moved…I beg of you, be gentle to your wife, give
her a kind word or two, and I'll be your friend forever, I'll even give you my
best troika.
SEREBRYAKOV: I thank you, but, forgive me, I don't understand you…
FYODOR IVANOVICH: Hm…you don't understand…Once I was returning
from a hunting trip, and there on a tree sat an owl. So I shot at him! He didn't
budge…so I let him have it again…And still he didn't budge…Nothing
would move him. He just sat there looking blank.
SEREBRYAKOV: What are you talking about?
FYODOR IVANOVICH: An old owl. *(Returns to the table.)*
ORLOVSKY: *(Listens.)* Ladies and gentlemen, quiet, please…It sounds like an alarm…
FYODOR IVANOVICH: *(Spotting a glow in the sky.)* Ay-ay-ay! Look at the sky!
What a glow!
ORLOVSKY: Heavens above, and we've been sitting here and not seeing anything!
DYADIN: Nice and cozy.
FYODOR IVANOVICH: *(Making the sound of a bugle.)* Ta-ta-ta! Quite an illu-
mination! It's near Alekseevskoye.
KHRUSHCHOV: No, Alekseevskoye is further to the right…It must be near
Novo-Petrovskoye.
YULYA: How terrifying! I'm afraid of fires!
KHRUSHCHOV: Yes of course, it's Novo-Petrovskoye.
DYADIN: *(Shouts.)* Semyon, run down to the pond, and see where the fire's com-
ing from. You might be able to see if from there!
SEMYON: *(Shouts.)* It's the Telibeevsky woods!
DYADIN: What?

SEMYON: The Telibeevsky woods!

DYADON: The woods —

A prolonged pause.

KHRUSHCHOV: I must go to where the fire is…Good-bye…Forgive me if I was rude — it's only because I've never felt as low as I feel today… There's such a heaviness in my soul… But, it doesn't matter…One must stand on one's own two feet. I won't shoot myself, nor will I throw myself under the wheel of this mill…I may not be a hero yet, but I'll shall be, one day! I'll grow eagle's wings, and fear neither the glow of the fire nor the devil himself! Let the forests burn to the ground — I'll plant new ones! And if my beloved doesn't love me, I'll find another! *(Rushes offstage.)*

YELENA ANDREEVNA: Good for him!

ORLOVSKY: Yes…"And if my beloved doesn't love me, I'll find another." I wonder what he meant by that!

SONYA: Take me away from here…I want to go home…

SEREBRYAKOV: Yes, it's time to go. The damp here is unbearable. Now where are my rug and my overcoat…

ZHELTUKHIN: Your rug's in the carriage, and your overcoat's here. *(Hands him the overcoat.)*

SONYA: *(Extremely agitated.)* Take me away from here…Take me away…

ZHELTUKHIN: At your service.

SONYA: No, I'll go with my godfather. Take me with you, Godfather, please…

ORLOVSKY: Come, my darling, let's go. *(Helps her with her coat.)*

ZHELTUKHIN: *(Aside.)* It's all so humiliating and degrading!

FYODOR IVANOVICH and YULYA put the crockery and napkins in the basket.

SEREBRYAKOV: I have a pain in my left foot…It must be rheumatism…I won't sleep again tonight.

YELENA ANDREEVNA: *(Buttons his coat.)* Darling Ilya Ilyich, please fetch me my hat and my cloak!

DYADIN: Right away! *(Exits into the house and returns with the hat and cloak.)*

ORLOVSKY: So the fire frightened you, my sweet! Don't be afraid, look, it's dying down. Soon, it will fade away…

YULYA: There's a half jar of cherry jam left…Oh, well, let's let Ilya Ilyich have it. *(To her brother.)* Lyonechka, carry the basket, please.

YELENA ANDREEVNA: I'm ready. *(To her husband.)* So come, take me like the statue of the *commendatore* in *Don Giovanni*, and we'll vanish into the depths of your twenty-six rooms! That is my destiny!

SEREBRYAKOV: The statue of the *commendatore*…Ordinarily I'd find the comparison amusing, but my foot hurts too much. *(To everyone.)* Good-bye, ladies and gentlemen! Thank you for your hospitality and pleasant company…It's been a lovely evening, the tea was delicious — everything, in fact, was superb, but forgive me, there is one thing I cannot accept and it is, namely, your backwater philosophy and attitude toward life. Ladies and gentlemen, we must do something! We can't live like this! We must do something… And that's it… Good luck. *(Exits with his wife.)*

FYODOR IVANOVICH: Let's go, sweetheart! *(To his father.)* Good-bye, Father! *(Exits with YULYA.)*

ZHELTUKHIN: *(Follows with the basket.)* This basket is heavy, damn it…I hate picnics. *(Exits and shouts offstage.)* Drive around, Aleksey!

ORLOVSKY: *(To SONYA.)* What are you sitting down for? Come on, my sweet…*(Goes with SONYA.)*

DYADIN: *(Aside.)* And nobody said good-bye to me… How delightful! *(Puts out the candles.)*

ORLOVSKY: *(To SONYA.)* So?

SONYA: I can't go, Godfather…I haven't the strength! I despair, Godfather…I despair! It's unbearable!

ORLOVSKY: *(Anxiously.)* What the matter? My sweet, my darling…

SONYA: Let's stay here for a moment.

ORLOVSKY: First it's "Take me away," then it's "Stay"…I don't understand you…

SONYA: I've lost all my happiness here tonight…I can't bear it…Ach, Godfather, why am I alive? *(Embraces him.)* Ach, if only you knew, if only you knew!

ORLOVSKY: Water, that's what you need, water…Come and sit down… Come…

DYADIN: What's going on? Sofya Aleksandrovna, darling… I can't bear it, I'm trembling all over… *(Tearfully.)* I can't bear to see you like this… Child…

SONYA: Ilya Ilyich, my dearest, take me to the fire? I beseech you!

ORLOVSKY: To the fire? Why? What do you want to do there?

SONYA: I beg of you, take me there, or else I'll go there myself. I despair… Godfather, I can't bear it, I can't. Take me to the fire.

KHRUSHCHOV rushes in.

KHRUSHCHOV: *(Shouts.)* Ilya Ilyich!

DYADIN: Here I am! What is it?

KHRUSHCHOV: I can't go by foot, give me a horse.

SONYA: *(Recognizing KHRUSHCHOV, exclaims joyously.)* Mikhail Lvovich! *(Goes to him.)* Mikhail Lvovich! *(To ORLOVSKY.)* Go away, Godfather, I must speak with him alone. *(To KHRUSHCHOV.)* Mikhail Lvovich, you said that you'd fall in love with someone else…*(To ORLOVSKY.)* Go away, Godfather…*(To KHRUSHCHOV.)* Well I am someone else now…I only want the truth… Nothing, ever, but the truth! I love you, I love you…I love you…

ORLOVSKY: Now that explains all this coming and going. *(Bursts out laughing.)*

DYADIN: Delightful!

SONYA: *(To ORLOVSKY.)* Go away, Godfather. *(To KHRUSHCHOV.)* Yes, yes, only the truth and nothing else… Speak, O speak…I already have…

KHRUSHCHOV: *(Embraces her.)* My darling!

SONYA: Don't go away, Godfather…When you declared your love, I almost expired from happiness, but I was still a captive of convention. What stopped me from responding is the very same thing that stops my father from smiling at Yelena. But now I'm free…

ORLOVSKY: *(Bursts out laughing.)* Together at last! Safe on the shores of love! I congratulate you. *(Bows low.)* Shame on you, shame on you both! You've dragged this thing out, chasing each other around in circles!

DYADIN: *(Embraces KHRUSHCHOV.)* Mishenka, my dear, how happy you've made me! Mishenka!

ORLOVSKY: *(Embraces and kisses SONYA.)* My sweetness, my little canary…My precious goddaughter…

SONYA bursts out laughing.

ORLOVSKY: There she goes again!

KHRUSHCHOV: Forgive me, I hardly know where I am…Let me have a word with her…Don't interfere, please…And don't go away…

Enter FYODOR IVANOVICH and YULYA.

YULYA: You're always talking nonsense, Fedyenka! Pure nonsense!

ORLOVSKY: Sh! Quiet, children! My son, the robber prince, is coming. Quickly, let's hide! Come on.

ORLOVSKY, DYADIN, KHRUSHCHOV, and SONYA hide.

FYODOR IVANOVICH: I left my whip and glove around here somewhere.

YULYA: But you're always talking nonsense!

FYODOR IVANOVICH: So?…What if I do? I don't want to go to your place now…First let's take a walk, and then we'll go.

YULYA: You bother me! Really, you do! *(Claps her hands.)* God, what a fool that Waffles is! He hasn't even cleared the table yet! Someone might have stolen the samovar…Ach, Waffles, Waffles, he seems quite old, and yet he's got the mind of a child!

DYADIN: *(Aside.)* Thank you kindly.

YULYA: As we were walking, I heard someone laughing…

FYODOR IVANOVICH: Some peasant women are bathing…*(Picks up a glove.)* Someone's glove…Sonya's, perhaps…Something's bitten Sonya today. She's in love with the Wood Demon. She's head over heels, it's so obvious, and he, the dummy, doesn't even see it.

YULYA: *(Angrily.)* Where are we going?

FYODOR IVANOVICH: To the pond…Come, let's go…There's no lovelier place in all the district…Such unspoiled beauty!

ORLOVSKY: *(Aside.)* That's my son, my handsome boy, and that great big beard of his…

YULYA: I heard the sound of someone's voice.

FYODOR IVANOVICH:
> "O marvelous spot of woodland wonder,
> Where water nymphs perch, and demons wander…"

We're here, old man! *(Claps her on the shoulder.)*

YULYA: I'm not an old man.

FYODOR IVANOVICH: Let's discuss things peaceably. Listen, Yulyechka. I have been through many trials and tribulations, I've walked through fire, and all that…I'm already thirty-five years old, and I have no profession whatsoever, save that of lieutenant of the Serbian Army and officer of the Russian reserves. I go from pillar to post, as they say…I want to change my life and, well…you see, I have this fantasy, that if I marry, then my life will be completely different…Marry me, will you? I'll never find anyone better than you…

YULYA: *(Embarrassed.)* Hm…You see…You ought to change your ways first, Fedyenka.

FYODOR IVANOVICH: Don't be coy! Answer me straight!

YULYA: I'm too embarrassed to…*(Glances around.)* Wait, someone might come, or might overhear us…Perhaps Waffles is listening from the window.

FYODOR IVANOVICH: There's no one here.

YULYA: *(Throws herself around his neck.)* Fedyenka!

SONYA bursts out laughing; ORLOVSKY, DYADIN, and KHRUSHCHOV start laughing, too, and clapping their hands and shouting: "Bravo! Bravo!"

FYODOR IVANOVICH: Tfoo! You frightened me! Where on earth did you come from?

SONYA: Congratulations, Yulyechka! And the same for me, too!

Laughter, kisses, noise.

DYADIN: Delightful! Delightful!

END OF PLAY

Chronology of the Plays

THE NIGHT BEFORE THE TRIAL   1890s

THE SEAGULL   1896
    a comedy in four acts

UNCLE VANYA   1899
    scenes from country life in four acts

THE THREE SISTERS   1901
    a drama in four acts

THE CHERRY ORCHARD   1904
    a comedy in four acts

Translator's note: The subtitles listed above are those given to the plays by their author. The dates of the final four full-length plays indicate their premieres.

Biographical Chronology:
Anton Pavlovich Chekhov

1860 January 17. Anton Pavlovich Chekhov is born in Taganrog, a town on the Azov Sea, son of a shopkeeper. (One of six children: Aleksandr, Nikolai, Anton, Masha, Ivan, Mikhail.) Of peasant lineage: His grandfather was a serf in the Voronezh province.

1869 enters grammar school, is required to work in his father's grocery store and to sing in the church choir along with his other siblings.

1876 Anton's father's bankruptcy forces the family to flee to Moscow; Anton is left behind to complete his education; supports himself by tutoring.

1877 sends his first serious full-length play, a lost manuscript whose title is purported to have been *Bezotsovshchina (Fatherless)* to his brother Aleksandr, along with several short comedic ones, which Aleksandr sends to journals for publication.

1879 passes his exams, joins his family in Moscow, enrolls in the medical school at Moscow University; to support his family and his education, begins writing sketches for humorous publications.

1880 first story published in *Strekoza (The Dragon Fly)*, a humorous journal; from 1880–87, writes over 400 stories and sketches for numerous journals under a variety of *"noms de plume."*

1881 completes his second full-length play (a.k.a. *Platonov*)

1882 begins to contribute stories regularly to the weekly *Oskolki (Fragments)* for a five-year period; its editor, Leykin, limits him to comedic sketches of less than 1000 words, signed primarily by Antosha Chekhonte; this becomes the main source of income for himself and his family.

1884 receives medical degree; begins to practice medicine; experiences his first lung hemorrhage; *Tales of Melpomena,* a collection of humorous short stories, is published.

1885 begins to contribute weekly to the *Petersburg Gazette* — no longer limiting him to strictly humorous pieces, and permitting him to write more lengthy stories; his collection *Motley Stories* is published; writes a dramatic study, *On the High Road.*

1886 invited to contribute to *Novoe Vremya (New Times)* by its prestigious publisher, Suvorin, enabling him to begin his more serious work and to publish under his true name with no space restrictions; experiences his second lung hemorrhage; writes *On the Harmful Effects of Tobacco;* continues writing dozens of short stories.

1887 premiere of *Ivanov* at the Korsh Theatre, Moscow, and then in St. Petersburg, with mixed and good reviews respectively; *At Twilight,* a volume of short stories, is published by Suvorin, establishing Chekhov as a writer of increased stature; writes *Calchas* (later retitled *Swan Song*).

1888 awarded Pushkin Prize in literature by the Imperial Academy of Sciences in St. Petersburg; premieres of *The Bear* and *Swan Song;* writes *The Proposal;* publication of a story, *The Steppe* in *The Northern Herald,* his first appearance in a so-called "thick journal," the serious monthlies of the Moscow literary establishment, further enhancing his stature as a writer; *Stories,* a volume of short stories, is published by Suvorin.

1889 writes *The Wedding;* premieres of *The Proposal* and *The Tragedian in Spite of Himself;* premiere of *The Wood Demon* in Moscow, which closes after three performance to uniformly negative reviews; death of his brother Nikolai of consumption; writes stories: *A Dreary Story, The Bet.*

1890 journeys across Siberia to the island of Sakhalin off the Pacific Coast of Siberia to study the penal colony; experiences symptoms of coughing, heart palpitations; writes stories: *The Horse-Thieves, Gusev.*

1891 travels in Western Europe; writes *The Jubilee;* writes story *The Duel,* beginning the period of the longer and more serious stories.

1892 journeys to Novgorod province to join the fight against famine; purchases his "estate" in Melikhovo, fifty miles south of Moscow, and moves from Moscow with his family; appointed honorary medical superintendent of Serpukhov, his district, in the fight against cholera; his notes on the Sakhalin journey are published in *Russian Thought;* writes stories: *Ward No. 6, The Grasshopper, In Exile, Neighbors, The Wife.*

1893 increased symptoms of his illness: coughing, heart palpitations, indigestion, headaches; writes stories: *An Anonymous Story, The Two Volodyas.*

1894 his cough worsens; writes stories: *The Black Monk, The Student, The Teacher of Literature.*

1895 completes *The Seagull;* first meeting with Tolstoy; writes stories: *The Murder, Ariadne, Anna on the Neck.*

1896 October 17: *The Seagull* premieres at the Aleksandrinsky Theatre in St. Petersburg; it is a critical failure; writes stories: *The House with a Mezzanine, My Life.*

1897 continues his humanitarian work in the Serpukhov district (Melikhovo), building schools (at his own expense), census taking; experiences a major lung hemorrhage; is formally diagnosed with consumption and advised by his doctors to move to the south; Stanislavsky and Nemirovich-Danchenko plan for the founding of the Moscow Art Theatre; Chekhov spends winter in France; writes stories: *Peasants, The Schoolmistress.*

1898 inaugural season of the Moscow Art Theatre; December 17: *The Seagull* is produced there with great success; Chekhov begins a relationship with actress Olga Knipper; performances of *Uncle Vanya* are well-received in the provinces; Chekhov shows interest in the Dreyfus affair; Chekhov's father dies; owing to his declining health, Chekhov buys a plot of land in Yalta and builds a house; writes stories: *Man in a Case, The Husband, Gooseberries, About Love.*

1899 sells Melikhovo and moves to Yalta with his mother and sister; sells all the rights for his works, past and future, to St. Petersburg publisher Marks; October 26: *Uncle Vanya* is produced at the Moscow Art Theatre; writes stories: *The Darling, The Lady with the Dog, On Official Duty.*

1900 spring: the Moscow Art Theatre comes to Yalta to visit the ailing Chekhov, and performs *Uncle Vanya* for Chekhov, with Gorky, Bunin, Kuprin, and Rachmaninov in attendance. Chekhov is elected member of the Academy of Sciences; writes stories: *In the Ravine, At Christmas-Time.*

1901 January 31: *The Three Sisters* premieres at the Moscow Art Theatre; May 25, Chekhov marries Olga Knipper.

1902 resigns from the Academy of Sciences in protest against exclusion of Gorky; writes story: *The Bishop;* completes the final revision of *On the Harmful Effects of Tobacco.*

1903 his health declines; elected president of the Society of Russian Literature; writes his last story: *The Bride.*

1904 January 17: Chekhov's forty-fourth birthday is honored at the premiere of *The Cherry Orchard*, his last play; April: leaves Russia for Germany with Olga Knipper, on doctors' advice. July 2: Chekhov dies at a spa at Badenweiler, German. Buried in the cemetery of the Novo-Devichy Monastery in Moscow.

Please note that the dates of his one-act and full-length plays are set forth in a separate chronology. I have included mention of a few of his almost five hundred short stories, to show that Chekhov wrote stories every year from the ages of seventeen to forty-three, a year before his death. The names of individual stories don't begin in this outline until 1889, since before then, they were so numerous and were published in collections.

Glossary

This glossary contains a brief explanation of selected literary, musical, historical, and cultural allusions in the plays. Its purpose is to enhance the understanding of the texts and their practical usage.

PLATONOV
ACT I

"Let me tell you…"

lyrics from a Russian "romanz" (romance), a popular song of the day.

summer solstice

the longest day of the year, occuring on June 22 or thereabouts, marking the beginning of summer.

women's emancipation

a popular and fashionable cause of the 1880s among the intelligentsia and educated landed gentry in Russia.

Marie Curie

(1867–1934) the Polish physical chemist and recipient of the Nobel Prize for chemistry. Chekhov indicates that Platonov continually teases Grekova, the little student of chemistry. I have taken an adaptor's liberty of choosing "Marie Curie" as a mocking *leitmotif* for this purpose. Since Marie Curie was actually seven years younger than Chekhov (1860–1904), my usage constitutes, technically, a historical inaccuracy. The choice of Marie Curie, however, seemed appropriate; and therefore I hope that readers will forgive a translator's indulgent anachronism for the sake of context.

"…don't disturb the geese…"

a paraphrase from the fable *The Geese* by the famous Russian fabulist Krylov (1769–1844).

lapin au vin blanc
> rabbit in white wine, a gourmet culinary dish (French).

ACT II

tout de suite
> right away (French).

"Tell her, my flowers ... "
> the beginning of Siebel's aria from Act III of *Faust* (1859), an opera by Gounod (1818–93).

ACT III

Kiev
> a city in the Ukraine, and a holy place of religious pilgrimages.

Don Juan
> the legend of Don Juan, the nobleman/womanizer, has been celebrated in many works of literature, including in Molière's *Don Juan* (1665) and Mozart's magnificent opera, *Don Giovanni* (1787). Chekhov refers to Don Juan in this play and again in *The Wood Demon;* he undoubtedly saw this opera, either in Taganrog or in Moscow.

à la chasse, mes amis
> "to the hunt, my friends" (French).

ACT IV

mouches volantes
> "flies" (French).

finita la commedia
> "the comedy is over" (Italian). Astrov also says this in the last act of of *Uncle Vanya.*

gospodi, pomilui
> "forgive us, O Lord" (from Russian church liturgy).

IVANOV
ACT I

kommen sie hier
> " come here" (German).

qui est-ce que c'est
> "who is this" (French).

mauvais ton
> "in bad taste" (French).

cher Nicolas
> "dear Nikolai" (French).

Tartuffe
> (1667), play by Molière: famous French dramatist (1622–73).

"Gevalt! Hek-skuse me"
> Shabelsky teases Anna Petrovna by speaking to her in a Yiddish accent.

"Little finch…"
> a Russian "tavern" song.

Aesculapius
> son of Apollo; the first physician, capable of restoring the dead to life. His powers angered Pluto, who convinced Jupiter to kill him; he was then placed among the stars.

ACT II

"In you I love my days of suffering…"
> a Russian "romance" (popular love song of the day), whose lyrics are a poem by Lermontov (1814–41, famous Russian nineteenth-century poet).

Dobrolyubov
> (1836–61) Russian journalist and critic; regarded by some as an originator of revolutionary activity in Russia.

Hegel

(1770–1831): German philosopher.

Bacon

(1561–1626): English philosopher, statesman, and jurist.

"Again before you I stand..."

a Russian *romanz* (romance), whose lyrics are the poem *Stansy (Stanzas)* (1841) by Russian poet V. I. Krasov.

Chatsky

sensitive and idealistic hero of *Wit Works Woe* (1822–24), a verse satire by the Russian playwright Griboedov (1795–1829). Chatsky returns to Moscow from traveling abroad to find that the Russian society, for which he had been nostalgic, had become reactionary, insipid, and petty.

Hamlet

Chekhov had a passion for Shakespeare and in particular for the play *Hamlet*, which he saw in Polevoy's Russian translation in Moscow in 1881 (he was then twenty-one) and about which wrote an ecstatic review.

ACT III

"Repetatur"

in this context, a toast meaning "Cheers."

guten appetit

"good appetite" (German).

"Doctor, O Doctor..."

probably a lyric from a popular contemporary vaudeville of the 80s.

Georges Sand

(1804–76): famous French novelist; a woman writer who defied the social conventions of the day.

"You fly to me..."

lyrics to a Russian "romance" of the day.

ACT IV

"rats in Gogol's play"

reference is to the characters Dobchinksy and Bobchinsky in *Inspector General* (1836), the comedy by Nikolai Gogol (1809–52), Russia's famous short story writer and novelist.

Schopenhauer

(1788–1860) German philosopher; chief expounder of pessimism; much admired by Chekhov.

THE WOOD DEMON
ACT I

"A writer toils through endless day
Yet hears he not a word of praise.
Though brow be knit, though mind be strained,
Nobody cares, so what is gained?"

Lines from the satirical poem *Other People's Views* (1794) by Ivan Dmitriev (1760–1837), poet, author of odes, elegies, verse tales), in which he satirizes the contemporary literary fashion of ode writing.

Humboldt, Edison, and Lassalle

Humboldt (1769–1859), German naturalist, traveler and statesman;
Edison (1847–1883), American inventor;
Lassalle (1835–1864), German socialist and disciple of Karl Marx.
Here, Uncle George is teasing Sonya with his sarcasm.

Trapezond

city in Turkey

"Your rule shall be divine, O royal mistress mine!"

Lines from Lermontov's narrative poem *The Demon* (1839), dealing with the love of a fallen angel for a mortal maiden. Lermontov (1814–41) was a leading Russian romantic poet and novelist, a Byronesque figure, killed at the age of twenty-seven in a duel.

ACT II

the tapping of the night watchman
The watchman taps on his lanterns with a stick, indicating that all is well.

" …lift your little finger"
a popular saying/custom that one could provoke another to laughter by raising one's little finger

"brüdershaft"
friendship (German).

ACT III

Lensky's aria from Eugene Onegin
At the top of Act III, Yelena plays the piano offstage. The piece she plays is form the opera *Eugene Onegin* (1877–78) by Tchaikovsky (1840–93), based on Pushkin's verse novel of the same name.

Circassian costume
a costume from the region in southern Russia, west of the Caucasus Mountains.

"manet omnes una nox"
"one night awaits us all" (Latin).

Lomonosov
(1711–65) Poet, scientist, educator, often called the "father of modern Russian literature." His odes are famous in Russian, eighteenth-century poetry.

ACT IV

"I'm in a state of *deshabilé*…"
meaning "I'm not dressed properly…" (French).

Ayvazovsky
(1817–1900) A popular and prolific nineteenth-century, Russian painter, famous for his marine subjects (his paintings numbered almost 6,000).

"Against my will to these sad shores
A mysterious force allures me …"

> This couplet comes from the dramatic poem *The Mermaid* (1832) by
> Pushkin (1799–1837), Russia's greatest poet.

"Sow the seeds of good and reason,
Sow them now for every season,
Russia thanks you from her heart!"

> These lines are found in the poem *To the Sowers* (1876–77) by Nekrasov
> (1821–78), the great Russian poet of the mid-nineteenth century.

"…there are more things in heaven and earth, Horatio,
Than are dreamt of in your philosophy!"

> These lines are from *Hamlet*, Act I, Scene V. More than any other work of
> literature, the play *Hamlet* — which Chekhov knew from Polevoy's
> Russian translation only — had a tremendous influence on Chekhov's
> theatrical imagination. He quotes from *Hamlet* throughout his plays, and
> *Ivanov* and *The Seagull* are deeply influenced by *Hamlet*.

"O marvelous spot of woodland wonder
Where water nymphs perch, and demons wander…"

> These lines are to be found in Pushkin's poem *Ruslan and Lyudmila*
> (1820), a long poetic fairy tale based on a popular seventeenth-century,
> Russian narrative.

Pronunciation Guide

For the actor, the most significant aspect of the pronunciation of Russian names is accentuation. This is indicated below by an accent mark (') following the stressed syllable in boldface. Once the actor masters this, the narrative will flow, and the names will provide the richness that resonates in the original Russian. Note that the Russian name and patronymic is used for formality in address. Occasionally, the patronymic is contracted in the dialogue (e. g. "Semyonovich" sometimes becomes "Semyonich"). In general, accented "a" sounds like "far," accented "e" sounds like "yet," and accented "o" sounds like "for". This guide is only approximate, since in Russian, some vowels change slightly based on whether they are accented or not, and based on their position in a given word.

PLATONOV

Character names:

Anna Petrovna Voynitseva
   An'-na Pe-**trov**'-na Voy-**nee**'-tse-va
   ("ee" as in the English word "seems")

Sergey Pavlovich Voynitsev
   Ser-**gey**' **Pav**'-lo-veech Voy-**nee**'-tsef (Serge = French)

Sofya Yegorovna
   So'-fya Ye-**go**'-rov-na (So-**fi**' = French)

Porfiry Semyonovich (Semyonich) Glagolyev (Pasha)
   Par-**fee**'-ree Se-**myon**'-o-veech (Se-**myon**'-ich) Gla-**go**'-lyef (**Pa**'-sha)

Gerasim Kuzmich Petrin (Gerasya)
   Ge-**ra**'-seem Kuz-**meech**' Pye-**treen**' (Ge-**ra**'-sya)

Marya Yefimovna Grekova
   Ma'-rya Ye-**fee**'-mov-na **Grye**'-ko-va

Ivan Ivanovich Triletsky
　　Ee-**van**' Ee-**va**'-no-veech Tree-**lyet**'-skee

Nikolai Ivanovich Triletsky (Kolya)
　　Nee'-ko-lai Ee-**va**'-no-veech Tree-**lyet**'-skee (**Ko**'-lya)
　　("lai" rhymes with English word "my")

Mikhail Vasilevich Platonov (Misha)
　　Mee-kha-**eel**' Va-**see**'-lye-veech Pla-**to**'-nof (**Mee**'-sha)
　　(Mi-**chel**' = french)

Aleksandra Ivanovna (Sasha, Sashenka)
　　A-lyek-**san**'-dra Ee-**va**'-nov-na (**Sa**'-sha, **Sa**'-shen-ka)

Osip
　　O'-seep

Yakov
　　Ya'-kof

Other names appearing in the text:

gospoldi pomilui
　　go'-spo-dee pa-**mee**'-loo-ee

Kharkov
　　Khar'-kof

Petya
　　Pe'-tya

Platonovka
　　Pla-**to**'-nov-ka

Voynitseva
　　Voy-**nee**'-tse-va

IVANOV

Character names:

Nikolai Alekseevich Ivanov (Nikolasha)
Nee'-ko-lai A-lek-**syey**'-e-veech Ee-**va**'-nof (Nee-ko-**la**'-sha)
("lai" rhymes with English word "my")
("syey" rhymes with the word "grey")
("Nicolas" — French pronunciation)

Anna Petrovna (Anyuta) (Sara Abramson)
An'-na Pye-**trov**'-na (A-**nyu**'-ta) (**Sa**'-ra **A**'-bram-son)

Matvey Semyonovich Shabelsky (Matyusha)
Mat-**vyey**' Se-**myon**'-o-veech Sha-**byel**'-skee (Ma-**tyoo**'-sha)
("oo" as in the English word "soon")

Pavel Kirilich Lebedev (Pasha) (Pashenka)
Pa'-vyel Kee-**ree**'-leech **Lye**'-bye-dyev (**Pa**'-shen-ka)

Zinaida Savishna (Zyuzyushka)
Zee-na-**ee**'-da **Sa**'-veesh-na (**Zyoo**'-zyoosh-ka)

Sasha (Aleksandra Pavlovna) (Shura) (Shurochka) (Sanyechka) (Sashenka)
Sa-sha (A-lek-**san**'-dra **Pav**'-lov-na) (**Shoo**'-ra) (**Shoo**'-roch-ka)
(**Sa**'-nyech-ka) (**Sa**'-shen-ka)

Marfa Yegorovna Babakina
Mar'-fa Ye-**gor**'-ov-na Ba-**ba**'-kee-na

Dmitry Nikitich Kosykh
Dmee'-tree Nee-**kee**'-teech **Ko**'-sikh

Mikhail Mikhailovich Borkin (Misha)
Mee-kha-**eel**' Mee-**khai**'-lo-veech **Bor**'-keen (**Mee**'-sha)
("khai" rhymes with the English word "why")
("Michel Michelich" — a corruption of French and Russian)

Avdotya Nazarovna
   Av-**do'**-tya Na-**za'**-rov-na

Yegorushka
   Ye-**go'**-roosh-ka

Pyotr
   Pyo'-tr

Gavrila (Gavryusha)
   Ga-**vree'**-la (Ga-**vryoo'**-sha)

Other names appearing in the text:

Barabanov
   Ba-ra-**ba'**-nof

Dobrolyubov
   Do-bro-**lyu'**-bof

Gerasim Nilich
   Ge-**ra'**-seem Nee-**leech'**

Korolkov
   Ko-rol-**kof'**

Mamasha
   Ma-**ma'**-sha

Mushkino
   Moosh'-kee-no

Ovsyanov
   Ov-**sya'**-nof

Plesniki
   Plyes'-ni-ki

Zaimishche
    Zai'-meesh-che

Zarevsky
    Za-**ryev'**-skee

THE WOOD DEMON

Cast of characters:

Aleksandr Vladimirovich Serebraykov
    A-lek-**san'**-dr Vla-**dee'**-mee-ro-veech Se-re-brya-**kof'**

Yelena Andreevna (Lyenochka)
    Ye-**lye'**-na An-**drey'**-ev-na (**Lye'**-noch-ka)

Sofya Aleksandrovna (Sonya, Sonyechka, Sofi)
    So'-fya A-lek-**san'**-drov-na (**Son'**-ya, **Son'**-yech-ka, So-**fee'**)

Maria Vasilyevna Voynitskaya
    Ma-**ree'**-ya Va-**see'**-lyev-na Voy-**neet'**-ska-ya

Yegor Petrovich Voynitsky (George, Georgenka)
    Ye-**gor'** Pye-**tro'**-veech Vay-**neet'**-skee (Zhorzh, **Zhorz'**-en-ka)
    (note: "George" and "Georgenka" are pronounced as if they were
    French names)

Leonid Stepanovich Zheltukhin (Lyonya, Lyonechka)
    Le-o-**need'** Stye-**pa'**-no-veech Zhel-**too'**-kheen
    (Lyo'-nya, Lyo'-nyech-ka)

Yulya Stepanovna (Yulya)
    Yoo'-lya Stye-**pa'**-nov-na

Ivan Ivanovich Orlovsky
    Ee-**van'** Ee-**va'**-no-veech Or-**lov'**-skee

Fyodor Ivanovich (Fedya, Fedyenka, Fedyushka)
Fyo'-dor Ee-**va**'-no-veech (**Fe**'-dya, **Fe**'-dyen-ka, **Fe**'-dyoosh-ka)

Mikhail Lvovich Khrushchov
Mee-kha-**eel**' Lvo'-veech Khroosh-**chof**'

Ilya Ilyich Dyadin
Ee-**lya**' Ee-**lyeech**' **Dya**'-deen

Vasily
Va-**see**'-lee

Semyon
Se-**myon**'

Other names appearing in the text:

Alekseevskoye
A-lek-**se**-yev-sko-ye

Dmitri Pavlovich
Dmee'-tree **Pav**'-lo-veech

Gerasim
Ge-**ra**'-seem

Kashkinazi
Kash-kee-**na**'-zee

Konstantin Trofimovich Lakedemonov
Kon-stan-**teen**' Tro-**fee**'-mo-veech La-ke-de-**mo**'-nof

Kuznetsov
Kuz-nyet-**sof**'

Lomonosov
Lo-mo-**no**'-sof

Novo-Petrovskoye
No-vo-Pye-**trov'**-sko-ye

Senka
Syen'-ka

Shimansky
Shee-**man'**-skee

Telibeevsky
Te-lee-**bye'**-yev-skee

Trezor
Tre-**zor'**

Yefim
Ye-**feem'**

Zhuchka
Zhooch'-ka

Selected Bibliography

The following sources were consulted for some of the biographical and literary information included in the introduction to this collection:

Chekhov, Michael. "Anton Chekhov and his Subjects," and "Tchekhov and the Theatre," in *The Life and Letters of Anton Tchekhov*, S. S. Koteliansky and Philip Tomlinson, transl. and ed. London: Benjamin Blom, 1925.

Frayn, Michael. *Introduction to Wild Honey*. New York: Signet, 1985.

Gilles, Daniel. *Chekhov: Observer Without Illusion*. New York: Funk & Wagnalls, 1968.

Korolenko, V. G. "Anton Pavlovich Chekhov," *Izbrannye Proizvedeniya*. Moskva, 1947.

Koteliansky, S. S. transl. and ed. *Anton Tchekhov: Literary and Theatrical Reminiscences*. London: Benjamin Blom, 1927.

Magarshack, David. *Chekhov the Dramatist*. London: John Lehmann, Ltd., 1952.

Rayfield, Donald. *Chekhov's Uncle Vanya and The Wood Demon*. Bristol, England: Bristol Classical Press, 1995.

Rayfield, Donald. *Anton Chekhov*. New York: Henry Holt and Company, 1997.

Simmons, Ernest J. *Chekhov: A Biography*. Chicago: The University of Chicago Press, 1962.

Valency, Maurice. *The Breaking String*. New York: Oxford University Press, 1966.

The texts of Chekhov's plays and the excerpts from his letters were newly translated from the Russian for this collection from the following:

Chekhov, Anton Pavlovich. *Polnoe sobranie sochineniy i pisem v tridtsati tomax.* Moskva, Izdatelstvo 'Nauka', 1974–82.

In addition to these, the following books are also recommended as source material for Chekhov's plays. They are only a few of the many sources available in English about Chekhov and his work:

Chekhov, Anton Pavlovich. *Chekhov: Four Plays.* Translated by Carol Rocamora. Lyme, N.H.: Smith & Kraus, 1996.

Chekhov, Anton Pavlovich. *Chekhov: The Vaudevilles.* Translated by Carol Rocamora. Lyme N.H.: Smith & Kraus, 1998.

Heim, Michael Henry and Simon Karlinsky, transl. and ed. *Anton Chekhov's Life and Thought: Selected Letters and Commentary.* Berkeley: University of California Press, 1975.

Hingley, Ronald. *A New Life of Anton Chekhov.* New York: Knopf, 1976.

Magarshack, David. *Chekhov: A Life.* New York: Grove Press, 1952.

Magarshack, David. *The Real Chekhov.* London: George Allen & Unwin, Ltd., 1972.

Miles, Patrick, ed. and transl. *Chekhov on the British Stage.* Cambridge University Press, 1993.

Pritchett, V. S. *A Spirit Set Free.* New York: Vintage, 1988.

Stanislavsky, Konstantin, transl. by J. J. Robbins. *My Life in Art.* London: Methuen, 1989.

Troyat, Henri. *Chekhov.* New York: Fawcett Colombine, 1986.

The Translator

Carol Rocamora, translator, director, and teacher, is a graduate of Bryn Mawr College. She received her M. A. and Ph.D. degrees from the University of Pennsylvania in Russian literature. She is the founder of the Philadelphia Festival Theatre for New Plays at the Annenberg Center, a nonprofit professional theatre, where she served as its Artistic and Producing Director from 1981–1994. In this capacity, she has worked with over 120 contemporary American playwrights in developing and producing their new work for the stage. At Festival Theatre, she directed many mainstage productions of new plays, and, in addition, directed the premieres of the new translations of Chekhov's major plays.

Dr. Rocamora has served on the faculties of Bryn Mawr and Haverford Colleges, and the University of Pennsylvania. She currently teaches theatre in the Dramatic Writing Program of New York University's Tisch School of the Arts. The first two collections of her translations, already published by Smith and Kraus, Inc., are: *Chekhov: Four Plays (The Seagull, Uncle Vanya, The Three Sisters, The Cherry Orchard)* (1996), and *Chekhov: The Vaudevilles* (1998).